Theoretical Approaches to Deviance: An Evaluation

Charles E. Frazier

University of Florida

CHARLES E. MERRILL PUBLISHING COMPANY
A Bell & Howell Company
Columbus, Ohio

Published by
Charles E. Merrill Publishing Company
A Bell & Howell Company
Columbus, Ohio 43216

This book was set in Primer.
The Production Editor was Linda Gambaiani.
The cover was designed by Will Chenoweth.

ISBN: 0-675-08657-4

Library of Congress Catalog Card Number: 75-18443

2 3 4 5 6 — 81 80 79 78 77 76

Printed in the United States of America

For
Lynn and Jason

Preface

This book is an attempt to bring together theory and reality. The theory involves theories of deviance. The reality involves the self-perceived life-histories of individuals who developed patterns of deviant behavior.

Reality is defined differently to each individual, but one tendency is common to us all. We all feel we know best why our own patterns of behavior develop. Only insiders know the real feelings, ideas, and intentions surrounding patterned action. If theories of behavior do not explain this insider reality—as the actors see and live it—they fail to be fully explanatory. This book applies theories of deviance to reality as perceived by individuals who are deviant. The general focus is on how well the theories fit the facts as conceived by the deviants themselves.

As it is usually studied, the sociology of deviance takes up the examination of some theories and some related research. But after reviewing different theories of deviance and the relevant research bearing upon them, students often lack a sense of direction and a sense of completion. They find the theories are often tight logical constructions which make good sense on paper. But reviewing the research literature tells them that there is something credible (supporting research) and something incredible (negating research) about all the theories. Frequently, they look beyond this for general conclusions and inquire which theory or set of theories is best, or which is most explanatory of deviance.

These are reasonable questions. But instead of good answers, the state of the field leaves instructors with only a variety of pat answers. "They are all good for some specific form of deviance or for certain phases of some form of deviance." Or, "they are all probably partly correct and we must continue to sort out the right parts." In spite of their potential truth and the fact that the state of the field offers nothing better than these sorts of answers, I doubt that instructors are ever comfortable in giving them or that students are satisfied in receiving them. This book asks the questions again and, while the answers are certainly not definitive, they are more developed and, hopefully, more satisfactory.

The major theories in the sociology of deviance are reviewed in part I of the book. Instead of focusing on specific theories, however, I have drawn on the most basic assumptions and the most general propositions underlying them. Combining those theories offering the same assumptions and the same general explanation of deviance, three distinct approaches (socialization, societal reaction, and control) are developed. Then in part II, the general theoretical approaches are compared to the life-history accounts given by career deviants on the emergence, patterning, and change of their deviance. Some of these life-history documents represent the kinds of cases each theoretical approach was designed to explain. Other cases illustrate the diversity of ways deviant behavior patterns develop. The most powerful approach is sought by examining the extent to which each approach is able to explain the development and change of deviant behavior patterns as the deviants relate them.

The life-histories were obtained from men who were incarcerated in prison at the time of the interviews with them. All names used in the quoted matter in this book are fictious and no other material from the interviews was used in a way that might identify any of the respondents.

I am grateful to Russell H. Levy of Illinois Division of Corrections, Warden Vernon G. Housewright, and Assistant Warden Don Hood of the Illinois State Penitentiary at Vienna for permitting my research and for their help in organizational arrangements at Vienna. Raymond Worley of the Florida Division of Corrections was helpful in arranging my research at the Reception and Medical Center and Florida State Prison at Lake Butler. I am grateful to Warden J. B. Godwin, Ken Snowver, and Colonel Adams at the Lake Butler facility for being receptive to my study and for making my research easy by finding space for me to work. The data collected in Florida were made possible by a grant from the Social Science Institute of the University of Florida.

The men who participated in this study, giving their time and their life-histories, did so because they thought the findings "might help someone sometime," or because they believed I could be trusted. I hope this work does not violate their trust and that I do not forget their noble motives.

There are several debts I have accrued over the past few years that I would like to acknowledge here. I owe much to Charles R. Snyder, Peter A. Munch, Jerry Gaston, and Robert Rossell for their interest and wise counsel on many matters. My understanding of sociology is better because of their tutelage.

I am grateful to Leonard Beeghley and Bill Sanders for commenting on selected chapters and to Tom Meisenhelder who read the entire manuscript. I am also grateful to Linda Gambaiani for her careful editing of this manuscript.

My greatest debt in this endeavor is to Lynn, my wife, who transcribed nearly 1,500 pages of taped interviews, typed the manuscript twice, proofread the drafts, and remained amazingly agreeable through it all. In many respects this book was a joint effort.

Contents

Appendixes

Part I

The Delineation of Theoretical Approaches to Deviance

Definitions and Purposes: An Introduction

1

This book is about deviance, theories that attempt to explain deviance, and the extent to which these theories explain the way deviance develops and changes. No single definition of deviance can be offered here that will satisfy all who are concerned with its broad personal and social effects. Sociologists differ greatly in their conceptions of deviance.[1] None is unquestionably true. All definitions serve more or less specific purposes.

Deviance is frequently defined as rule-breaking. One definition holds that any act that violates the conduct norms of the group is deviant.[2] Another considers that deviance is any act that violates the institutional "expectations which are shared and recognized as legitimate within the social systems."[3] Another views as deviant any behavior which goes against the rules of dominant culture.[4] Still another suggests that only those acts which violate the most important of conventional norms are to be considered deviant.[5] The assumption in each of these definitions is that we may apply some known and commonly accepted standard in determining what is deviant and what is not.

Other sociologists observe that who does the behavior, how it is done, and under what circumstances are all factors taken into account in deciding what is actually regarded as deviant behavior. They look, not at the rules, but at the way a particular behavior is reacted to by others. Rules are not abstract things that exist in and of themselves. They are formed and applied in interaction and through the reactions of others to our behaviors. For these sociologists acts that are reacted to negatively by others are deviant.[6] Rule-breaking behaviors that are ignored or rationalized away by those that observe them are not really deviant.[7] The actor is not considered a deviant person and therefore the behavior is not the proper subject matter for the study of deviance. Real deviance, by this definition, is behavior in response to being labeled as a deviant actor and comes from playing the role of a deviant.[8]

There is no magic in any of these definitions. In the first group of definitions an abstract and arbitrary set of standards is used to separate deviant from nondeviant behavior. The second group of definitions places the burden on social reaction— what gets by without negative response is not deviant and what does not is deviant. In all of the definitions, someone other than the person doing the behavior, and maybe someone or some group or groups not familiar with the actor's circumstances and customs, does the defining of what is deviant. We know, of course, that each person or each group cannot make and attend to its own rules in total exclusion of the consideration of other groups. Society would be chaotic if that were the case. But, at the same time, we know that frequently we engage in behaviors that violate general rules or that others define negatively which are perfectly appropriate to ourselves and to our peers. Clearly, no present definition of deviance is sufficient to satisfy all our concerns and interests. Each one is given with a specific purpose in mind.

When calculating rates of deviance in a population, for example, it is convenient to use an arbitrary definition of behaviors which fall outside acceptable limits. We do this by assuming that everyone marches to the same drummer, or, at least, that everyone should be responsive to a single set of rules. Our purpose here is different. Rather than considering how many people break some set of rules, we are concerned with how deviant behavior develops and changes in the life-histories of individual actors. So another definition of deviance is offered, not to clutter an already crowded field, but to fit specific purposes.

Deviance, as defined for this work, is a process where a form of behavior, subjectively perceived as deviant by the actor, emerges, stabilizes, and disappears in individual histories. In this context deviance is not just behavior that violates some rule, however important, nor is it just behavior that is labeled by others as rule-breaking. *Deviance is,* for our purposes, *behavior that violates the standards of the person performing the act, the perceived standards of some person or some group that is important to that actor, or both.* This is a definition that puts the emphasis on the actor's own perceptions of the quality of his conduct. A deviant act may not be reacted to negatively by others, it may or may not be known about by others. Whether an act is or is not reacted to, and is or is not known about, individuals will usually regard as deviant any conduct in which it is perceived that their own standards or the standards of significant others have been violated. The more important the standards violated are to the actor, or the more important the holders of the standards violated are to the actor, the more severely the actor will judge his own conduct. Judith Lorber found, in studying illness as a form of deviance, that many individuals defined what they did as deviant even though no one else knew about it. They either believed it really was deviant themselves or they recognized that significant others would believe that if they knew about it.[9] In the study of the development of deviant behavior patterns reported in part II of this book, eighty-one persons with histories of specific kinds of deviance were interviewed. In these cases the respondents recounted as part of their deviant histories both acts which they believed violated the standards of significant others but not their own, and acts that violated their own standards but not those of significant others. They also included acts unknown to others, and therefore not reacted to overtly, and acts that were both known about and reacted to as deviant.

Most theorists of deviance, whatever their specific purpose, ultimately get around to a consideration of deviance as it forms a stable part of an individual's action patterns. Less permanent behaviors, deviant or otherwise, are not generally of interest to sociologists. Our purpose is like that of other theorists in the consideration of patterned deviant behavior, but it is different in two ways. First, we are interested in two additional phases of the deviance process—the emergence and the abandonment of deviant behavior patterns. Second, we are interested in how social forces believed to induce deviance work in the private worlds of deviant actors.

Deviance as seen here proceeds through three phases—emergence, patterning, and change. These three phases of deviance will be discussed at length in chapters 6, 7, and 8. Therefore, for the moment, it should suffice to note that *emergence* refers to the first instances of deviant behavior. *Patterning* refers to the point when any particular form of deviance becomes a normal part of individual behavior tendencies. *Change* or *abandonment* of deviant behavior patterns pertains to the point where the actor discontinues the behavior. The thrust of the book deals with how deviant behavior is portrayed to begin, stabilize, and stop in major sociological theories, how deviance develops and changes in real world cases, and how well the former explain the latter.

The book is presented in two parts. In part I, three broad theoretical approaches, socialization, societal reaction, and control, are outlined. What we call the socialization approach includes theories of deviance from the "cultural transmission," the "anomie," and the "culture conflict" traditions. The central thesis of this approach is that individuals come by values, through normal socialization processes or through precarious socialization processes, that ultimately determine and shape their deviance. The societal reaction approach includes theories from what is generally referred to as the labeling school. The focus of these theories is on the effect of negative social reactions on individual rule-breakers and their behaviors. Theories included to make up the control approach are all basically extensions or elaborations of Emile Durkheim's view that, when uncontrolled, individuals are more prone to deviance. The central thesis of this approach is that deviance is a result of ineffective social controls.

In the three following chapters the socialization, societal reaction, and control approaches are developed by looking at several major theories which rest upon the same basic assumptions and which offer the same general explanations of social deviance. Each theory is reviewed independently to sort out (1) the assumptions that are made about the nature of social action and personality and (2) the theoretical statements that refer to the emergence, patterning, and change phases of a deviant career. At the same time, each of the three sets of theories is considered in broad terms, with an eye to developing general propositions which depict the overall approaches. Appendix A elaborates the basic assumptions underlying each specific theory and identifies the general proposition on emergence, patterning, and change offered to characterize each of the three approaches.

The works and the authors included in this review do not represent an exhaustive list. Rather, we have attempted a portrayal of three important approaches to the study of deviance by including representative works from many of the most influential writers in the field of the sociology of deviance. Other important theories that do not fit one of the three approaches or that do not imply an explanation of individual behavior patterns are left out.

Each of the theories considered in the following chapters was originally intended to explain only a certain form or phase of deviance. The reader may wonder, in subsequent chapters, how they can be held accountable for failure to explain things for which they were not intended. This concern is unnecessary in that no single theory is at issue here—no single theory is being tested. Rather, the theories reviewed in chapters 2, 3, and 4 are used to get at the assumptions and basic positions upon which each general theoretical approach rests (see Appendix A). In short, these individual theories are used only as bases from which to infer what is fundamental to each general approach. The socialization, societal reaction, and control approaches, then, are to become our concern as alternative explanations of deviance and as the subject of our evaluation.

In part II of this book the three theoretical approaches are put to work in an effort to determine their comparative explanatory power when pitted against life-history accounts of the development and change of deviance. Chapters 6, 7, and 8 are analyses of the emergence, patterning, and change phases of deviance. The analysis involves considering the relative utility of the socialization, societal reaction, and control approaches as explanations of life-history accounts of real deviants.

The life-history documents were collected through intensive interviews by the author, in an ongoing study of the development and change of deviance. All of the respondents had previously manifested at least one pattern of some form of deviance and all were imprisoned at the time of their interviews. Several different forms of deviance patterns were found among these respondents including mental illness, drug addiction and abuse, homosexuality, alcoholism, and a variety of forms of property crimes. The particular form of deviance, however, is unimportant to us. Our interest throughout this work will be with the way deviance emerges, stabilizes, and changes and the extent to which the broad theoretical approaches developed in part I explain that process. In the last chapter we offer some observations in an attempt to lay groundwork for a general theory of the deviance process.

Notes

1. For more elaborate discussions of the different conceptions of deviance utilized by sociologists see, for example, Jack P. Gibbs, "Conceptions of Deviant Behavior: The Old and the New," *Pacific Sociological Review* 9 (Spring 1966): 9–14; Earl Rubington and Martin S. Weinberg, eds., *Deviance: The Interactionists Perspective* (New York: Macmillan, 1968), pp. 1–12; Howard S. Becker, *Outsiders: Studies in the Sociology of Deviance* (New York: Free Press, 1963), pp. 1–18 and 121–34; and Ronald L. Akers, "Problems in the Sociology of Deviance: Social Definition and Behavior," *Social Forces* 46 (June 1968): 455–65.

2. Thorsten Sellin, *Culture, Conflict, and Crime* (New York: Social Science Research Council, 1938), pp. 42–44.

3. Albert K. Cohen, "The Study of Social Disorganization and Deviant Behavior," in *Sociology Today,* ed. Robert K. Merton, Leonard Broom, and Leonard S. Cottrell (New York: Basic Books, 1959), pp. 461–84.

4. Walter Miller, "Lower Class Culture as a Generating Milieu of Gang Delinquency," *Journal of Social Issues* 14 (1958): 5–19, and Ronald Akers, *Deviant Behavior* (Belmont, Calif.: Wadsworth, 1973), p. 8.

5. Ruth Shonle Cavan, "The Concepts of Tolerance and Contraculture as Applied to Delinquency," *Sociological Quarterly* 2 (1961): 243–58, and Marshall B. Clinard, *Sociology of Deviant Behavior,* 3rd ed. (New York: Holt, Rinehart & Winston, 1968), pp. 25–28.

6. Becker, *Outsiders,* p. 9.

7. Thomas Scheff, *Being Mentally Ill* (Chicago: Aldine, 1966), p. 50.

8. Edwin M. Lemert, *Social Pathology* (New York: McGraw-Hill, 1951), pp. 75–76.

9. See Judith Lorber, "Deviance and Performance: The Case of Illness," *Social Problems* 14 (Winter 1967): 302–10.

The
Socialization
Approach

The basis of the socialization approach is formed by three important theoretical traditions in the sociology of deviance—the cultural transmission, the anomie, and the culture conflict. While these traditions are unique in many respects, the underlying assumptions and the explanations of patterned deviance are basically the same. That is, in the final analysis, all three traditions portray deviants as those who come to internalize values that encourage their deviance. In this chapter, we will consider each of six different theories separately and then combine their common tenets which make up the socialization approach.

We will be concerned with how the emergence, patterning, and change of deviant behavior may be explained by each of the theories. In many cases, theoretical positions on these three phases of deviance are not explicit in the theories, but this presents no major problem for our purposes. Where theoretical positions were not clearly spelled out in the works discussed, we have inferred a logically consistent statement to fit the particular phase of deviance being considered. This was necessary most frequently for the change phase of deviance.

Cultural Transmission Theory

Theories of the cultural transmission tradition grew out of studies by sociologists at the University of Chicago which began in the 1920s and continued through the 1950s. The original idea was that deviant behavior was learned in the transfer of culture to the individual from his social setting. Values favorable to deviance were prominent and considered normal in certain segments of the society. Individuals socialized in these particular segments were believed to take on deviant behavior patterns as naturally as those who developed conventional patterns.

Shaw and McKay

Probably the clearest statement on the causes of the emergence of deviant behavior from the early works of the cultural transmission tradition comes from Clifford R. Shaw and H. D. McKay. Shaw, for example, describes how participation in one's social world conditions the individual so that initial conduct is the product of accepted parts of the culture.

> Through participation in the activities of ... [his or her] social world, beginning in such intimate groups as the family, the play group, and the neighborhood, the *original activities* of the ... [individual] *are conditioned and organized and come to assume the character of well defined attitudes, interests, and behavior trends.*[1] (Italics added)

Here Shaw points to the initial sources of socialization and the permanent impact of this process on the individual's dispositions and behavior. Shaw believed that socialization into deviant values was characteristic of deteriorated and disorganized sections of cities. It was here that conventional traditions, neighborhood institutions, and public opinion, which usually effect control over the behavior of individuals, were lacking. And this was where a high rate of delinquency and adult crime, various forms of stealing, and many organized delinquent and criminal gangs were prevalent.[2] In these circumstances a powerful influence "tends to create a community spirit which not only tolerates, but actually fosters, the gradual formation and crystallization of deviant behavior traits."[3] At this point Shaw considered deviant behavior to be "fixated" or, in other terms, deviant behavior was an aspect of the personality.

This view that deviance comes to be *fixated* in the individual's behavior tendencies and personality pervades all the works of Shaw and McKay. However, this does not mean change was considered impossible. It is apparent that Shaw and McKay believed change of individual behavior could be achieved.[4] The most important ingredients of change, in their view, involved removing the individual from the environment that produced the deviant behavior and the establishment of new associations in conventional social groups.[5] Through involvement in conventional groups and isolation from deviant groups the deviant would take on new values and new behaviors consistent with conventional standards.

Sutherland

Edwin H. Sutherland's work follows in the tradition of the "Chicago School" and represents the most systematic and successful attempt to formulate a general theory in cultural transmission terms. The theory, called differential association, was designed to explain criminal behavior. However, the basic principles of this theory apply equally well to other forms of deviance.

Considering the three phases of deviance process in Sutherland's theory, we see that emergence comes about because an excess of values favorable to the violation of the law or other rules have been internalized by the individual.[6] This is the essence of the principle of differential association. If an individual's associations with others are differentially distributed in the direction of those with values favoring deviant behavior, the individual will acquire deviant values and engage in deviant behavior. Behavior becomes patterned as deviant if the "frequency," "duration," "priority," and "intensity" of associations are weighted heavily in the direction of contact with values favorable to rule violation. But if one's associations are weighted more heavily toward definitions favorable to compliance with the rules, conventional behavior patterns will develop. As Sutherland and Donald R. Cressey put it, a "person inevitably assimilates the surrounding culture unless other patterns are in conflict."[7]

In this theory, as well as in Shaw and McKay's, the processes through which the individual begins and patterns deviant behavior are no different from the processes whereby others begin and pattern conventional patterns of behavior.[8] The patterning of a certain form of deviant behavior seems to be a simple matter of specialized socialization, through differential association, with deviant groups and individuals whose values are favorable to that particular type of deviance.[9] For example, one learns pickpocketing by differential association with pickpockets or those who value it and drug use through differential association with drug users or those whose values are favorable to it.

Sutherland's position on changing deviant behavior patterns can be seen best by examining the work of his student and collaborator, Donald R. Cressey. In Cressey's attempts to apply differential association theory to the idea of change in deviant behavior patterns three points are clear. Change entails (1) some form of desocializing process whereby the individual disavows internalized deviant values, (2) assimilation of the deviant into law-abiding nondeviant groups and society, and (3) resocialization in terms of nondeviant values.[10] Desocialization and resocialization are discussed in detail in chapter 8.

Anomie Theory

A second theoretical tradition that relies on the principle of socialization as a factor in explaining deviant behavior is anomie theory. The term anomie refers to the breakdown in or the imperfect development of society which induces deviant behavior patterns. Socialization, however, is not as straightforward a factor in anomie theory as it was in cultural transmission theory. Moreover, there are two different conceptions of anomie and they have both served as bases for theories of deviance.[11] We will consider one conception here and one in chapter 4. Theories of anomie to be considered in this chapter began in 1938 with Robert K. Merton's classic essay, "Social Structure and Anomie" and continued through the 1960s in the works of Albert K. Cohen, and Richard Cloward and Lloyd Ohlin. It was not Merton's intention to consider our problem of how behavior emerges and becomes patterned in individual histories. He was concerned with explaining rates of deviance in the whole society. Merton's theory is included here because it has become a basis for other socialization theories that imply the emergence and patterning process.

Merton

For Merton, deviant behavior may be regarded as a symptom of a disorganized society.[12] That is, when the *cultural system* is not coordinated with the *social system,* society is what Merton calls "malintegrated." The *cultural system* consists of goals and prescribed means of achieving the goals common to all members of the society. In the American society Merton argued that monetary and material success was a universal goal. The *social system* in any society consists of the way culturally prescribed means for achieving goals are distributed to all segments. When all members of a society share the same goals but the legitimate means for achieving the goals are not equally available or not available at all to some segments, society is malintegrated and high rates of deviance may be expected.

This is easily seen in the United States. The common cultural goal for Americans is monetary and material success. However, the legitimate institutionalized means for achieving success such as inheritance, education, high-paying occupations, and access to loans for speculation are not equally available to all segments of society. Obviously the lower socioeconomic groups have less accessibility to these means to success. American society is in this sense malintegrated.

Merton suggests that even those who do not have realistic opportunities of reaching cultural goals acquire them nonetheless. And it is these persons and groups that the social structure exerts pressure upon to engage in deviant rather than conforming behavior.[13]

Merton's theory does not consider directly the question of how deviant behavior emerges, becomes patterned, and changes in individual histories. But he does make clear, in a later work, that he believed values favorable to deviance emerge and come to support individual patterns of deviance: "I assume that the structure constrains individuals variously situated within it to develop cultural emphases, social behavior patterns and psychological bents."[14] In other words, individuals develop values and behavior patterns relative to their location in the social structure. Some, because they have little or no access to institutionally acceptable means of achieving success, develop and later become motivated by values favorable to deviant behavior. Deviant behavior becomes patterned in a continually malintegrated society and individuals develop "psychological bents" toward deviant modes of behavior.

For Merton then, it is essentially socialization that is at the root of individual deviance. But the process was not spelled out in his original theory. However, the later theories of Cohen and Cloward and Ohlin did take up the issue by combining Merton's sociostructural theory of deviance with the cultural transmission theory of Sutherland. In both theories there is an attempt to spell out the process through which individuals in certain groups come to develop deviant behavior patterns.

Cohen

The view Albert K. Cohen presents of the social factors involved in the emergence of deviant behavior is, generally speaking, a restatement of Merton's 1938 essay.[15] Cohen believes where opportunities for achieving goals are blocked, or where a history of blocked opportunities have caused people to be too poorly equipped to take advantage of the limited opportunities available, deviance is likely. Individuals will either reject or react negatively toward the aspects of culture that represent sources of the problem or barriers to problem solutions.[16] They will then substitute goals and values they can live with more comfortably. These substituted goals and values "may permit or require behavior that violates the norms of conventional society; they may justify or demand deviant behavior."[17]

To this point Cohen adds little to what is explicit in Merton's essay. He goes on, however, to point out that an acceptable and successful solution to problems brought about by a malintegrated society requires a collective response. It takes groups to develop values favorable to deviant behavior. Cohen describes the emergence of a subculture as the origin of these values.

> A number of people, each of whom functions as a reference object for the others, must jointly arrive at a new set of criteria and apply these criteria to one another. For this to happen, people with similar problems, . . . because they occupy similar positions in the social structure, must be able to locate one another and communicate with one another. They can then sound one another out, make tentative and exploratory moves in new directions, experience the feedback, and— if the feedback is encouraging—go on to elaborate what becomes a new and in some respects deviant subculture. *In persuading one another through this "conversation of gestures," one creates social support for his own inclinations, and thereby helps persuade himself.*[18]
> (Italics added)

In other words, the malintegration in society tempts the individual who is blocked from legitimate opportunities to achieve cultural goals. In the process of communication with others with similar problems, support grows for developing new values favorable to deviance. A subculture is formed based on these values, and the individual's inclinations for employing deviant means are supported in the group.

Deviant behavior becomes patterned for Cohen as the deviant values of the subculture are internalized and followed by individual members. Deviant values are internalized through socialization in differential association with other members of the subculture. With this formulation, Cohen brings together the socialization dimension of deviant behavior, which is characteristic of the cultural transmission tradition, and the anomie tradition's emphasis on the pressure placed on those at the bottom of the social heap.[19]

Cohen considers the personality an important factor in the patterning of deviant behavior.[20] Lower-class individuals especially are pressured into a situation where they have a reaction formation. That is, instead of pursuing cultural goals that are relatively out of reach to them, they develop negative values conducive to deviant behavior. The deviance of these individuals is often malicious and nonutilitarian in the sense that it is not designed to achieve general cultural goals such as monetary success.

The circumstances under which individual deviant behavior patterns will change for Cohen would require at least desocialization, removal from the subcultural support of deviance, and resocialization in terms of nondeviant values.

Cloward and Ohlin

Finally, Richard Cloward and Lloyd Ohlin formulated a theory in the anomie tradition adding to, and amending, Merton and Cohen. Their influential work brings the cultural transmission and anomie traditions and role theory together in a theory of delinquent gangs. Generalizing their view to deviant behavior we see that deviants tend to be persons who have been misled to expect opportunities because of their own perceived potential ability to meet the formal criteria for success. That is, they feel capable but when the system fails to fulfill their expectations by providing opportunities for being evaluated as a success they feel it is an injustice.[21] Their response to injustice leads to deviance.

This feeling of injustice operates to weaken motivations for accepting the legitimacy of official societal norms. In turn, weakened motivation permits the individual to accept alternative values and patterns of conduct. The sense of injustice grows into alienation, which cancels out obligation to established rules and encourages the person to emulate other, normally deviant, role models.

It is the discrepancy between feeling capable and the limited legitimate opportunities available to be able to compete equally with others that produces a sense of alienation. For example, the person may feel smart and ambitious but cannot get a good job or cannot afford higher education in order to compete equally with others. The individual perceives his probable failure to meet accepted criteria for success (good job and education) as an injustice in the structure rather than a personal deficiency. He is at this point alienated and an emergent deviant. There is no obligation to conventional norms. He is free to join with others in a deviant solution to the problem without great concern about the moral validity of personal or group actions.[22] The deviant actions may take one of a variety of forms depending on possibilities in the neighborhood and surroundings for learning and performing specific deviant roles.[23] If there are organized groups of thieves around, patterned theft is likely. If extortion and the rackets are prominent in the neighborhood, racketeering is likely.

The factors contributing to the patterning of deviant behavior of whatever form are (1) continued influence of the initial cause (i.e., a perceived sense of injustice) and (2) the availability and social support of a subculture of deviant peers.[24] The first is clear when Cloward and Ohlin note that the situation which provokes the deviant's sense of injustice provides advanced justification for *subsequent acts of deviance.* The second point is based on both differential association and role theory. Individuals are likely to emulate and become socialized into the deviant roles that are available in the immediate environment.

Clearly then, the generalized view to be derived from this work is that the emergence of deviant behavior is caused by the "perception" of unjust opportunity blockage. Patterning follows from a continued sense of alienation and socialization into deviant values with others in the same situation. Changes in the rate of deviance may result if individuals perceive openings in the opportunity structure.[25] Change at the individual level, however, implies change in the personality structure. As in previous socialization theories, once the behavior is patterned, the personality of Cloward and Ohlin's deviant is organized around values favorable to deviance. Therefore, change of individual deviance likewise would entail desocialization, removal from group support, and resocialization.

Culture Conflict

The final theoretical tradition to be considered as a part of the socialization approach is culture conflict. Like cultural transmission and the works following Merton in the anomie tradition, culture conflict theory was developed specifically to explain crime and delinquency. Thorsten Sellin's theory of crime in 1938 was the first prominent statement of the culture conflict thesis.[26] To the culture conflict theorist behavior patterns of all forms are learned within distinct cultural groups. But some behaviors become defined as criminal or deviant.

Behavior comes to be defined as deviant when (1) the distinct behavior of one group is regulated by the law or rules of another, (2) a person or a group moves into a culture with different conduct norms, or (3) when the borders of groups overlap so that each culture defines the behavior of the other in terms of its own laws and rules. Behavior patterns then are not deviant in the culture which generates them. They become deviant when measured by the standards of another culture. Perhaps the most prominent example of culture conflict theory in the past two decades can be attributed to Walter Miller.[27]

Miller

In 1958 Walter Miller formulated another influential theory of delinquent behavior. The theory emerges from Miller's analysis of gang delinquency in the lower-class culture. The primary thesis of Miller's theory is that the major motivation to "delinquent" behavior engaged in by members of lower-class corner groups involves a positive effort to achieve states, conditions, or qualities valued within their own significant culture. We may generalize this statement to include a more broadly conceived notion of deviant behavior. Then Miller's theory suggests that deviants are motivated to their misconduct by desires to achieve certain states, conditions, or qualities rewarded in their cultures. They learn, or are socialized to value, these cultured emphases.

Behaviors which bring on the culturally valued states or conditions are acceptable within the culture, but they may be defined as deviant by the larger, more dominant culture. The lower-class boys Miller studied were socialized in a habitat with standards and expectations that demanded certain characteristic behavior. The behavior was deviant because the moral and legal system reflected another more dominant value system, namely that of the middle and upper classes. To take an example, it is a value in the lower class for youths to be tough. In order to demonstrate toughness, lower-class youths may fight frequently and over small matters. The dominant middle-class value system defines fighting as generally undesirable. Behavior designed to achieve reward within the lower-class culture is reacted to as deviant by middle-class dominated institutions. The lower-class boy's behavior is deviant because it is designed to seek reward in one culture while being defined differently by another culture. The patterning of deviant behavior in Miller's theory follows directly from being socialized into the lower-class culture, which is an autonomous subculture that happens to be at variance with the dominant culture. Learning the ways and values of one's immediate significant culture explains both the emergence and the patterning of deviant behavior. This is the case because Miller's deviant internalizes and therefore is constantly motivated by the values of his culture. Much of the behavior a lower-class person patterns will be deviant because it will conflict with the more dominant value system. Miller's characterization of deviants tends to portray them as almost mindless of the existence of the dominant value system. Unlike Cohen's and Cloward and Ohlin's deviant, Miller's does not reject or react to the dominant system in patterning forms of deviance except insofar as they cope with and resist the police who patrol their territory.[28]

Considering how deviant behavior patterns change, we must infer what Miller's position would be. Miller implies a static view of personality which depicts the deviant as one committed to a way of life. Therefore, any successful change from deviant behavior patterns would first require specific desocializing efforts involving the devaluation of internalized values. In addition, removal of the deviant from the cultural milieu that supported deviant behavior would be essential to permanent change. Finally, the individual would have to be resocialized in terms of the values of the dominant culture.

Summary of the
Socialization Approach

Whatever the character of the general causes of rates of deviance in groups, the socialization approach views the internalization of values as the ultimate force causing deviant behavior in individuals. Values and beliefs favorable to deviance may be acquired two ways in socialization theories. First, they may be directly transmitted from the culture within which one is socialized or from differential association with persons and groups holding deviant values.[29] Second, values favorable to deviance may be induced precariously in malintegrated societies. That is, disorganized societies may give way to the development of values favoring deviance in the groups disadvantaged by it.[30] In the final analysis then, all the theories of this approach find internalized values responsible for both deviant behavior and deviant behavior patterns. Patterns of behavior are sometimes buttressed by positive group support and values which are, either normally (as in the works of Shaw and McKay, Sutherland, and Miller) or precariously become (as in the works of Cohen, and Cloward and Ohlin), a prominent part of the individual's character. Hence, deviant patterns are continued, justified, and rationalized by deviant persons. In each theory of the socialization approach, basic beliefs and, therefore, substantial parts of the personality structure must be changed in order to effect a change or disengagement from the behavior patterns of individuals. Further, it is implied that some form of therapeutic intervention, such as individual or group psychotherapy, is required to bring about the abandonment of beliefs favorable to deviance and the resultant deviant behavior and patterns.

Notes

1. Clifford R. Shaw, *The Natural History of a Delinquent Career* (Chicago: University of Chicago Press, 1931), p. 224.

2. Ibid., pp. 225–29.

3. Ibid.

4. Ibid., pp. 232–34; Clifford R. Shaw, *The Jack-Roller* (Chicago: University of Chicago Press, 1930), p. 183; Clifford R. Shaw, H. D. McKay, and J. F. McDonald, *Brothers in Crime* (Chicago: University of Chicago Press, 1938), pp. 340–49.

5. Shaw, *The Jack-Roller*, p. 183.

6. Edwin H. Sutherland and Donald R. Cressey, *Principles of Criminology* (Philadelphia: J. B. Lippincott, 1966), p. 85.

7. Ibid., p. 82. Cressey seems to consider "differential association" less well suited for explaining how a person becomes a criminal than for explaining the distribution of criminal behavior. See Donald R. Cressey, "Epidemiology and Individual Conduct" in *Delinquency, Crime, and Social Process,* ed. Donald R. Cressey and David A. Ward (New York: Harper & Row, 1969), p. 569.

8. See, for example, Shaw, *The Jack-Roller* and *Natural History,* Shaw, McKay, and McDonald, *Brothers in Crime;* Clifford R. Shaw and H. D. McKay, *Juvenile Delinquency in Urban Areas* (Chicago: University of Chicago Press, 1942); and Sutherland and Cressey, *Principles of Criminology.*

9. Edwin H. Sutherland, *The Professional Thief* (Chicago: University of Chicago Press, 1937).

10. Donald R. Cressey, "Changing Criminals: The Application of the Theory of Differential Association," *American Journal of Sociology* 61 (September 1955): 116–20. Also see Rita Volkman and Donald R. Cressey, "Differential Association and the Rehabilitation of Drug Addicts," *American Journal of Sociology* 69 (September 1963): 129–42.

11. In one conception, the condition of "anomie" frustrates the normal individual who has internalized the norms of his culture. Frustration then necessitates behavioral adaptations, some of which may be deviant. This is the basis of Robert Merton's "Social Structure and Anomie," *American Sociological Review* 3 (October 1938): 672–82; Albert K. Cohen's *Delinquent Boys: The Culture of the Gang* (New York: Free Press, 1955); and Richard Cloward and Lloyd Ohlin's *Delinquency and Opportunity: A Theory of Delinquent Gangs* (New York: Free Press, 1960) which are included here as part of the socialization approach. In the second conception, "anomie" is viewed as an obstruction to, or dislocation of, effective control norms. The result here is that the individual is more prone to deviant modes of behavior. Talcott Parsons' model of deviance in *The Social System* (New York: Free Press, 1951), pp. 249–325; H. Warren Dunham's "Anomie and Mental Disorder" in *Anomie and Deviant Behavior,* ed. Marshall B. Clinard (New York: Free Press, 1964), pp. 128–57; and Charles R. Snyder's *Alcohol and the Jews* (New York: Free Press, 1958) are examples of applications of this conception of anomie to forms of deviance. This latter conception of anomie also forms the basis for the works grouped into the control approach to deviance considered in chapter 4.

12. Merton, "Social Structure and Anomie."

13. Robert K. Merton, "Social Structure and Anomie," in *Social Theory and Social Structure* by Merton (New York: Free Press, 1968), p. 213. In a related work, Cloward and Ohlin's *Delinquency and Opportunity,* p. 118, the authors note that it is the "perception" rather than the realities of malintegration by the individual that prompts deviant behavior.

14. Merton, *Social Theory and Social Structure,* p. 177. For an interpretation of Merton's assumptions about the human actor see Marshall B. Clinard, ed., *Anomie and Deviant Behavior* (New York: Free Press, 1964), p. 31.

15. Cohen notes this several years after the publication of his book *Delinquent Boys.* See Albert K. Cohen, *Deviance and Control* (New York: Prentice-Hall, 1966), p. 107.

16. Cohen, *Delinquent Boys,* p. 28.

17. Cohen, *Deviance and Control,* p. 107.

18. Ibid., p. 108.

19. Ibid.

20. Cohen, *Delinquent Boys,* p. 69.

21. Cloward and Ohlin, *Delinquency and Opportunity,* p. 117.

22. Ibid.

23. Ibid., pp. 170–86.

24. Ibid., pp. 118–26.

25. Ibid., p. 211.

26. See Thorsten Sellin, *Culture, Conflict, and Crime* (New York: Social Science Research Council, 1938).

27. Walter Miller, "Lower Class Culture as a Generating Milieu of Gang Delinquency," *Journal of Social Issues* 14, no. 3 (1958) : 5–19.

28. David Matza, *Delinquency and Drift* (New York: John Wiley, 1964), p. 35.

29. This is the case for all the works cited for Clifford R. Shaw and H. D. McKay; for Sutherland and Cressey's *Principles of Criminology;* and for Miller's "Lower Class Culture as a Generating Milieu."

30. See Cohen, *Delinquent Boys,* and Cloward and Ohlin, *Delinquency and Opportunity.* Don C. Gibbons characterizes this process of developing deviant values as a by-product of "position discontent" in the Cloward and Ohlin formulation and as a by-product of "status discontent" in Cohen's theory. See "Observations on the Study of Crime Causation," *American Journal of Sociology* 77 (September 1971) : 262–78.

The
Societal
Reaction
Approach

3

Societal reaction theories are concerned with the effects negative social reactions have on individual behaviors and self-conceptions. Some important works in societal reaction theory are not covered here because they do not deal with the questions concerning the behavior patterns of deviant actors. These omitted works address the question of how people and behaviors come to be labeled deviant but not the effects of this process on the behavior and identity of individuals.[1] Nor do they address the questions dealing with the origins of behavior or the reasons patterns of deviant behavior develop and change. Each of the works included in this section addresses the patterning phase of deviant behavior directly, and in some works the consideration of emergence and change is implicit. When these phases are not implicit, as in the case of socialization theories, we have attempted to infer a picture of emergence and change that is consistent with the tenets of the theory under consideration.

The societal reaction thesis suggests that real deviance is primarily the result of acceptance of, and conformity to, negative expectations inherent in labels that are applied when one is reacted to as deviant. These theories began receiving wide attention in the 1960s. But when considered

retrospectively, it must be recognized that the social psychological aspects of the societal reaction thesis were clearly stated as
early as 1938 by Frank Tannenbaum.[2] Except for minor refine-
ments and qualifications, the major points of more recent theories are at least implicit in Tannenbaum's formulation. Edwin
H. Lemert's and Howard S. Becker's debt to Tannenbaum for
their later theories is as clear, if not as acknowledged, as that
of Cloward and Ohlin to Merton.[3] Erving Goffman, Thomas
Scheff, and Richard Quinney also have contributed significantly to the identification and explanation of negative social
reaction and its effects upon individual behavior.[4]

The societal reaction thesis has a more sporadic history than
the "internalized beliefs" thesis of the socialization approach.
Nevertheless, it will be seen that a persistent theme revolving
around the societal reaction process has bothered sociologists
of deviance for some time. Our discusussion begins with Tannenbaum and chronologically unfolds the development of the
societal reaction thesis in the works of its major proponents.

Tannenbaum

To Tannenbaum, the behaviors defined as deviant arise out of
the conflict between a group and the community at large. In
other words, individual behavior, while adjusted to a certain
group, may be rendered "maladjusted" to the larger society
because that group is at war with the larger society.[5] For the
children of such groups, behavior defined as deviant is mostly
random movement in a world with attitudes and organized
institutions that stamp and define their activities: "What one
learns to do, one does, if it is approved by the world in which
one lives."[6]

The patterning of deviant behavior follows a conflict over
values between the rule-breaker and the community where
there are two opposing definitions of the situation. To the rule-
breaker, in the beginning, the behaviors he has engaged in may
be acceptable, harmless, or of minor import. To the community, however, these behaviors may, and often do, take on the
form of nuisance, evil, or deviance, with a demand for control,
admonition, chastisement, or punishments.[7]

> As the problem develops, the situation gradually
> becomes redefined. The attitude of the community
> hardens definitely into a demand for supression. There is
> a *gradual shift* from the definition of the specific acts as
> evil *to a definition of the individual as evil*, so that all

his acts come to be looked upon with suspicion. In the process of identification his companions, hang-outs, play, speech, ... all his conduct, the personality itself, becomes subject to scrutiny and question. From the community's point of view, the individual who used to do bad and mischievous things has now become a bad and unredeemable human being. From the individual's point of view there has taken place a similar change. He has gone slowly from a sense of grievance and injustice, of being unduly mistreated and punished, to a *recognition that the definition of him as a human being is different* from that of other boys in his neighborhood, his school, street, community. *This recognition on his part becomes a process of self-identification and integration with the group which shares his activities.* It becomes, in part a process of rationalization; in part, a simple response to a specialized type of stimulus. *The young delinquent becomes bad because he is defined as bad and because he is not believed if he is good. There is a persistent demand for consistency* in character.[8] (Italics added)

All of this comes about through the "dramatization of evil," clearly the most frequently cited and probably the most important portion of Tannenbaum's book. In brief, this excerpt from Tannenbaum represents an important antecedent to the societal reaction theories which followed in the next three decades. In the following statement Tannenbaum emphasizes the role of societal reaction or, as he calls it, "tagging" in the making of the patterned and career deviant.

The first dramatization of the "evil" which separates the child out of his group for specialized treatment plays a greater role in making the criminal than perhaps any other experience. It cannot be too often emphasized that for the child the whole situation has become different. A new and hitherto non-existent environment has been precipitated out for him.

This process of making the criminal, therefore, is a process of *tagging,* defining, identifying, segregating, describing, emphasizing, making conscious and self-conscious; it becomes a way of stimulating, suggesting, emphasizing, and evoking the very traits that are complained of. If the theory of relation of response to stimulus has any meaning, the entire process of dealing with the young delinquent is mischievous in so

far as it identifies him to himself or to the environment
as a delinquent person.

The person becomes the thing he is described as being.
Nor does it seem to matter whether the valuation is
made by those who would punish or by those who would
reform.[9]

Generalizing from Tannenbaum's views of criminal patterns
and careers to deviance as a broad category, it is clear that the
"tagging," or societal reaction, process is the major force in
affixing deviant patterns and self-conceptions. In similar fash-
ion the agents and agencies of enforcement, punishment, and
reform lend to the continuing development of individual deviance. This is the case because, as Tannenbaum states, "the
emphasis is upon the conduct disapproved of."[10] The very en-
thusiasm of these efforts defeats their aim. "The harder they
work to reform evil, the greater the evil grows under their
hands. The persistent suggestion, with whatever good intentions, works mischief, because it leads to bringing out the bad
behavior that it would suppress."[11] Tannenbaum also suggests
a way to alleviate this problem: "The way out is through a
refusal to dramatize the evil. The less said about it the better.
The more said about something else—still better."[12]

It can be inferred from Tannenbaum that the way to change
deviant behavior patterns is to de-emphasize the deviant quality of the individual and his behavior.[13] Moreover, Tannenbaum suggests that there should be a marked emphasis on the
conforming behavior of individuals. Dramatizing of the evil
tends to precipitate circumstances of isolation which, in turn,
force the individual into companionship with the similarly defined, thus providing a means of escape and security. If this
occurs, the problem of change is more problematic—it now
involves the social world of deviants.[14] Therefore, de-empha-
sizing deviance and reconfirming the usual good behavior of
individuals stands a better chance of inducing conformity in
subsequent behavior than emphasizing the negative, serious,
and dangerous components of one's momentary deviance.

Lemert

After Tannenbaum, the next significant contribution to societal reaction theory was Edwin Lemert's *Social Pathology.*
This work was not recognized widely as an important contribution to sociology and to the development of the societal reaction

orientation until the mid-1960s. To Lemert the original causes or antecedents of initial deviant behavior are many and diverse.[15] These causes may be grouped in three major categories: (1) the social; (2) the cultural; and (3) the psychological.[16] For example, sometimes deviant behavior is "a product of differentiating and isolating processes" where the individual's deviant behaviors and status as a deviant "... [are] caused by his maturation within the framework of a social organization and culture designated as 'pathological' by the larger society."[17] This sort of unconscious process in socialization operates throughout the individual's life-history. Organic irregularities constitute a second source of deviation. A third source of deviation "results from the special way in which social and cultural influences impinge upon and interact with normal hereditary qualities of the person. Often this type of deviation is symptomatic of deep-lying intrapsychic conflicts or arises out of conflicts over major role identifications."[18] Even this psychologically induced deviation, which assumes an integrity and momentum of its own, has its origin in social and cultural contexts. Finally, Lemert points out that:

> Situations have a compelling force and may cause persons to transgress rules of conduct to which they have rigidly adhered in the past and which presumably have been incorporated as part of their personality structures.[19]

It is clear from this that Lemert generally views social and cultural forces as the primary source of social deviation including psychologically symptomatic deviation.

Lemert's work is most widely known for the conceptual distinction made between primary and secondary deviance. These definitional concepts are particularly germane to this study in that they represent roughly the distinction made in chapter 6 between primary emergence and secondary emergence as two focal areas of explanation. To Lemert deviations are not significant, from a sociological viewpoint, "... until they are organized subjectively and transformed into active roles and become the social criteria for assigning status. The deviant individuals must react symbolically to their own behavior aberrations and fix them in their socio-psychological patterns."[20]

Primary deviance in other words has only marginal implications for the psychic structure of the individual, since it does not lead to symbolic reorganization at the level of self-regarding attitudes and social roles.[21] As a result of the overt or covert problems created by consequent societal reaction to his primary deviance, a person begins to employ his deviant behavior or a role based upon it as a means of defense, attack, or adjustment. This is secondary deviation.[22] The development of secondary deviation usually follows a sequence of interaction along the approximate lines:

> ... (1) primary deviation; (2) social penalties; (3) further primary deviation; (4) stronger penalties and rejections; (5) further deviation, perhaps with hostilities and resentment beginning to focus upon those doing the penalizing; (6) crisis reached in the tolerance quotient, expressed in formal action by the community stigmatizing the deviant; (7) strengthening of the deviant conduct as a reaction to the stigmatizing and penalties; (8) ultimate acceptance of deviant social status and efforts at adjustment on the basis of the association role.[23]

Lemert presents an example of how primary deviation may eventuate in secondary deviation which is produced as a result of social reaction.

> As an illustration of this sequence the behavior of an errant schoolboy can be cited. For one reason or another, let us say excessive energy, the schoolboy engages in a class-room prank. He is penalized for it by the teacher. Later, due to clumsiness, he creates another disturbance and, again he is reprimanded. Then, as sometimes happens, the boy is blamed for something he did not do. When the teacher uses the *tag* "bad boy" or "mischief maker" or other invidious terms, hostility and resentment are excited in the boy, and he may feel that he is *blocked in playing the role expected of him. Thereafter, there may be a strong temptation to assume his role in the class as defined by the teacher,* particularly when he discovers that there are rewards as well as penalties deriving from such a role.[24] (Italics added)

It is important to point out here that there must be a spreading corroboration of a sociopathic or deviant self-conception and social reinforcement at each step in the process.[25] That is to say, an increase in one's deviant self-conception is dependent upon an increase in, or a hardening of, negative social reaction.

With regard to change, Lemert leaves us with both the problems characteristic of the socialization theories, as noted in chapter 2, and the unique problem of the societal reactionist—how to reduce the effect of unofficial and official negative reaction inherent in informal treatment and in legal and professional processing by control agencies.[26] Lemert's model of personality has both static and processual (or dynamic) components.[27] The structured part of the personality requires the type of intervention typical of the socialization theorist to effect change in, or abandonment of, patterned deviant behavior. In addition, the major societal reaction problem of neutralizing the effect of the unplanned imposition of stigmatizing and degrading symbols in control situations must likewise be eliminated. These latter processes give unintended but critical meaning to deviant conduct that, in many instances, is the cause of dramatic redefinitions of the self in undesirable directions.[28] Abandonment of specific patterns of behavior, then, must be preceded by change in the personality structure as well as elimination of stigmatizing social labels.

Becker

Howard S. Becker's *Outsiders* is often credited with sparking the popularity and increased attention given to the societal reaction perspective in the study of social deviance. While this is most probably the case, it is important to note that Becker's formulation is primarily a restatement of ideas firmly laid by Tannenbaum and Lemert.

The question of emergence, to Becker, follows and is important only after one explains the question as to how the person comes to be in a situation where deviance, of a particular type, is available to the actor.[29] Then the question of the causes of one's "willingness" to engage in the behavior may be asked.

Becker assumes that most people frequently experience impulses to engage in behavior in violation of the rules.[30] By contrast, the socialization theorist assumes that only those prone to become patterned deviants have such impulses. The individual who chooses not to pursue the deviant impulse is "able to check that impulse by thinking of the manifold consequences action on it would produce for him."[31] Conventionally defined persons, for example, must not indulge their interests in deviant behavior because much more than the pursuit of immediate pleasure is involved; their job, their family, and their reputation may seem to depend on their continuing to avoid temptation. Becker's position implies that those who are in possession of conventional (or nonrule-breaker type) definitions are constrained by these definitions and the fear of losing them. The negative proposition derived from this is that deviant behavior is more likely to emerge (1) in those cases where the individual either possesses so few, weak, or unimportant conventional definitions as to be nonconstraining or (2) in cases where the individual is already defined negatively in enough ways as to induce a self-fulfilling prophecy—"I will do what others expect me to do." If this sort of extrapolation is permitted, we see that Becker's theory, like Lemert's, implies the feasibility of explaining primary deviance as a result of negative inducements through societal reaction processes. That is, persons inheriting negative labels (such as those in the lowest socioeconomic groups) may behave deviantly in conformity to the prevailing expectations that they cannot do otherwise.[32]

Explicitly, however, Becker assumes that deviant behavior may emerge in only two ways. First, as a result of the individual never having become entangled in alliances with conventional society:

> He may, thus, be free to follow his impulses. The person
> who does not have a reputation to maintain or a
> conventional job he must keep may follow his impulses.
> He has nothing staked on continuing to appear
> conventional.[33]

Second, since most people are sensitive to conventional codes of conduct, they must deal with their sensitivities in order to engage in the rule-breaking act for the first time. Thus, the individual rationally neutralizes these sensitivities by providing valid (to the individual, at least) justifications for the behavior.[34]

One aspect of the way initial forms of behavior become patterned is through the learning of motives and interests in the course of interaction with more experienced deviants.[35] This process is elaborated in detail in Becker's frequently cited study "Becoming a Marihauana User."[36] Nevertheless, one of the most crucial steps in the process of patterning rule-breaking behavior is likely to be the experience of being caught and publicly labeled as a deviant. Whether the individual continues in deviant behavior "depends, not so much on what he does, as on what other people do, on whether or not they enforce the rule he has violated."[37] If there is a social response to the individual, "being caught and branded has important consequences for one's further social participation and one's self-image."[38] Social response operates to generalize the symbolic value of the initial act, so that "people automatically assume" that the individual possesses other undesirable attributes associated with the deviant act. In other words, recognition of the initial deviant act evokes the application of a *master status* which proves to be more important than other statuses. One will then be identified as a deviant first before other identifications are made. As Becker says:

> Treating a person as though he were generally rather than specifically deviant produces a self-fulfilling prophecy. It sets in motion several mechanisms which conspire to shape the person in the image people have of him.[39]

When the individual is then cut off from participation in conventional groups, he "finds it difficult to conform to other rules which he had no intention or desire to break, and perforce finds himself deviant in these areas as well."[40] Furthermore when "the deviant is caught, he is treated in accordance with the popular diagnosis of why he is that way, and the treatment itself may likewise produce increasing deviance."[41] Hence, the application of a generalized deviant label (or what Becker calls a master status) in the process of interaction pushes the individual into a position where only deviant acts are acceptable or where further deviance alone fulfills expectations. At this point the individual may find it comfortable to join a deviant group. If this occurs, deviant activity may be rewarded and routinized, and the individual may develop a deviant identity.

In summary, Becker understands deviance as passing through four states: (1) situation of availability; (2) the initial act; (3) continuance of the behavior; and (4) formation of a deviant career where the individual moves into a deviant group and cuts ties and identifications with the conventional world.[42]

Change or abandonment of behavior patterns, for Becker, may occur rationally at any stage in the process of development but most easily at the beginning stages. Career deviants may find that after change of their behavior people still treat them as though they were deviants. This leaves the individual with the final choice, to pursue a deviant career as a result of continued negative reaction or to maintain the change to conventional patterns in spite of the unaccepting reactions.

Goffman

Perhaps the most penetrating analyses of social reaction processes have been done by Erving Goffman. His writings are among the most important in modern sociology. But looking at Goffman's work for explanations of emergence, patterning, and change reveals few firm statements of position and leaves much to be inferred.[43] For instance, Goffman does not directly address the problem of initial cause, but it may be inferred that he generally recognizes four main sources from which primary behavior arises: situational determinants, cultural determinants, identity building, and stress.[44] The following excerpt suggests that the situation of the individual often renders even bizarre behavior, such as that symptomatic of mental illness, understandable in terms of rational and normal psychological adjustment:

> ... the craziness or "sick behavior" claimed for the
> mental patient is by and large a product of the
> claimant's [labeler's] social distance from the situation
> that the patient is in, and is not primarily a product of
> mental illness.[45]

Regarding cultural determinants, Goffman notes that some initial behavior, specifically symptomatic of mental illness but generalized here to apply to all deviance, is a product of compliance to the norms of a subculture that is already judged deviant for ethnocentric or political reasons.

> Ordinarily the pathology which first draws attention to
> the patient's condition is conduct that is "inappropriate
> in the situation." But the decision as to whether a given

act is appropriate or inappropriate must often necessarily be a lay decision, simply because we have no technical mapping of the various behavioral subcultures in our society, let alone the standards of conduct prevailing in each of them. Diagnostic decisions, except for extreme symptoms, can become *ethnocentric*, the server judging from his own culture's point of view individuals' conduct that can really be judged only from the perspective of the group from which they derive. Further, since inappropriate behavior is typically behavior that someone does not like and finds extremely troublesome, decisions concerning it tend to be *political*, in the sense of expressing the special interests of some particular faction or person rather than interests that can be said to be above the concerns of any particular grouping, ...[46] (Italics added)

Goffman also suggests that initial deviance might be a natural product of attempts to claim a certain sort of identity or character in some social settings.[47] A youth in an area of high rates of gang delinquency may steal or fight in ways involving high risks and danger in order to gain a favorable identity as an emerging delinquent.[48] The action is willful and is perceived as a reflection of character.

Finally, in an attempt to qualify the static view of personality, Goffman suggests that the initial cause of symptomatic mental illness is sometimes merely a result of temporary emotional upset in a stressful situation.[49] Even gross symptoms psychiatrically judged as pathological are, in some instances, transitory results of stress situations, not upsurges in a defectively structured personality.

Like Tannenbaum, and Lemert before him, Goffman regards the beginning of deviant behavior, in a significant sense, as separated from similar behaviors which have not been labeled, as occurring when "some *complainant*, some figure . . . takes action against the offender."[50] If this action turns out to be an effective move, the crucial factor in the patterning of deviant behavior has occurred, because this is the social beginning of the person's career regardless of where one might locate the psychological beginning.[51] That is to say, regardless of the origins of a form of behavior, or specific symptomatic attributes of it, the important factors determining the course of an individual's behavior and self-concept are a part of the societal reaction process. An effective social reaction serves not only to evoke continuance of certain forms of behavior but also to precipitate changes in one's self-concept. The form that changes in behavior and self-conceptions will take "is based on culturally derived and socially ingrained stereotypes."[52] In other words, these changes in behavior and self-concept will fit other socially meaningful categories—deviant categories.

Discussing how professionals and officials, but generalized here to other labelers, contribute to a process by which individuals are defined as, and subsequently become, deviant, Goffman says:

> I am suggesting that the patient's nature is redefined so
> that, in effect if not by intention, the patient becomes the
> kind of object upon which a psychiatric service can be
> performed. So to be made a patient is to be *remade* . . . .[53]
> (Italics added)

Stated generally, as a result of societal reaction individual rule-breakers are redefined to the extent that they often become the kind of deviant they are defined as being. Goffman clearly believes that often the effect of imposed negative definitions by high-ranking labelers "requires" the person to take the same view of himself.[54] Goffman's discussion of the effects of being treated as a mental patient serves as an extreme example of the potential power he accords societal reaction processes.

> Persons who become mental-hospital patients vary
> widely in the kind and degree of illness that a
> psychiatrist would impute to them, and in the attributes
> by which laymen would describe them. But once started
> on the way, they are confronted by some importantly
> similar circumstances and respond to these in some
> importantly similar ways. Since these similarities do not
> come from mental illness, they would seem to occur in
> spite of it. It is thus a tribute to the power of social
> forces [societal reaction] that the uniform status of
> mental patient cannot only assure an aggregate of
> persons a common fate and eventually, because of this, a
> common character, but that this social reworking can be
> done upon what is perhaps the most obstinate diversity
> of human materials that can be brought together by
> society.[55]

True, this remaking and reworking of the character of individuals occurs in the mental institution where conditions are almost totally controlled but, nevertheless, Goffman is suggesting that uniformity of treatment can induce common patterns of response among groups containing the widest assortment of multiformities, those in an asylum. This is not to say that human fabric is so totally malleable as to allow infinite molding and remolding of essential character; rather, it seems Goffman is saying that the definition of the situation that prevails in mental hospitals and that may prevail elsewhere encourages similar rational, expedient, and expected responses from those who are inmates. Significantly similar responses are witnessed by inmates in other total institutions such as prisons, army training camps, monasteries, and "old folks" homes.[56]

Goffman's view of the patterned deviant, as portrayed here, is substantially a product of definitions imposed by empowered agents. The deviant, therefore, becomes what he is defined as being by force of circumstances when the negative social reaction is sustained in exclusion of contradictory definitions of the situation. When the single definition of the situation as deviant is disrupted, by conflicting definitions, behavior may change.[57] Thus, there are alternatives available to the individual in negotiating self-conceptions when more than one definition of the situation exists. The source of conflicting definitions may be in the variety of significant others, in the structured circumstances, or in one's self.

The ability to change is, for Goffman, ultimately located in the rational capacity and processual quality of the "self" as defined by Goffman. Therefore, given alternative definitions of one's "self" and that situational opportunities for playing non-deviant roles are available, the matter of change is largely a rational choice.

Scheff

Thomas Scheff's 1966 book, *Being Mentally Ill*, represents one of the most systematic theories within the societal reaction approach.[58] While specifically intended to explain some forms of mental illness, it is examined here as a general theory of deviance from a societal reaction perspective. Scheff views the emergence of initial deviant behaviors as having diverse sources: organic, psychological, external stress, or volitional acts of innovation or defiance.[59] These behaviors are relatively unimportant, however, since their rate is extremely high and since most such behavior is *denied;* that is, unrecognized, ignored, or rationalized in a patterned form of inattention by others.[60] In other words, everyone violates social rules and for various reasons, but these rule-breaking behaviors are usually routinely dismissed or *denied* in the course of interactions with others.[61]

Since rule-violating behavior is extremely prevalent among the "normal" population and is usually transitory, we must ask what accounts for the small proportion of individuals who go on to patterned deviance? Stated differently, what causes the initial rule-breaking behavior to become patterned? To Scheff the most important single factor in the patterning of deviant behavior is the societal reaction.

The process of patterning of rule-breaking may follow if there is a crisis in which the deviance of an individual becomes a public issue.[62] If either the rule-breaking or the circumstances surrounding it evoke a readiness to act on the part of others, a crisis has developed. Then the traditional stereotypes of any particular form of deviance become the guiding imagery for action, both for those reacting to the deviant and, at times, for the deviant actor. Therefore, when enforcement agents and others around the deviant react in uniform ways, in terms of these traditional stereotypes, what was originally amorphous and unstructured rule-breaking tends to crystallize in conformity to these expectations. The deviant's behavior becomes similar to the behavior of other deviants classified in the same categories, and stable over time.[63]

When publicly labeled, a rule-breaker becomes highly *suggestible* (psychologically receptive) and may accept the proffered role of a particular kind of deviant as the only alternative.[64] The deviant role or label operates at two levels. At first labeling merely gives a name to rule-breaking or fits behavior into commonly understood categories. If the behavior becomes an issue, and is not ignored or rationalized away, continued labeling may create a pattern of behavior in conformity with the stereotyped expectations of others. To the extent that the deviant role becomes a part of the deviant's self-conception, the ability of the individual to act in nonexpected ways may be impaired under stress, resulting in behaviors conforming to common stereotypes.[65]

The deviant individual assumed by Scheff is the product of labeling processes which (1) fit the behavior into a public stereotype, (2) render the individual psychologically receptive to the deviant role proffered by the reactors, and (3) finally force conformity to the expectations of others to be deviant in stereotypic ways. Societal reaction is not regarded as the only cause of patterned deviant behavior but, to Scheff, it is regarded as the single most important cause.[66]

Critics often ask what determines how long and how severe the negative societal reaction will be. Scheff identifies seven variables which have an effect upon societal reactions to rule-breakers: (1) the *degree* of rule-breaking; (2) the *amount* of rule-breaking; (3) the *visibility* of rule-breaking; (4) the *relative power* of the rule-breaker as compared to the reactors; (5) the *social distance* between the rule-breaker and the reactors; (6) the *community tolerance level* for rule-breaking; and (7) the degree of *availability in one's group or culture of nondeviant roles* to play.[67] If all, or some combination, of these factors stack up negatively around a given actor's rule-breaking, societal reaction can be predicted. However, there is no established equation to suggest the precise number or combination of these contingencies necessary to evoke a societal reaction.

The critics' interest is probably misdirected because it is not the absolute number, intensity, or combination of these contingencies that influences social reaction and ultimately personal identities. Rather, it is the way these contingencies form a part of an interactional system and influence the behavior of both the actor and the reactors that organizes their causal power. As Scheff says:

> ... These contingencies are causal only because they
> become part of a dynamic system: the reciprocal and
> cumulative inter-relation between the rule-breaker's
> behavior and the societal reaction. For example, the
> more the rule-breaker enters the role of the [deviant], the
> more he is defined as [deviant]; but the more he is
> defined as [deviant], the more fully he enters the role,
> and so on.[68]

At each stage in the action-reaction process the aforementioned variables or contingencies play a prominent part, influencing the shape and intensity of the responses of both the deviant and the definers.

While the path to stablized deviant behavior patterns is the result of a dynamic process for Scheff, the factors contributing to patterned deviance seem almost deterministic. That is, once the process of labeling is in motion the effects are to produce deviance and in a way that the deviant personality becomes fixed. If the social contingencies all stack up the wrong way, the individual's role behavior is predominantly *determined* by the stereotyped role expectations of others. The individual's conformity to these expectations is involuntary and the accompanying personality change is firmly implanted.

Change or abandonment of behavior patterns taken on by necessity would, because of Scheff's conception of an involuntary actor, require a positive reverse of the labeling process which produced the patterned deviance. Such a positive labeling process would involve replacing negative reactions and stereotypic deviant definitions of the individual with positive reactions and definitions of character. This is not too unlike what was earlier referred to as "resocialization" as an implied mechanism for change in the socialization view. A basic difference between the two views of change is related to the processual model of personality posited by Scheff and other societal reactionists, making change somewhat easier than is the case for the static model of personality, assumed by socialization theorists. The latter requires some sort of therapeutic intervention to break down the deviant personality structure prior to the building of a new one. Changing negative to positive reactions would not need to be done under therapeutic circumstances to change Scheff's deviant.

Quinney

Richard Quinney's theory of the social reality of crime represents a more recent and somewhat different version of the societal reaction orientation.[69] To Quinney, the conception of crime, the formulation and application of laws, and the changing nature of crime is the product of a highly integrated social and legal process. We may extend his views here to apply to deviance in general.

The content of any rule-breaking behavior to Quinny is learned in the normative systems of certain social and cultural settings.[70] While the content of social action differs greatly for people in a heterogeneous society, it all represents the behavior patterns of certain segments of that society.[71] Within the context of a segmentally organized society, the individual learns a variety of group and individual action patterns. The general content of social behavior is shaped in these social and cultural settings, but individual actions are ultimately the result of personal rational choice.[72]

In essence, the individual "learns about" his social world rather than "learning it" in the sense that it directs his behavior. That is, the person learns about different forms of conduct but this learning does not compel him to behave in any specific way. To Quinney, human behavior is intentional, in pursuit of selected goals, and engaged in with an awareness of the possible consequences of the choices made as compared to alternative behaviors.[73] Both the sociocultural settings and the reactions of other persons influence the continuing behavior of the individual.

During the interactions between those empowered to define deviants and those defined as deviant, the latter may develop deviant action patterns partly because they are negatively defined.[74] More specifically, the person may develop a way or pattern of behaving, including a supporting style of life, and a self-conception that takes its reference from the deviant definitions implied in negative social reaction.[75] These patterns continually develop as the deviant moves from one experience to another. It is the development of these patterns that gives the deviant's behavior its own substance in relation to the negative definitions. That is, the deviant constructs individual action patterns (1) while participating with others in particular social and cultural structures and (2) as a result of the reactions of others to individual behaviors.

The patterning of deviant behavior, then, depends in part on the substance (deviant or nondeviant) of (1) structured opportunities, (2) learning experiences, (3) interpersonal associations and identifications and, in part, on the continued experience of being defined as deviant and thus succumbing to deviant self-concepts.[76] Quinney, like other societal reaction theorists, implies the greater importance of social reaction processes over structural inducements in the development of deviant behavior patterns, although the influence of the latter is not ignored.

> ... those who have been defined as criminal begin to conceive of themselves as criminal as they adjust to the definitions imposed upon them, they learn to play the role of the criminal. Because of others' reactions, therefore, persons may develop personal action patterns that increase the likelihood of their being defined as criminal in the future. That is, *increased experience*

with criminal definitions increases the probability of developing actions that may be subsequently defined as criminal. (Quinney's italics)

Thus, both the criminal definers and the criminally defined are involved in reciprocal action patterns. *The patterns of both the definers and the defined are shaped by their common, continued, and related experiences. The fate of each is bound to that of the other.*[77] (Italics added)

Regarding change, three possibilities emerge from Quinney's work. First, it might be suggested from the statement above that change in the behavior of the criminally defined implies a prior change in the activities of the definers. Confounding this problem, however, is the point that the opposite would also have to be true—to change the definitions the deviant must first change. It is logically possible, of course, for either the defined or the definers to begin the process. But the abandonment of deviant behavior patterns, at one level of analysis, seems to imply the reverse of the process through which they were developed. That is, a gradual redefinition process where a slight change for the positive in one (say the deviant's behavior) would bring about a slight positive change in the other (in this case, the negative feelings on the part of the definers); to further induce change in the former, and so on, until the deviant behavior patterns and negative definitions disappear.

It must be remembered, as a second possibility, that Quinney's model of social action is voluntaristic. This adds another level of analysis and an unpredictable dimension to the consideration of change. A view of change, inferred from Quinney, yields the following possibilities. The deviant may well respond positively to positive changes in definition. Equally plausible is the possibility that the deviant would, for whatever reasons, elect to remain a deviant in spite of positive definitions from others. For example, one reason for not responding to positive social reactions would be that the benefits of deviance may be worth the costs of deviant status. Or a third and final possibility is that the deviant may decide to change or disengage from behavior patterns and self-conceptions in spite of the deviant stigma expressed in the reactions of others.[78]

Summary of the Societal
Reaction Approach

The theme of this approach centers around the societal reaction process. As it is the internalization of beliefs (whether normally or precariously derived) which ultimately shapes deviant behavior patterns in the socialization approach, it is the societal reaction process which precipitates and shapes patterns of deviant behavior in the societal reaction approach. The crucial factors, for societal reaction theorists, in the explanation of patterned deviance revolve around the application of deviant labels and their effects on individual behavior patterns and self-conceptions. The source, severity, persistence, and exclusiveness (in terms of how widely the label is applied in the individual's circles of associations and contacts) of the societal reaction determine the effectiveness of bringing on conformity to the expectations inherent in the label.

There is considerable diversity in this approach regarding the degree of voluntarism involved in the individual's conformity to deviant role expectations. In both Scheff's and Lemert's versions of societal reaction, for example, the involuntary aspects of role-playing are strongly emphasized. The other works of this orientation presume a more conscious, calculated and purposive quality with regard to behaviors in conformity to applied deviant labels.

In summary, it is the view of these theorists that whatever the origin of first instances of deviant behavior, its patterning is more a result of societal reaction processes than any other set of factors. In addition, for purposes of testing alternative themes in societal reaction theories against those in the socialization approach, a general proposition explaining emergence and change of deviant behavior was proposed. Change or abandonment of deviant behavior patterns was shown to entail a calculated choice possible within the limits of alternatives blocked by labeling processes. That is, one may disengage from deviant behavior patterns if the labeling processes have not precluded all nondeviant alternatives. A theory of the emergence of deviant behavior was shown to be implicit, although grossly underdeveloped, in the works of some societal reactionists such as Lemert, Goffman, and Becker. Initial acts of deviant behavior emerge as a result of conformity to expectations inherent in ascriptive labels attached to certain individuals negatively differentiated from the definers.

Notes

1. The particular works omitted are Austin T. Turk, *Criminality and Legal Order* (Chicago: Rand McNally, 1969); Kai T. Erikson, *Wayward Puritans: A Study in the Sociology of Deviance* (New York: John Wiley, 1966); and Thomas S. Szasz, *The Myth of Mental Illness* (New York: Harper & Row, 1961). These works represent a structural as opposed to a social psychological approach to societal reaction theory. All of the works included in this chapter depart from a social psychological perspective.

2. Frank Tannenbaum, *Crime and the Community* (New York: Ginn, 1938), pp. 1–33.

3. See Edwin H. Lemert, *Social Pathology* (New York: McGraw-Hill, 1951), pp. 1–98, and Howard S. Becker, *Outsiders: Studies in the Sociology of Deviance* (New York: Free Press, 1963).

4. Erving Goffman, *Asylums: Essays on the Social Situation of Mental Patients and Other Inmates* (New York: Doubleday, 1961); Thomas J. Scheff, *Being Mentally Ill: A Sociological Theory* (Chicago: Aldine, 1966); Richard Quinney, *The Social Reality of Crime* (Boston: Little, Brown, 1970).

5. Tannenbaum, *Crime and the Community*, pp. 8–9. Material adapted from this work for the following discussion is used by permission of Columbia University Press. In definitional consideration of deviance Tannenbaum's position is essentially the same as the culture conflict theorists, see Miller, "Lower Class Culture as a Generating Milieu of Gang Delinquincy," *Journal of Social Issues* 14, no. 3 (1958): 5–19; and Thorsten Sellin, *Culture, Conflict and Crime* (New York: Social Science Research Council, 1938).

6. Tannenbaum, *Crime and the Community*, p. 11.

7. Ibid., pp. 17–18.

8. Ibid. Used by permission of Columbia University Press.

9. Ibid., pp. 19–20. Used by permission of Columbia University Press.

10. Ibid., p. 20.

11. Ibid. A markedly similar view is found in George Herbert Mead's "The Psychology of Punitive Justice," *American Journal of Sociology* 23 (1917–1918): 577–602.

12. Tannenbaum, ibid.

13. This de-emphasis of deviant behavior while emphasizing the usual conforming behavior of the individual is a common everyday practice. Thomas Scheff referred to it as "denial" which means that observers frequently refuse to recognize rule-breaking as deviance for some people and circumstances. See Scheff, *Being Mentally Ill*, pp. 80–83. Walter R. Gove later called the same process "normalization." See his "Societal Reaction as an Explanation of Mental Illness: An Evaluation," *American Sociological Review* 35 (October 1970): 873–84.

14. Tannenbaum, *Crime and the Community*, pp. 20–21.

15. Lemert, *Social Pathology*, p. 75.

16. Ibid., p. 17.

17. Ibid., p. 73. Used by permission of McGraw-Hill Book Company. This is essentially the culture conflict idea as espoused by Miller and Sellin.

18. Ibid., p. 37. Used by permission.

19. Ibid., pp. 37–38. Used by permission.

20. Ibid., p. 75. Used by permission.

21. Ibid., p. 17.

22. Ibid., p. 76.

23. Ibid., p. 77. Used by permission.

24. Ibid. Used by permission. The term "tag" was first employed by Tannenbaum (1938) and has exactly the same meaning as "label" has in the work of Becker (1963); Scheff (1966); and Quinney (1970).

25. Lemert, *Social Pathology*, p. 77.

26. Ibid., pp. 70–71.

27. Ibid., p. 23.

28. Ibid., pp. 70–71.

29. Becker, *Outsiders*, p. 23. Material adapted from this work for the following discussion is used by permission of the Macmillan Company.

30. Ibid., p. 26.

31. Ibid., p. 27.

32. The potential of negative pre-labeling as an explanation of primary deviance has been suggested by Charles E. Frazier and Thomas D. McDonald, "Societal Reaction Theory: Postulates and Their Evaluation" in *Alternative Structures and Values*, ed. Swaran S. Sandhu (Moorhead, Minn.: Moorhead State College, 1973), pp. 49–60; Edwin M. Schur, *Labeling Deviant Behavior* (New York: Harper & Row, 1971); and Robert K. Merton, *Social Structure and Social Theory*, rev. ed. (New York: Free Press, 1957), pp. 421–36. Also, Milton Mankoff's conceptualization of "ascribed rule-breaking" may be expanded to include a general tendency to pre-label in social relationships. See his "Societal Reaction and Career Deviance: A Critical Analysis," *The Sociological Quarterly* 12 (Spring 1971): 204–18.

33. Becker, *Outsiders*, p. 28. Used by permission. This position is discussed more fully by Jackson Toby, "Social Disorganization and Stake in Conformity: Complimentary Factors in the Predatory Behavior of Hoodlums," *Journal of Criminal Law, Criminology and Police Science* 48 (1957): 12–17.

34. Becker, *Outsiders*, p. 28. See also Gresham Sykes and David Matza, "Techniques of Neutralization: A Theory of Delinquency," *American Sociological Review* 22 (December 1957): 667–69, for an elaboration of several techniques of neutralizing commitments to conventional norms.

35. Becker, *Outsiders*, p. 30.

36. Ibid., pp. 41–58. Originally published in the *American Journal of Sociology* 9 (November 1953): 235–42.

37. Ibid., p. 31. Used by permission. While the most crucial factor in the patterning process, to Becker, is "societal reaction" (the response of others to the rule-breaker) he admits (1) that even if there is no societal reaction the individual may label himself ("act himself, as the enforcer") and (2) that there may be cases like those described by psychoanalysts in which the individual really wants to get caught and perpetuates, or patterns, his deviant behavior in such a way as to almost assure that he is caught.

38. Ibid., pp. 31–32. Used by permission.

39. Ibid., p. 34. Used by permission.

40. Ibid. Used by permission.

41. Ibid. Used by permission.

42. Ibid., p. 42.

43. Erving Goffman, *Asylums; The Presentation of Self in Everyday Life* (New York: Doubleday, 1959); *Stigma: Notes on the Management of Spoiled Identity* (Englewood Cliffs, N.J.: Prentice-Hall, 1963); and "Where the Action Is," in *Interaction Ritual,* by Goffman (New York: Doubleday, 1967), pp. 149–270.

44. For some other cases Goffman concedes the plausibility of personality defect as a partial explanation of primary deviant behavior. See his *Asylums,* p. 363; "The Moral Career of the Mental Patient," *Psychiatry* 22 (1959): 124; and *The Presentation of Self,* p. 77. There are also behavior categories explicitly noted by Goffman that are created by students of behavior and then studied by them. See *Stigma,* p. 140. Initial deviance is, in still other instances, the result of a person's inability to meet the prescriptions of norms due to physical or social attributes. The person's deviance, then, is based on his "condition not his will, on conformance not compliance." See *Stigma,* p. 128.

45. Goffman, "Moral Career," p. 124. Used by permission of the journal.

46. Goffman, *Asylums,* pp. 363–64. Used by permission of Doubleday & Company. Goffman notes in this work that the process he is exploring may be broadly applied to all forms of deviancy (pp. 319–20).

47. Goffman, "Where the Action Is," pp. 149–70.

48. Carl Werthman, "The Function of Social Definitions in the Development of Delinquent Careers," in President's Commission on Law Enforcement and Administration of Justice, *Task Force Report: Juvenile Delinquency and Youth Crime* (Washington, D.C.: Government Printing Office, 1967), pp. 155–70. Werthman's excellent analysis of gang delinquency using Goffman's conception of *action* was pointed out to the author by Bill Sanders.

49. Goffman, "Moral Career," p. 125.

50. Ibid., p. 126. Used by permission of the journal.

51. Ibid.

52. Change in self-conception and behavior may result from one's own perception of the offense and self-labeling as well as from overt societal reaction processes. See Goffman, "Moral Career," p. 125. Used by permission of the journal.

53. Goffman, *Asylums,* p. 379.

54. Ibid., p. 150.

55. Goffman, "Moral Career," p. 124. Used by permission of the journal.

56. Goffman, *Asylums,* pp. 1–125.

57. Goffman, *Presentation of Self in Everyday Life,* p. 254.

58. Scheff, *Being Mentally Ill.*

59. Ibid., p. 40.

60. Ibid., pp. 47–48. Material adapted from this work for the following discussion is used by permission of Aldine Publishing Company.

61. It must be noted here that Scheff is explicit in pointing out that the rule violations to which he refers are diverse kinds of violations for which culture provides no explicit label. As we have used it here, Scheff's "residual rule-breaking" is generalized, with this qualification, to include all rule-breaking. As in discussing previous theories, certain qualifications are ignored in order to infer more general propositions about deviance broadly conceived. See ibid., p. 34.

62. Ibid., p. 82.

63. Ibid.

64. Ibid., p. 88.

65. Ibid., p. 92.

66. Ibid., pp. 93–94.

67. Ibid., pp. 96–97.

68. Ibid., pp. 97–98. Used by permission.

69. An early statement of the theory of the social reality of crime was presented at the annual meeting of the American Sociological Association in 1968. The first revision appears in Jack Douglas, ed., *Crime and Justice in American Society* (Indianapolis: Bobbs-Merrill, 1970). The second revision, which is considered here, appears in Quinney's *The Social Reality of Crime* (Boston: Little, Brown, 1970).

70. Assumed within Quinney's theory is Sutherland's differential association theory. However, unlike Sutherland, Quinney does not assume the automatic internalization of a differentially represented set of values. The individual is capable of considering and engaging in other behaviors which break with the established normative system. This view assumes that once an awareness of self is gained by being a member of society, a person is able to choose actions in contrast to being propelled by internalized values. Adapted from Richard Quinney, *The Social Reality of Crime*, pp. 13–20. Copyright © 1970 by Little, Brown and Company (Inc.). Reprinted by permission of the publisher and the author.

71. Ibid., p. 207. Adapted with permission.

72. Ibid., p. 13. Adapted with permission .

73. Ibid., p. 14. Adapted with permission.

74. Ibid., p. 21. Adapted with permission.

75. Ibid., p. 274. Adapted with permission.

76. Ibid., p. 21. Adapted with permission.

77. From Richard Quinney, *The Social Reality of Crime*, pp. 21–22. Copyright © 1970 by Little, Brown and Company (Inc.). Reprinted by permission.

78. Adapted from Richard Quinney, *The Social Reality of Crime*, pp. 13, 14, 20, 207, 274. Copyright © 1970 by Little, Brown and Company (Inc.). Reprinted by permission.

Control
Theory

In modern control theory, deviance is not
caused, it is made possible. The possibility for
deviance results from the inability of societies
or groups to prevent its occurrence, that is, to
effect social control. While this theoretical
position is rooted in at least eighty years of
sociological history, it remains less well
delineated as a general approach to the study
of deviance than either the socialization or the
societal reaction framework.[1]

For present purposes, we are interested in
the formulations of sociologists who have
employed a control thesis to some form of
deviance. Six theorists are examined in the
following pages. They are Emile Durkheim,[2]
Albert Reiss, F. Ivan Nye, David Matza, Walter
Reckless, and Travis Hirschi. Their works are
concerned with three different forms of
deviance—suicide, crime, and delinquency.
They all agree, however, that when the hold
of societies and groups on individuals is
weakened, neutralized, or broken, deviance
results. This proposition was brilliantly
presented by Emile Durkheim in his classic
study of suicide, and most subsequent work in
the control tradition has been, to a large
extent, influenced by Durkheim. While his
influence is less emphatically acknowledged
presently among writers in the control
tradition than it is among some socialization

theorists, Durkheim's work is a clearer antecedent for control theory than Merton's classic "Social Structure and Anomie" and those who followed the conception of anomie presented by him. Both control theory and socialization theory of the Merton variety claim a basis in Durkheim's anomie theory. Still, the theoretical tradition started by Merton is called anomie while the theory more closely approximating the original Durkheimian conception of anomie is called control theory. This curious situation will be discussed in more detail later in this chapter.

The beauty of control theory, from Durkheim's conception of anomie onward, is that, essentially, it is as much a theory of conformity as it is a theory of deviance. Human action, under normal conditions of social organization, is seen to be regulated by social norms, and deviance is considered minimal precisely because behavior is regulated. But when the social organization is for some reason disrupted, the control force of norms is weakened or broken, leaving human beings unregulated and thereby free to deviate. This is the central idea underlying the theories of the control approach.

Durkheim

The background Durkheim developed for control theory centers around his consideration of anomie. Anomie is usually translated into English as normlessness, but it is best understood as a state of societal deregulation where norms are ineffective as sources of social control. This concept was first considered in the *Division of Labor in Society,* but Durkheim's analysis of it was only incidental and his consideration was limited to seeing anomie as an abnormal state of society.[3] A more deliberate and careful consideration of anomie came with Durkheim's classic study of suicide, published in 1897. The groundwork for modern control theory may be seen to be clearly elaborated in Durkheim's sociological interpretation of the data he collected for this study.

Durkheim concluded, in general terms, that variable qualities in the state of society itself are causally related to suicide rates. Variations in (1) the degree of social integration and (2) the extent to which society effects its moral authority on individuals are both used to explain fluctuations in rates of suicide. In the former instance, Durkheim found low rates of suicide in highly integrated religious, domestic, and political society.[4] It would be easy to explain this in religious societies if we consider that the special nature of religious sentiments may have a moderating influence on suicide. But Durkheim did not accept this specific explanation because the same reasoning could not be used to explain his general findings—since domestic and political societies, when they were strongly integrated, produced the same results.

Integration was ultimately the crucial variable used to explain general findings. The higher the degree of integration of social groups, the lower will be the rates of suicide.[5] Phrased negatively, when society is disintegrated, suicide rates are high because individuals become detached from social life. The more detached individuals are from social life, the more likely they are to recognize no social rules of conduct, and, in turn, the more likely is suicide. Durkheim's interpretation of this part of his data led him to call this type of suicide egoistic.

> Society cannot disintegrate without the individual simultaneously detaching himself from social life, without his own goals becoming preponderant over those of the community. . . . The more weakened the groups to which he belongs, the less he depends on them, the more he consequently depends only on himself and recognizes no other rules of conduct than what is founded in his private interests. If we agree to call this egoism, in which the individual ego asserts itself to excess in the face of the social ego and at its expense, we may call egoistic the special type of suicide springing from excessive individualism.[6]

In essence, Durkheim tells us that disintegrated groups cannot constrain individual conduct and that the more disintegrated the groups, the more likely the occurrence of deviance.

Another part of Durkheim's data led him to the problem of society's moral authority being ineffective as a control over individual behavior. Although similar to the problem of disintegration, this matter receives separate attention when Durkheim considers anomic suicide. Basically, he argued that suicide may occur in rates higher than the average over a long period of time if the discipline of socially given moral norms is broken down. This part of Durkheim's data indicated that variations in the rate of suicide were concomitant with the business cycle.[7] For example, states of economic panic and depression were accompanied by increases in suicide rates beyond the average rates over a long period of time. The data also showed that the suicide rate increased at times of unusual prosperity. While common logic offered an explanation for the relationship between economic depression and suicide, the tendency for suicides to increase in times of unusual prosperity defied this same common-sense reasoning. Why would a condition of prosperity produce higher suicide rates?

The explanation Durkheim offered was that in both conditions of economic depression and of unusual prosperity, large numbers of persons are thrown with relative suddenness out of adjustment with certain important features of their social environment.[8] Or put differently, society's moral authority in terms of its ability to regulate behavior was weakened or broken down, resulting in individual confusion, frustration, and a loss of a sense of security and orientation in knowing what the rules are. This state is called anomie by Durkheim, and it represents a much expanded version of his earlier use of the concept in the *Division of Labor in Society.* Under conditions of anomie, rates of suicide increase.

In broad terms, we may generalize Durkheim's proposition to all forms of deviance, using suicide as an extreme case. Durkheim argued that when unregulated by society's moral authority, individual behavior will be unlimited and will follow basic appetites and personal interests. Being unlimited, basic appetites and personal interests constantly surpass the means at an individual's command and, consequently, these desires cannot be quenched.[9] In this disorganized state, rates of deviance and suicide increase.

This is a point at which Durkheim's discussion of anomie may be seen to differ from Merton's conception. Durkheim considered the source of goals and desires to be a product of individual appetites and personal interests when society was in a state of anomie.[10] By contrast, Merton considered the source of goals that expressed group and individual wants to be learned from the cultural system. Merton's view on this point seems to bear closest resemblance to Durkheim's discussion of suicide resulting from economic disasters.[11] Here Durkheim does imply that some goals are a product of a stable social system in his suggestion that individuals are confronted with an adjustment problem requiring them to reduce their earlier (and presumably culturally induced) expected requirements, restrain their previous unusual needs, and learn greater social control.[12] But, even though Merton's theoretical thesis is close to this particular discussion in Durkheim, it does not reflect the full depth and range of Durkheim's conception of anomie.[13]

In another prominent part of Durkheim's consideration of anomic suicide, he looks at the effects of economic prosperity on suicide rates. Here the source of individual and group desires (or cultural goals in Merton's terms) for which means are unavailable is the condition of anomie itself. Anomie here is a state of societal deregulation whereby individuals are not regulated by the usual constraining influence of a well-ordered society. Unregulated individuals set their own goals based on basic appetites and personal interests which inevitably surpass the available means for their accomplishment. While Merton alludes to the problem of escalating goals in his essay, the heart of his position was that goals were learned in the cultural system, not, as Durkheim believed, dictated by individual whim and interests. It is this latter emphasis that seems to be the central thrust and characteristic strength of Durkheim's work. When society is in a state of deregulation individuals are unregulated by it and in turn are controlled only by their own whims and self-interests. The basic difference between Durkheim's anomie and Merton's adaptation of it, then, is that the individual had to learn the cultural goals to be pressured into deviance in Merton's conception of anomie, while the individual needed only to be human and uncontrolled for deviance to occur in Durkheim's view.

Another difference between Durkheim's and Merton's theories may be seen even if we grant the bases of Merton's inferences from *Suicide*. That is, Merton's hypothesized pressure toward deviance focuses on a different social stratum than Durkheim implies in his discussion. Merton's essay suggests the lower classes are more apt to feel adjustment problems and, therefore, pressure toward deviance because institutionalized means to commonly shared goals are relatively unavailable to them. For Durkheim, the group most directly disadvantaged under conditions of economic depression or panic are the most prosperous classes. His argument was that those who were socially influential and economically comfortable before an economic disaster would be more likely to experience adjustment problems after it, because under conditions of anomie, the means are no longer available for them to retain their earlier learned desires or goals.

Together these differences shed some light on the reason two characteristically distinct theoretical traditions have evolved from what really is Durkheim's one theory.[14]

Our attention must now shift back to summarizing Durkheim's anomie theory as the seedbed for the control approach to deviance. Durkheim summarizes and synthesizes his two interpretations of suicide in the following way:

> Man's characteristic privilege is that the bond he accepts
> is not physical but moral; that is social. He is governed
> not by a material environment brutally imposed on him,
> but by a conscience superior to his own, the superiority
> of which he feels. Because the greater, better part of his
> existence transcends the body, he escapes the body's
> yoke, but is subject to that of society.
>
> But when society is disturbed by some painful crisis [e.g.,
> economic depression] or by beneficent but abrupt
> transitions [e.g., economic prosperity], it is momentarily
> incapable of exercising this influence; thence come the
> sudden rises in the curve of suicides.[15]

This means that, when something happens to break down society's ability to regulate individuals through moral norms, they are neither disciplined to restrict their needs and requirements nor are they controlled in terms of their desires and personal interests. Without society's control, rates of deviation may be expected to increase.

Robert Merton's brand of anomie theory is partially reflective of but not fully consistent with the sense of Durkheim's theoretical discussion of anomie. What is left out by Merton is accented as a basis in what has come to be called control theory in the sociology of deviance. The thrust of Durkheim's argument, and that of modern control theory, revolves around the idea that deviance occurs not so much because it is caused but more because individuals are not controlled or regulated by society. It is conformity, not deviance, for the control theorists that is the unnatural human condition. Therefore, conformity must be caused, and if it is not, deviance is inevitable. In the control theories considered in the following pages, deviance is seen to be a natural product of broken, weak, or neutralized external and internal controls. In short, deviance is the result of the failure to produce conforming members of society. Consequently, deviance is not caused, it is natural. Nothing needs to propel or drive human beings into deviance, it follows from lack of control.

Reiss

Following Durkheim's conceptualization of anomie, the control thesis was theoretically emphasized again by Albert Reiss, first in a doctoral dissertation in 1949 and then published in an article two years later.[16] Reiss argued that delinquency can be seen to result from the failure of personal and social controls to produce behavior in conformity with the legal norms of the social system.[17] This meant delinquency, or more generally deviance, could be expected when personal and social controls were absent or too weak to produce behavior in conformity to conventional norms.

Reiss recognized three sources of control that, if effective, would bring about behavior in conformity with the conventional norms of the social system: (1) community and institutional controls; (2) primary group controls; and (3) personal controls. Neighborhoods and residential areas were community-based sources of control. The school was the most prominent example of an institutional source of control. Primary group control was seen to rest exclusively with the family. In turn, the development of personal controls and the exercise of social control over the child were seen to be functions of primary groups.[18] It follows then that, for Reiss, personal control is the product of internalizing norms of social groups which have nondelinquent group expectations. General social control is present when communities, neighborhoods, and schools and similar conventional institutions are effective in obtaining conformity with their norms.[19]

Both the emergence and the patterning of deviant behavior are consequences of ineffective social and personal controls. There are four conditions in which ineffective controls may result in deviance: (1) if previously established controls are broken down; (2) when there is an absence of definite social rules among important reference groups; (3) when there is a conflict in social rules among important reference groups; or (4) when the individual has not internalized conventional control norms.[20]

It should be made clear that the fourth condition identifying insufficient control to prevent deviance does not imply that, because the individual has not internalized control norms, there has been an internalization of deviant norms. Rather, the individual may not have internalized any norms whatsoever. The person is simply uncontrolled and, therefore, may deviate. This is a point of distinction from socialization theories that presume a person who does not internalize conventional norms must internalize deviant norms.

Reiss found the general thrust of his theory confirmed by official juvenile court data on 1,110 probationers between the ages of eleven and seventeen. The weaker the personal and social controls, the greater the chances were that an individual would engage in deviant behavior. Reiss' data suggest a lack of personal controls is more crucial than a lack of social controls in opening the way to deviance. The explanation of change by control theory is different from either of the former theoretical approaches. Control theorists posit no internal personality factors or identifications that must be eliminated before change may occur. Since it is a lack of controls, especially personal controls, that permits deviance, for control theoreists, change may be seen to follow from either the establishment of new controls or the strengthening of old ones. While Reiss did not address the question of change, it is clear, by inference, that an alteration of primary group affiliations in the direction of strengthening ties would produce stronger personal controls and could effect a change from deviant behavior patterns. In other cases, a change in community, school, or neighborhood could result in stronger social control on the individual and contribute to the abandonment of deviant behavior patterns.

It must be remembered here, that in control theory, the deviant has not internalized values favorable to deviance. Rather, control theorists simply assume insufficient amounts of social control or internalized control norms. Therefore, the control theorists are not faced with the problem of ridding the individual of internalized deviant values that socialization theorists are when considering change.

Nye

In 1958, F. Ivan Nye published a study of delinquency departing from the control perspective.[21] Nye recognized two ways of approaching the study of delinquency or, in general terms, the study of deviance. One was to assume that any form of deviant behavior is *produced* by specifiable motivations; and the other was to assume that deviant behavior occurs in the *absence* of controls or if controls are ineffective.[22] The first approach is based on the positive learning thesis characteristic of the socialization theories discussed in chapter 2. The second approach distinctly fits the control thesis as delineated earlier in this chapter.

Nye accepted that instances of deviant behavior sometimes would be the combined results of positive learning of deviant values and ineffective social control. However, he argued that such cases will be comparatively rare and that most delinquent behavior (and by extension deviance in general) is the result of insufficient social control, broadly defined.[23]

Nye's formulation of control theory recognizes four mechanisms of social control, which when absent or weak permit deviant behavior: (1) *direct control* which is imposed from without by means of restriction and punishment; (2) *internalized control* which is exercised from within through conscience; (3) *indirect control* that is correlative to affectional identification with parents and other nondeviants; and (4) control through wide availability of routes to goal and need satisfaction.[24] This set of control devices differs somewhat from those presented by Reiss. For Reiss, social controls are external to the individual while personal controls involve internalized norms developed in primary group socialization. Nye, on the other hand, saw all social control as in part a measure of the effectiveness of socialization processes of social groups, especially the family.[25]

The production of conformity, and therefore the avoidance of deviance, follows from effective controls on individuals. All social groups begin their efforts at control immediately upon entry or admission of new members. In most cases, probably some degree of all four sources of control identified by Nye function simultaneously throughout social life.[26] However, in some cases, the balance of the problem of social control will no doubt rest with a single source. In this sense, the control devices may be seen to operate somewhat independently.

For example, socializing a new member into a group takes the form of instilling the goals and values of the group into the individual's conscience. This is related to, but also somewhat independent of, affectional ties between the individual and group members. In spite of the degree of success in socialization, the affectional ties are an independent source of control. Direct control exercised by parents as well as by institutions and agencies such as the school and police represents another potentially independent source of control. Finally, parental preparation for alternative routes to need satisfaction represents still another potentially independent source of control.

One may not be controlled by internalized control norms, affectional ties with nondeviant others, or direct control through parental restriction. But, if alternative nondeviant routes to need satisfaction are available and the individual is prepared to use them, it is possible, according to Nye, that this will constitute sufficient control. An individual may enjoy circumstances where needs may be met without resorting to deviance. The wasteful spending by the wealthy youth on one day does not preclude prospects for satisfying monetary needs the next day because even thriftlessness does not exhaust his financial resources. Those in less prosperous circumstances may have no legitimate or legal alternatives to need satisfaction on a day following lavish spending. Therefore larceny and other deviant alternatives are more likely resorts for some than for others. While the independent operation of sources of control is possible, Nye argues that whatever the degree of effectiveness of any single source of control, some minimum of each of the other controls is probably necessary also.[27]

Nye's work represents a systematic evaluation of control theory and the effects of family relationships on delinquent behavior. He argues that most criminal behavior is the result of a failure of controls.[28] The research reported by Nye focuses exclusively on variables revolving around parent-adolescent relationships. The family is considered to be the single most important mechanism for exercising social control over adolescents.[29] A most impressive general finding is that of the more than 300 tests of relationships considered by Nye, some 95 percent were in the direction supportive of control theory.[30]

Matza

David Matza, in 1964, published a reaction to the almost wholesale acceptance by sociologists of socialization theories of delinquency in his *Delinquency and Drift*.[31] In this important work, Matza proposed an alternative explanation of juvenile delinquency called drift theory which is most appropriately classified within, and as an extension of, the control tradition. While there are a number of significant contributions in this work that go beyond our purposes here, we should point out that this book is an important piece in the development of phenomenological sociology as well as an expansion of social control theory.[32]

We will be concentrating on Matza's contribution to control theory. Control theory had been solidly criticized for being incomplete. It was argued that deviance could not be assumed to be an automatic human resort when social control is weak.[33] Or as Matza interpreted the criticism, apparently the removal of social control is not sufficient to explain the occurrence of deviance. There must be something that intervenes between lack of control and deviance. Motivation, pathology, practicality; something, it was argued, must produce deviance—it cannot simply occur. But it was precisely this simplistic view of deviance that Durkheim so effectively argued. When social controls are absent or weak, human behavior is shaped by self-interests, not social standards, and it therefore has a high probability of being defined as deviant or fitted into deviant categories.

Matza acknowledges the plausibility of the Durkheim argument, but he also accepts the view of the critics that something needs to precede moving into delinquency.[34] A major part of his theoretical work deals with the development of the concept *will* as an inducement to deviance once the moral bind of society is broken down or weakened. Another part of Matza's theory of drift deals directly with the breakdown of social control; that is, how the moral bind of society is rendered ineffective in controlling individual behavior.

We may see the structure of Matza's theory most clearly by focusing on his basic conceptual scheme. The theory was formulated to explain gang delinquency but we will generalize it here to pertain to a broader range of deviant forms of behavior. Two concepts, neutralization and subterranean convergence, explain how the failure of society's moral bind on some individuals is possible. Subterranean convergence refers to the blending of the conventional culture with the subculture of deviants in a way that conventional values offer subterranean support for deviance. Society's moral grip on individuals is neutralized by employing conventional reasoning to behavioral infractions. For example, conventional reasoning often excuses insane persons from true responsibility and guilt. Taking this reasoning and extending it to meet private needs, an individual may be freed from moral constraint by disclaiming responsibility because drugs, alcohol, or even anger has produced temporary insanity.[35]

Matza argues that the delinquent is forever exposed to the precepts of conventional and deviant cultures. The norms of both invite conformity. In order to engage in an infraction, conventional norms must be neutralized. Neutralization permits violation of conventional norms without surrendering allegiance to them. The norms may be simply evaded rather than rejected. Neutralization is made possible by subterranean convergence and is essentially an unwitting extension of legal and conventional excuses for infractions that mentally frees the actor from the moral constraint of and permits conformity to deviant norms.[36] The reverse is necessary also when a member of a subculture of deviance engages in certain forms of conventional behavior. Exemption from or neutralization of deviant expectations is necessary. An example would be the deviant youth who excuses himself from a gang fight by claiming the necessity of keeping a young brother home and safe from other gangs. The appeal to family responsibility exempts the youth from gang obligations.

Neutralization breaks the moral bind of conventional society on the actor, but it does not assure deviant action. Rather, it produces *drift* or a state where the actor has been freed from social controls but lacks either the position, the capacity, or the inclination to rationally choose a deviant act.[37] Something must intervene here to induce deviance or else inaction and conventional behavior are as probable as infraction. Matza introduces the concept of *will* as the missing element in traditional control theory. *Will* provides the thrust, motivation, or impetus to deviance.[38] But *will*, like *drift*, must be set in motion or activated.

The activation of the decision to engage in a deviant act may follow from an assurance that it is technically feasible, that the actor is capable of performing the act. Neutralization has already provided the moral feasibility. For a deviant act to become technically feasible an actor must learn to manage the action (do the act) and overcome any apprehension about performing it. Most delinquent acts require little more than the learning that is available to all youths. For that matter, most deviance may be performed sufficiently with stock knowledge available to us all. Usually, confidence about ability to perform an act negates, to a large extent, anticipatory trepidation which might deter the act.[39]

The second way a motivation or *will* to deviance may be produced is through a sense of fatalism. In this case, deviance provides a means to restore a sense of control over one's destiny. Fatalism refers to a feeling of being pushed around or that events involving the actor personally are being directed by others. This feeling may produce massive desperation leading the individual to engage in actions that might restore a sense of personal control over his destiny. Deviant actions represent a large category of actions capable of giving the actor a sense of control over events. Even if the actor is caught in a transgres-

sion, it was a self-initiated act that caused the events of apprehension and punishment.[40] And the actor takes satisfaction
even when the result is punishment. Thus, it is will, activated
by preparation or desperation, that provides the impetus for
deviance once social controls are neutralized.

Matza's theory may be summarized by the diagram shown in
figure 1.

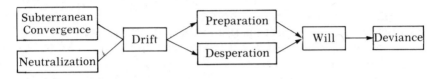

Figure 1

Drift is a state of being freed from society's moral grip by the
combined influence of subterranean convergence and neutralization. *Drift,* however, does not automatically result in deviance. The uncontrolled individual must be induced to commit
and repeat deviant acts; that is, there must be a *will* or motivation to deviate. *Will* may be activated by either preparation or
desperation assuring the decision to deviate.[41]

The deviant, to Matza, is halfway between the involuntary
actor posited by the socialization theorists and the largely rational actor posited by some societal reactionists. The human or-
ganism is neither propelled by internal beliefs nor is it an
unencumbered calculator of its social destiny. The personality
is not basically formed nor is it free of social or internal constraint. To see, then, how one is released from bonds of social
control and thrust into deviance, it is necessary to analyze the
deviant actor in the natural context where conventional and
deviant cultures converge. Here we find Matza's *drifter* who is
always between convention and deviance, "responding in turn
to the demands of each, flirting now with one, now the other,
but postponing commitment" to either.[42]

Reckless

Another development in support of control theory evolved from
a series of studies directed by Walter C. Reckless. This research
demonstrated the importance of self-factors in explaining
differential response to deviance. Reckless and his colleagues
had been bothered by the inability of socialization theories to
account for why some persons do and some do not succumb to

the conditions of social disorganization, differential association with criminal models, blocked opportunity structures, or
subcultural pulls.[43]

Reckless' theory is called containment theory and posits, like
that of Reiss and Nye, both external and internal sources of
control. It is generally assumed the individuals can be made to
conform to social norms. Societies, and particularly nuclear
groups, attempt to hold their members within the limits of
accepted norms and laws. The holding power of societies and
groups on their members is the basis of external containment.
Nuclear groups and small organizations do more of the job of
providing external constraint against deviance than does
larger society. The person who finds a sense of belonging, acceptance, ego bolstering, and support in nuclear groups and
small organizations is more apt to follow social norms than one
who does not have such integrating elements.[44] Reckless indicates that external containment is probably never completely
effective but it is no doubt maximized under general social
"conditions of isolation, homogeneity of culture, class, and population," and where nuclear groups have a strong hold on individual members.[45]

External containment, therefore, represents the capability of
society and smaller groups to hold the behavior of individuals
within the bounds of accepted norms and laws. Inner containment, the internal complement, refers to elements internal to
the self which affect control over one's behavior. As social relations become more impersonal, as society becomes more diverse, and as individuals spend larger portions of time away
from intimate nuclear groups, internal containment becomes
more and more essential in affecting social control.[46] In folk
communities and highly integrated and isolated social groups
inner containment is largely unnecessary. But serious deviance
is not a problem in such societies and groups. Deviance that
offends the moral order is more a characteristic of modern,
industrial, and urbanized societies like our own.

Reckless' interest in inner containment centers around four
components of the self which give it strength to resist deviance,
that enable an individual to be contained conformingly in modern society. The first of the components of inner containment
is a favorable self-concept. The person who has a favorable
(meaning conventional and conforming) self-concept is apt to
behave in accord with conventional norms. Goal orientation is
the second component. This pertains to the orientation of a
person toward socially approved goals. The person oriented

toward conventional goals, such as education, job improvement, savings, and help for others has the capability for inner
direction, conforming to conventional norms.[47]

The third self-factor that contributes to inner containment is
frustration tolerance. Frustration tolerance refers to a capability to withstand adversity, pressure from others, and disap-
pointment or failure without resorting to deviance. The fourth
and final element of inner containment is norm retention. As
Reckless puts it, norm retention may be seen to consist of retention of, adherence to, commitment to acceptance of, identification with, legitimation of, and defense of values, norms, and
laws. Deviance may occur if an individual becomes alienated
from or neutralizes previously internalized ethics, morals, and
values. We then have *norm erosion* which releases the individual from the moral bind of formally internalized principles.[48] In actual cases, all four of the components of inner
containment overlap and complement each other. Self or inner
containment is, in large part, assumed to be an aspect of personal development. It is a self-management system that results
naturally if the internalized models of behavior are conventional and conforming.[49]

The question that occupied Reckless and his colleagues was:
who, and under what conditions, is more or less likely to display
or become involved in deviance? Reckless puts together an explanatory model described as a series of concentric circles as
shown in figure 2.

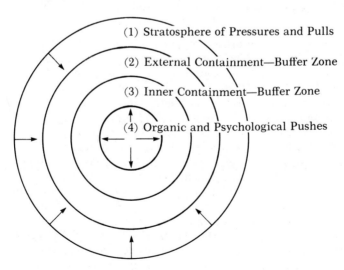

(1) Stratosphere of Pressures and Pulls

(2) External Containment—Buffer Zone

(3) Inner Containment—Buffer Zone

(4) Organic and Psychological Pushes

Figure 2

In the outer circle (1) is the social stratosphere of pressures and pulls. In the next circle (2), coming from outside to inside, lies the buffer of external containments —the person's groups and organizations. Then there is the circle (3) of inner containment—the self. Finally, there is the innermost circle (4) of organic and psychological pushes. Circle (2) is the external containing buffer, if and when it is strong enough. Circle (3) is the internal containing buffer (the self), if and when it is strong enough. The pressures and pulls are exerted for the most part in a sphere outside the nuclear containing groups, such as the family or organizations. Pressures consist of adverse living conditions (relative to region and culture), such as poverty, unemployment, economic insecurity, group conflicts, minority group status, lack of opportunities, inequalities. Some break through the weakness in the buffer of circle (2). Some of the pressures are diluted or diverted by circle (2). Those that break through the buffer of group containment confront the person head on. If he has the strength to fend them off, the buffer in circle (3) holds. If not, he succumbs to deviance and violation of law. The same can be said for the pulls which also are located in circle (1). The pulls draw the person away from his original way of life and accepted forms of living. Pulls consist of prestige individuals, bad companions, delinquency or criminal subculture, deviant groups, mass media, propaganda. They must break through the buffer (2) (outer containment) and break through also the buffer of circle (3) (the self).

In addition to the pressures and pulls which batter at outer and inner containment, there are the organic and psychological pushes which batter the self. These are located in circle (4), the innermost circle. Some of the pushes which are rather uncontainable are extreme restlessness and discontent, marked inner tensions, extreme hostility and aggressiveness, aggrandizement and need for immediate gratification, extreme suggestibility, strong rebellion against authority, strong feeling of inadequacy and inferiority, guilt reactions, mental conflicts, anxieties, compulsions, phobias, organic impairments ..., psychoses. Many of these pushes are too strong for the self to handle or for nuclear groups such as the family. ... The buffers of circle (2) and circle (3) can parry ordinary disappointments, frustrations, restlessness, but they are no match for the big thrusts.[50]

In this account of containment theory Reckless suggests that a strong external and internal containment is not sufficient to insulate individuals against all social and psychological inducements to deviance. There are many pressures and pulls both outside and inside the individual that may overpower even the strong conventional self entrenched in containing nuclear groups and organizations. However, such overwhelming social and psychological forces toward deviance are infrequent in comparison to ordinary social pressures and pulls toward deviance. Containment is a theory to explain this latter larger set of causes of deviance. It cannot explain the former.[51]

Of the two sources of social control, external and internal containment, Reckless, like Reiss and Nye, gives the greatest strength to internal controls within the individual.[52] External containment is a product of membership in well-integrated conventional groups and organizations. Internal containment is largely the result of successful internalization of conventional norms and values.[53] In most instances, deviant behavior emerges and becomes patterned only if both levels of control are weak or neutralized, though some deviance may follow from the weakening of either external or internal containment.[54] Change may come about if an individual is moved from a free environment to a controlled environment, or if attachment to conventional reference groups yielding a sense of belonging and worth is effected. In general, it is the building up of an inner and outer containment which will enable an individual to resist social pressures, temptations, normal restlessness, and dissatisfactions which ordinarily produce deviance.[55]

Hirschi

A final contribution to control theory to be considered is Travis Hirschi's *Causes of Delinquency.*[56] This work enjoys a dual distinction among the contributions to control theory. There are two reasons for this. First, it is the clearest statement available on the variations in the control approach. Second, it presents some of the most compelling data to be found in support of control theory.

Hirschi's approach to control theory is perhaps more congruent with the Durkheimian formulation than any of the more recent variants of the control thesis. Like his predecessors, Hirschi identifies elements of the bond to conventional society—

the bond that constrains individuals to conform. There are four such elements described by Hirschi: attachment; commitment; involvement; and belief.

† The way societies or social groups effect control over their members is a basic concern to all control theorists. For it is the lack of whatever effects control that frees individuals to deviate. Control theorists, since Durkheim, have generally posited that some sources of control rest inside the individual and some are an aspect of group control effected from without. Hirschi does not place any critical emphasis on internal sources of control. Reiss, Nye, and Reckless, on the other hand, assume that there is some internalization of control norms and that they operate as a continuing source of control even when external control is weak or lacking altogether. Attachment is the nearest to internalization of Hirschi's four elements of the bond to society. For Hirschi, the essence of internalization of norms, however, lies in the degree of attachment of the individual to others, not in the personality.

Hirschi recognizes that an individual's attachment to others is not the equivalent of the socialization theorists' conception of internalization. However, when attachment is combined with belief (the fourth element of the bond to society), he believes there is only a small amount of implied internal control left unaccounted for by his concepts. The basic difference between Hirschi's position and the traditional sociological conception of internalization is that Hirschi assumes even *conscience* is largely an aspect of continuing personal relationships—not a dimension of *personality*.

Hirschi's position on internal control is much like that in Durkheim's early work. The importance of, and the manner in which, Durkheim viewed individuals' attachment to society may be seen in the following:

> The bond that unites them with the common cause
> *attaches* them to life and the lofty goal they envisage
> prevents their feeling personal troubles so deeply. There
> is, in short, in a cohesive and animated society *a
> constant interchange of ideas and feelings from all to
> each and each to all, something like a mutual moral
> support,* which instead of throwing the individual on his
> own resources, *leads him to share in collective energy
> and supports his own when exhausted.*[57] (Italics added)

For Hirschi, then, like Durkheim, the greater the degree of attachment to others the more likely one is to be bound by their norms.[58]

The second element of the bond to society is commitment. Commitment refers to the extent to which individuals accrue goods, reputations, and prospects that might be endangered by deviance.[59] That is, a person is committed when costs and risks of deviance exceed the potential gain or satisfaction from deviance.[60]

Involvement is the third element of the bond identified by Hirschi. The extent to which one is involved in conventional activities affects the extent one is controlled by conventional expectations. The individual who is deeply engrossed in conventional activities is tied, in large part, to schedules, meetings, plans, and working hours, to the extent that the opportunity to commit deviant acts is rarely available.[61] Involvement is seen to prevent the time and place for deviance.

The final element of the bond that may hold a person to group norms is belief. Hirschi assumes there is variation in the extent to which individuals believe they should obey the rules of society. He does not accept the assumption of socialization theorists that deviants have beliefs favorable to deviance while conventional people hold beliefs unfavorable to deviance. Nor does he accept the Mertonian view that strong identification with conventional beliefs are indirectly related to the commission of deviant acts. Rather, Hirschi assumes that when the person's beliefs in the validity of social rules are weakened, the probability that deviance will occur is increased.[62]

In summary, when the general bond that holds individuals to society or to conventional norms is weakened or broken, the individual is then free to deviate. There is no suggestion by Hirschi that one must deviate at this point. It is simply more probable that one will deviate when the elements of the bond are weak than it is when individual attachment, commitment, involvement, and beliefs are strongly conventional.

Unlike his recent predecessors, such as Nye and Reckless, Hirschi does not emphasize the internalization of social control norms. Rather he suggests that effective conscience, the personal result of internalization, is basically a product of the strength and continuance of attachments to conventional others.[63] Also, unlike Matza, Hirschi does not posit a motivation to deviance. He gets around the problem of motivation to deviance by assuming a rational component to social action paired with the assumption that deviant acts are frequently easier, faster, more convenient and perhaps even more fun than conformity to the rules.[64] Therefore when controls are weak or broken there is no need to look for a special or pathological motivation to deviance. It may be simply the reasonable, expedient, or fun thing to do under the circumstances.

If this can be said to represent the source of emergence into the first instance of a deviant act, the continued lack of control or weak control and unrestrained personal interests are sufficient to induce patterning of deviance. The most apparent inference we may make about change is that a change in deviant behavior patterns will follow with the introduction of effective control. For Hirschi effective control means a high degree of attachment to others, commitment to conventional society, and a belief in the legitimacy of social rules.[65] Becoming an active member of one or more highly integrated conventional groups or institutions may provide a basis for all the elements of the bond. We will see, in part II of this book, cases of deviant careers that begin and end with variations in the effectiveness of social control.

Notes

1. The term social control is interpreted differently in modern sociology. Lewis Coser and Bernard Rosenberg, for example, consider the internalization of social norms, as discussed in selected works by Emile Durkheim, George Herbert Mead, Sigmund Freud, and Jean Piaget, to reflect the social control thesis. Others see social control as the ability of societies and groups to exercise control over their members from without. The theories discussed in this chapter interpret social control both ways and sometimes internal and external control are combined in the same theory. See Lewis Coser and Bernard Rosenberg, *Sociological Theory* (New York: Macmillan, 1969).

2. We are primarily interested in Durkheim's early work in the *Division of Labor* (1893) and *Suicide* (1897), and his development of the concept of anomie. For a different perspective on social control and Durkheim's later work dealing with internal as opposed to external constraint, see Coser and Rosenberg, *Sociological Theory*, p. 98. Coser and Rosenberg deal mainly with Durkheim's paper on "The Determination of a Moral Fact," a later work, which was first read before the French Philosophical Society in 1906. It was published later in a collection of essays; see Emile Durkheim, *Sociology and Philosophy*, trans. D. F. Pocock (Glencoe, Ill.: Free Press, 1953). Also see Stephen R. Marks, "Durkheim's Theory of Anomie", *American Journal of Sociology* 80 (September 1974): 329–63, for an elaborate discussion of the way anomie weaves through Durkheim's later works.

3. Talcott Parsons, *The Structure of Social Action,* vol. I (New York: Free Press, 1937), p. 334.

4. Emile Durkheim, *Suicide,* trans. John H. Spaulding and George Simpson (New York: Free Press, 1951), p. 208. Material adapted from this work for the following discussion is used by permission of the Macmillan Company.

5. Ibid., p. 209.

6. Ibid. Used by permission.

7. Parsons, *Structure of Social Action,* p. 334.

8. Ibid., p. 335.

9. Durkheim, *Suicide,* p. 247.

10. Durkheim reasoned that when society is broken down in a state of anomie, the natural tendency for individual goals and desires to know no limits except those in the individual would be eventuated. For a similar interpretation of Durkheim see Marshall Clinard, *Anomie and Deviant Behavior* (New York: Free Press, 1964), p. 11.

11. Durkheim, *Suicide,* pp. 241–76.

12. Ibid., p. 252.

13. See Durkheim, *Suicide,* pp. 241–76. Clinard, *Anomie and Deviant Behavior,* p. 10; Reece McGee, *Social Disorganization in America* (San Francisco: Chandler, 1962), pp. 34–36; and Marvin B. Scott and Roy Turner, "Weber and the Anomic Theory of Deviance," *Sociological Quarterly* 6 (Summer 1965): 5–14, express views of anomie similar to the one used in the present work.

14. The view that Durkheim's analysis of various forms of suicide reflects one rather than two theories is well argued by Barclay D. Johnson, "Durkheim's One Cause of Suicide," *American Sociological Review* (December 1965): 875–86.

15. Durkheim, *Suicide,* p. 252. Used by permission.

16. Albert J. Reiss, Jr., "The Accuracy, Efficiency and Validity of a Prediction Instrument" (Ph.D. diss., University of Chicago, 1949) and "Delinquency as the Failure of Personal and Social Controls," *American Sociological Review* 16 (1951): 196–207.

17. Ibid., p. 196.

18. Ibid., p. 198.

19. Ibid., p. 201.

20. Ibid., p. 207.

21. F. Ivan Nye, *Family Relationships and Delinquent Behavior* (New York: John Wiley, 1958).

22. Ibid., p. 3.

23. Ibid.

24. Ibid., p. 5.

25. Ibid., p. 9n.

26. Ibid., p. 157.

27. Ibid.

28. Ibid., p. 5.

29. Ibid.

30. Ibid., p. 155. Roughly half of these relationships were not significant at the .05 level with a two-tailed test of significance. However, the direction of the relationship was almost always consistent with the control theory hypothesis.

31. David Matza, *Delinquency and Drift* (New York: John Wiley, 1964).

32. Matza developed more fully his phenomenological perspective in a later work. See David Matza, *Becoming Deviant* (Englewood Cliffs, N.J.: Prentice-Hall, 1969).

33. Albert K. Cohen and James F. Short, "Research in Delinquent Subcultures," *Journal of Social Issues* 14 (1958): 20–37.

34. Matza, *Delinquency and Drift*, p. 182. Material adapted from this work for the following discussion is used by permission of John Wiley & Sons, Inc. and the author.

35. Ibid., pp. 60–62.

36. This conception of neutralization was first presented in 1957 by Gresham Sykes and David Matza, "Techniques of Neutralization: A Theory of Delinquency," *American Sociological Review* 22 (December 1957): 664–70. In 1964 Matza elaborated the process of neutralization in *Delinquency and Drift*, pp. 69–184.

37. Matza, *Delinquency and Drift*, p. 29.

38. Ibid., p. 181.

39. Ibid., pp. 186–88.

40. Ibid., pp. 188–91.

41. Ibid., pp. 181–91.

42. Ibid., p. 28. Used by permission.

43. Walter C. Reckless, *The Crime Problem*, 4th ed. (Englewood Cliffs, N.J.: Prentice-Hall, 1967), p. 446. Material adapted from this work for the following discussion is used by permission of the publisher.

44. Ibid., pp. 470–71.

45. Ibid., pp. 471–72. Used by permission.

46. Ibid., p. 475.

47. Ibid., pp. 475–76.

48. Ibid., p. 476.

49. Ibid.

50. Walter C. Reckless, *The Crime Problem*, 4th ed. © 1967. (Prentice-Hall, Inc., Englewood Cliffs, N.J.), pp. 479–80. Used by permission.

51. Ibid., pp. 477–80.

52. Simon Dinitz, Frank R. Scarpitti, and Walter C. Reckless, "Delinquency Vulnerability: A Cross Group and Longitudinal Analysis," *American Sociological Review* 27 (August 1962): 517.

53. Reckless, *The Crime Problem*, pp. 469–76.

54. Ibid., p. 478.

55. Ibid., p. 481.

56. Travis Hirschi, *Causes of Delinquency* (Berkeley: University of California Press, 1969).

57. Durkheim, *Suicide*, p. 210. Used by permission.

58. Hirschi, *Causes of Delinquency*, p. 18.

59. Ibid., p. 19.

60. This idea has been more aptly called "stake in conformity" by Jackson Toby in his "Social Disorganization and Stake in Conformity: Complementary Factors in the Predatory Behavior of Hoodlums," *Journal of Criminal Law,*

Criminology, and Police Science 48 (1957): 12–17. Howard S. Becker elaborates essentially this same idea in *Outsiders: Studies in the Sociology of Deviance* (New York: Free Press, 1967), p. 27. Also, see Scott Briar and Irving Piliavin, "Delinquency, Situational Inducements, and Commitment to Conformity," *Social Problems* 13 (1965): pp. 34–45, for added support for the "stake in conformity" thesis.

61. Hirschi, *Causes of Delinquency,* p. 22.

62. Ibid., pp. 23–26.

63. Ibid., pp. 18–19.

64. While Hirschi does not hypothesize an intervening motivation between a breakdown in control and deviance, he does assume rational decision intervenes to make deviance more likely. This view is very close to one presented recently by Briar and Pilavin, "Delinquency, Situational Inducements, and Commitment to Conformity," pp. 34–45.

65. Involvement, the fourth element of the bond, was found not to be as important in Hirschi's data as he had assumed. See his *Causes of Delinquency,* p. 230.

Part II

An Empirical Evaluation

Evaluating Theoretical Approaches to Deviance

5

In part I of this book it was argued that there are at least three distinct sociological approaches to the explanation of deviance—the socialization, the societal reaction, and the control approaches. Each approach rests on somewhat different assumptions about the nature of social action and personality, and each approach generates different explanations of the emergence, patterning, and change of deviant behavior. The questions that occupied us in previous chapters centered around (1) how sociologists explain deviance and deviant behavior, (2) to what extent the various theories may be said to be essentially competing or alternative explanations reflective of broad sociological approaches, and (3) what general and comparable propositions may be derived to represent the explanation of deviance offered by each approach. In part II we turn our attention to questions dealing with the credibility of the approaches. We will inquire about the extent to which the theories explain the lives and actions of real deviants and about the relative explanatory power of these three alternative approaches.

But to say that we are interested in evaluating the credibility of major theoretical approaches requires some discussion of established theory testing strategies and the problems and prospects of evaluations based on these strategies.

Theory Testing

Questions bearing on the validity of theories in the social sciences are most commonly addressed through a hypothesis testing method. The researcher formulates some hypotheses, tests the hypotheses with systematically obtained data, and, after analyzing the data, interprets the extent to which the findings support or call into question the specific hypotheses and the theory from which they were derived. The theory is considered to be more credible if the hypotheses are supported by the data, or it is thought to be less credible if the hypotheses are not supported in the data.[1] Sociologists employing this strategy derive much information that leads to better insights into the phenomena under study and constructive amendments of the theory under test. But, in spite of the fact that the hypothesis testing procedure as it is customarily employed is important, indeed crucial, to theory building in any discipline, it is at the same time inadequate for purposes of evaluating competing theoretical approaches.

Hypothesis testing strategies generally are aimed at testing only one theory, and more often than not, only a few of the many hypothesized relationships necessary to hold the theory together are tested in any one study. Even if the usual scope of sociological studies were to be expanded, it would be difficult, if not prohibitive, to test the comparative validity of competing theories.[2]

At the same time, conclusions drawn from single theory hypothesis testing studies have no implications for evaluating the validity of competing theories. Evidence in support of the theory under test, in such studies, intuitively lends support to it.[3] But this same evidence derived from single theory hypothesis testing studies cannot be used in the evaluation of competing theories that were not represented in the conceptualization and design of the studies.[4] The fact is that there is substantial research evidence in support of all the theories examined in this study. But evidence in support of one theory does not negate the possibility that the alternative aspects of competing theories might similarly be shown to be valid. Therefore, the practice employed by some sociologists of amassing evidence in support of one theory to invalidate another theory neither disproves it, nor does it bear in any way upon the overall validity of the competing theory.[5]

Strictly speaking, there is no strategy in the social sciences, such as the crucial experiment used in the physical sciences, which will give one result if one of the alternative theories under consideration is correct and a different result if another is true.[6] In spite of the relative inability of our methods to solve such problems, social scientists remain interested in determining the comparative explanatory power of their theories. And such evaluation is important to the development of better explanations of social phenomena and should be continued, but only with appreciation for philosophical rules of truth, canons of logic, and an awareness of the inherent limits of our methods.

Evaluating Alternative Theoretical Approaches

We have seen in earlier chapters that the general explanations of how deviant behavior emerges, becomes patterned, and changes are fundamentally different in the socialization, societal reaction, and control theories. In addition, it has been suggested above that standard research strategies in social science are not adequate to provide a basis for evaluating the comparative explanatory strength of these approaches. So now the problem of how to evaluate the credibility of these alternative explanations must be dealt with. The problem has two phases. The first phase involves the collection of data in a way that avoids the imputation or assumption of theoretical import by the researcher of any factor in advance of knowing its subjective meaning. The second phase involves the application of these data to the question of the relative explanatory power of the three approaches.

In the present evaluation study we were concerned with the extent to which actual instances of deviant behavior patterns developed and changed in accordance with the explanations of three major theoretical approaches in sociology. In addition, we were interested in examining cases of deviant career development in a way that would reveal factors that might emerge as causal forces even if they were not theorized to be important, and therefore not earmarked for specific observation, by any of the three approaches. This meant the empirical observations had to be made without precluding the emergence of either (1) factors posited to be important in the three theoretical approaches or (2) factors not previously considered to be theoretically important by any of the theories under consideration.

To this end, the data for this study were obtained through intensive life-history interviews with individuals who had manifested a pattern of some form of deviant behavior, usually theft and drugs. The interviews were structured to obtain self-perceived life-histories. There were no prephrased questions making up an exact interview schedule,[7] but the interview focus was broadly organized around a chronology of (1) memorable events, (2) relationships with other persons, (3) self-conceptions, (4) deviant acts, (5) perceptions of deviant acts and reactions from others to them and to the person, and (6) appraisals of the general circumstances of life. These points were considered at several different life stages. The period from the respondent's earliest memories to the time of the last interview was covered. The interviews drew upon the perceptions of the persons who were considered, and who often considered themselves, to be deviant. It was their story, their perceptions, and the subjective meanings they had of events, relationships, and self-conceptions that made up their life-histories. The assumption here is that it is the perceptions of events, circumstances, and forces of life that are held by the actors that influence behavior, not what others perceive these forces to be, nor any other facts that escape the perception of the actor. Therefore, for purposes of this study, the important and causal facts of an individual's deviance were assumed to be best known by the deviants themselves.[8] A complete discussion of the methodology and procedures used in this research is in Appendix B.

In brief, the way we have chosen to address the first phase of the problem of testing alternative theories, that of collecting suitable data, is through obtaining self-perceived life-histories. As to the second phase of the problem—how to use these data in a way that allows us to evaluate the relative explanatory power of alternative theories—we were guided by what Howard S. Becker refers to as the "negative test" utility of life-history data.[9] That is, life-history documents may be used as empirical cases with which theories may be compared. As we have used them in this study, life-history documents are a base against which the underlying postulates and the general propositions of broadly conceived theoretical approaches may be evaluated.

When used as a negative case, we ask if the empirical facts of the life-histories can be explained by the theories under consideration. If they cannot, then the case serves to point out the weakness of the theories. It does not, however, mean that the theory is invalid or that the theory does not explain any cases at all. Rather it means, by looking at cases that cannot be explained by our theories, that we may be instructed as to how the theories may be amended or expanded to explain a broader class of cases. For example, if other factors not identified in the theories operate in ways that cause the emergence, patterning, or change of deviant behavior, any approach offered as a general explanation of deviance that overlooks these factors should be, at least, revised or expanded to include them.

The life-histories are used in another way also. Several life-histories represent very close approximations of model cases for each theoretical approach. If the underlying postulates and general propositions of an approach are not founded in these archetype cases—to which they purport to be applicable—then the theories which make up the approach must be considered less credible. Or if, in these cases to which any particular approach is most applicable, the theoretically important factors are present but do not operate as they are described in the theories making up the approach, the relevant propositions must also be considered less credible.

In the next three chapters several life-history accounts of the development and change of deviance are presented and analyzed. The procedure employed in this evaluation looks at these empirical cases in an effort to see not only what is consistent with the hypotheses derived from any particular set of theories but also what is important in the case that is not a consideration for theories making up one of the approaches. If something is at work in the development of deviant behavior patterns that is not recognized in a theory, it can be added to considerations of the viability of that theory. We will inquire as to whether what is supposed to be present and operating in cases of deviant careers is there in fact—and whether all that is present and operating in the development of deviance can be explained by the theoretical approaches under consideration. In the latter instance, if factors or influences not conceptualized in the approach cannot be explained by it, we have identified a weakness and have moved a step closer to knowing how this set of theories may be made more accurate.

Chapter 6 examines the question of etiology or the emergence of the first instances of deviant behavior. Chapter 7 deals with the patterning of deviant behavior. Change or abandonment of patterned deviance is considered in chapter 8.

Notes

1. Actually our evaluation of a theory is safest if the data do not support the hypotheses. Then we may suggest the theory is rendered less credible. But when the data support the hypotheses we must always recognize that there are also numerous other possible explanations of the phenomena not covered by the theory or the research. See Arthur L. Stinchecomb, *Constructing Social Theories* (New York: Harcourt, Brace, and World, 1968), p. 18.

2. It is extremely difficult to test all the crucial relationships from several different theories in the same hypothesis testing study—and in a way that the support of one would imply the rejection of another. Travis Hirschi's *Causes of Delinquency* (Berkeley: University of California Press, 1969) is one of the best of the available efforts in this direction. But even in this well-designed study, the operational definitions are more fair to one theory than to another. See, for example, the way Hirschi treats the concept of internalization and his operationalization of "attachment."

3. Stinchecomb, *Constructing Social Theories*, p. 18.

4. Abraham Kaplan, *The Conduct of Inquiry* (San Francisco: Chandler, 1964), p. 313. To use evidence from research and surveys that do not directly test the propositions of the theory under consideration ignores the philosophical truth that the way we conceptualize facts (i.e., evidence) depends to a very large extent on the theories which play a part in their cognition.

5. An example of overstated conclusions about an alternative theory may be seen in Walter Gove, "Societal Reaction as an Explanation of Mental Illness: An Evaluation," *American Sociological Review* 35 (October 1970): 873–84. Gove examines some data that were in support of the medical model of mental illness but that were not obtained from studies specifically designed to test labeling theories as an alternative. Then he suggests, erroneously, that the labeling theory of mental illness is false because it is not confirmed in the studies he considered.

6. Stinchecomb, *Constructing Social Theories*, p. 54.

7. While some researchers believe unstructured interviews are best suited for strictly exploratory studies, if it is the respondent's perceptions and subjective meanings that are being sought, the unstructured interview is best no matter what type of study. See Norman K. Denzin, *The Research Act* (Chicago: Aldine, 1970), p. 127.

8. This assumption is deeply rooted in the methodology of symbolic interactionism. What individuals perceive to be real is indeed what influences their behavior. See George Herbert Mead, *Mind, Self, and Society* (Chicago: University of Chicago Press, 1934); Herbert Blumer, *Symbolic Interactionism: Perspective and Method* (Englewood Cliffs, N.J.: Prentice-Hall, 1969); and Bernard N. Meltzer and John W. Petras, "The Chicago and Iowa Schools of Symbolic Interactionism" in *Human Nature and Collective Behavior: Papers in Honor of Herbert Blumer,* ed. Tamotsu Shibitani (Englewood Cliffs, N.J.: Prentice-Hall, 1970).

9. See the introductory essay to the 1966 edition of Clifford R. Shaw's *The Jack-Roller* (Chicago: University of Chicago Press, 1966), pp. v-xviii. Also, see Denzin, *The Research Act,* p. 257, for a discussion of the evaluation utility of life-history data.

The
Emergence of
Deviant
Behavior

The study of the emergence of initial acts of deviant behavior is called etiology. In recent years, this general question of how deviant behavior emerges has been, in large part, avoided,[1] assumed to be sufficiently answered,[2] or overlooked in favor of addressing questions of patterning or questions dealing with the behavior of those who define behavior as deviant.[3] Moreover, sociologists who have continued to concern themselves with questions of etiology have devoted an inordinate amount of attention to the prominent motivational and genetic theories of emergence.[4] Progress on the question of emergence, then, has, for the most part, stopped. But, even in the past, sociologists generally passed by this question quickly to answer questions about deviant *careers, patterns, roles, lifestyles, behavior systems, gangs,* or *subcultures.*[5]

In spite of the scant attention given to etiology in the past and the drift away from it today, it remains an important area of study for sociologists interested in explaining the phenomena of behavioral deviation. The socialization approach considers original cause an integral aspect of subsequent deviance. Etiology is important to the societal reaction theorists because a closed system of explanation, the ultimate purpose of theory, can be developed only if the question of primary emergence is addressed. Moreover, the cumulative effect of negative reactions is a crucial concern of societal reactionists. Therefore, the first instance of deviance may mark the beginning of labeling or it may be the result of prior labeling through normal social differentiations. Control theorists address the question of etiology more forthrightly than either of the other approaches. Since control theory assumes deviance to result from lack of effective control, the difference between the causes of the first act and subsequent instances of deviance can be only a matter of variation in the extent to which control is lacking.

The question of etiology, then, is germane to all of the approaches considered here. Indeed, it is important for any perspective in the study of deviance.[6] Each of the approaches considered in this analysis has been constructed from a number of specific theories by deriving underlying postulates, generalizing specific propositions, and inferring theoretical positions where they are implicit or absent. A fully credible approach to deviance must offer a total explanation of the phenomenon, not simply an account of one facet of it. A total explanation, we have argued, must account for the emergence, patterning, and change or abandonment of deviant behavior within the same theoretical framework. The case materials cited in this chapter are organized around the question of how well any of the three approaches explain etiology.

Etiology has been said to connote two distinct levels of explanation. Lemert distinguished between original cause, "the origins of the initial aberrant conduct," and effective cause, "the immediate cause in a delimited sequence of events."[7] This is like explaining why a youth steals candy the first time as one level and why he steals candy every day after school as a second level. The two explanations are probably different. Following Lemert's lead, the emergence of deviant behavior is similarly dichotomized in this analysis. *Primary emergence* refers to events, perceptions, and circumstances deemed important to the subject in explaining the first remembered instances of deviant behavior. *Secondary emergence* refers to events, circumstances, conditions, and conceptions subjectively perceived as important in explaining the emergence of *subsequent delimited patterns* of deviant behavior. Both the original involvement and the subsequent involvements in deviant behavior are important in understanding one's life-history at any point in time.[8] *Primary emergence,* or "original cause," is considered in this chapter. *Secondary emergence,* or "effective cause," and the subsequent deviant behavior patterns are examined in chapter 7.

Alternative Explanations of Emergence

It was shown in chapter 2 that the general proposition which represents the position of the socialization approach on the question of primary emergence assumes the internalization of norms and values. Deviant behavior emerges as a result of internalized norms and values which shape the perception and ultimately the behavior of individuals. The norms and values that are internalized by the individual are called *positive* since they reflect the norms and values of the individuals and groups expressing them. In short, the individual, one way or another, comes to hold values favorable to engaging in deviant behavior.

Analysis of the societal reaction theories in chapter 3 yielded the following general proposition: Deviant behavior emerges as the result of an individual's acceptance of and conformity to *negative behavior expectations* inherent in labels imposed prior to initial acts of deviant behavior. These expectations are *negative* in that they refer to behaviors regarded as deviant by the individuals and groups expressing them.

The control approach position on primary emergence is distinguished, in chapter 4, from both the socialization and societal reaction in that it is not something that stimulates deviance that is thought to cause deviant behavior. Rather, it is the absence or the weakness of something to prevent deviance that is important for control theorists. When the controls that bind individuals to groups and societies are absent, weakened, or neutralized, deviance may result.

The central question addressed in this chapter inquires to what extent these propositions explain the cases of primary emergence from life-history accounts. In general, the data show that neither the socialization, the societal reaction, nor the control approach accurately explains the full variety of sources of primary emergence. One case in which each approach is shown to be clearly plausible in explaining the emergence of initial deviant behavior is illustrated here. The preponderance of cases of primary emergence is not sufficiently explained by any one of the approaches. Of those instances not explained by the socialization, the societal reaction, or the control approach, some are sufficiently explained by other estalished theories and some fall outside the explanatory range of contemporary theories altogether.

In the following pages life-history accounts of primary emergence are divided into four groups: (1) those explicable in terms of the socialization approach; (2) those explainable in terms of the societal reaction approach; (3) those fitting the control approach; and (4) those cases that require either other theoretical frameworks or additional theorizing beyond established formulations. The plausibility of the socialization approach, in explaining the primary emergence of deviance in some cases, is demonstrated in the next section. The working definition of initial or first instances of deviance was the first remembered instance of a behavior that the respondent considered to be deviant, or that he felt others whose opinions and reactions he valued would have considered deviant had they known of it.

The reader will observe that what is deviant for one respondent may not be for another by this operational definition. It may appear to be excessively subjective to the point of overlooking common and shared values on the propriety of certain behaviors. In fact, however, it is a social definition. No normally functioning individual has a completely individualistic conception of morality. Our subjective sense of morality is shaped and altered in social interaction and is always more than individualistic. For purposes of the present study it would make no sense to define deviance as something beyond the actor's subjective meaning world—because it is within these social confines that individual social action is shaped.

The Socialization Approach

Of seven cases where the emergence of deviant behavior fits the socialization model, one stands out most clearly. This respondent's emergence into deviance is archetypal of the socialized deviant. His life-history closely resembles characterizations made in the early works of socialization theorists.

Don Catelli[9] grew up in a section of a large midwestern city where illegal and extralegal activity was usual. Don's parents separated at an early age and he had no significant contact with his real father from earliest memory. His step-father from age three was a career thief and Don knew it. Don himself had been involved in some kind of stealing as far back as he could remember. When he was seven years old he was arrested for a burglary of a storage shed and he distinctly recalled another burglary during the same year.

Don's childhood through early adolescence was marked by frequent involvement in some form of theft. In fact, this pattern of variable thievery continued, interrupted only rarely by incarceration in jail or prison or brief periods of change, through the rest of his thirty-five years. The central theme of his life-history revolves around one basic ambition—to be a *resourceful thief.* This ambition along with the associational network of Don's early life suggests compelling evidence for the plausibility of the commitment thesis underlying the socialization approach. That is, Don's case suggests to us that individuals may become committed to values favorable to deviant behavior and then be propelled into behavior that will actualize their values.

We will look at a period from the respondent's earliest memories to early adolescence in order to examine sources of his primary emergence into deviance. The life-history material on this period in Don's life invites the conclusion that this is an example of *cultural transmission* and especially *differential association* processes in their purest form.[10] More generally, this case supports the credibility of the socialization approach. The excerpts from the life-history document that follow make up an abridged account of this respondent's first involvements in deviant activity. The materials are presented with a minimum of commentary and a brief discussion follows this section. This particular life-history is also illustrated in the two subsequent chapters dealing with patterning and change. General conclusions are discussed in chapter 9.

Some clarifying notes are necessary for the reader before beginning the presentation of the life-history data. There is no one acceptable convention or format for presenting data of the sort presented here. The following is an explanation of the meaning of these symbols as used throughout the next three chapters. Parentheses are used to continue a line of thought verbally unfinished by the respondent and to clarify a personal pronoun or the meaning of a word or an expression. A quotation within parentheses or brackets is used to clarify the intended meaning of a comment by using the respondent's own definition taken from another part of the interview. Brackets are used to convey the investigator's interpretations, to note nonverbal communication, and to inject clarifying commentary. Quotes are used in the text of a passage to identify a conversa-

tion or dialogue reported by the respondent or to signify instances where the respondent is "thinking out loud" or
commenting to himself (e.g., "Drugs are really dumb," I
thought to myself).

In the following dialogue Don describes how he became
aware of his father's means of livelihood and the circumstances under which he was initially exposed to values favorable to theft.

> INTERVIEWER: [Before his father's background was
> known.] What were your parents' feelings about
> "stealing"?
>
> DON: Well, my mother and father never encouraged it,
> but *I knew he was a thief.*
>
> INTERVIEWER: You knew it at this time (when you were
> seven years old)?
>
> DON: Yeah, I knew it by friends and that. *There was
> always jokes, "Aw, he's* (Don) *going to be a burglar too,"
> you know, and uh, things like that.*
>
> . . . my father's friends (always teased me about
> becoming a burglar)—his friends were always around
> and everything. They were all thieves and burglars, so it
> was kind, uh, (always present), . . . all our clothes were
> bought from a fence [someone who deals in stolen goods],
> and uh, this is all I remember really. There was no, . . . *I
> just don't remember an honest situation.*
>
> . . . as far back as I can remember I guess my father,
> well, (would say) " Jesus, get up with that mathematics
> and you'll be able to work in the *book joints.*" "I'll see
> that you do all the books for the *book joints,*" you know,
> stuff like that. Or, "Jesus, you're small" and this or that,
> "you'll make a good burglar," you know.

Don was very much impressed with his father's versatility in
stealing. Recalling his father's activities during World War II
he says:

> I had seen shotguns, machine guns (in the house) so I
> remember these things. We were told to leave the room
> or whatever, but I can remember people that were there.
> I guess they had "cut a booty" [split the proceeds of a
> theft or a "hustle"] or whatever . . . they had stolen. I

remember once there was whole room full of silver dollars. And it was always stuff like that, you know, as far back as I can remember.

By age ten Don was well into the style of life he saw in the actions of his father and his father's associates. Although Don's father never encouraged his deviant activities overtly, he was well aware that Don was molding himself after him. His father's family and brothers and sisters were all, except one who was in the taxicab business, in one racket or another. In addition, they all lived in the same apartment building. Don knew what was expected of him and began plying his trade very early in life. The versatility of his father to come up with a profit was emulated by Don.

I was pretty cocky. ... I was beginning to be very *resourceful* ... and I was doing things then that the other kids wouldn't be doing for years, you know.

I could become very occupied with stealing, it was ... something I plotted and planned. ... Uh, but, I don't remember having any particular need to steal. I mean it wasn't (that I needed to steal to have things).

(I) had all (I) wanted. I mean Dad had that much money and he gave us [Don and his brother] anything we wanted. And we always had more money (than any of the other kids in the neighborhood) ... he was pretty generous that way. I remember sometimes he'd give us enough to take the neighbor kids to the movies.

I was always stealing—and I did it on my paper route and yet I was responsible as far as a newspaper guy. Boy, I got my route out. They could always depend on it. But I would steal right along the way ... in the city (at that time, it was customary) ... to hang bags on the corner and you put a dime in and got a paper. Well, that was my route ... (too). I went right around with it and emptied all the bags along the way ... they caught up with me there.

As a result of being caught for this he was probated to report to the police station every week and was required to make restitution. From age seven to ten Don had frequent contacts with the police. The contacts had no damaging effect on him, however:

> I knew my Dad would be there and work it out and ... I
> think they (the police) were afraid of him. Either they
> were conniving with him ... or (they) grew up in the
> same neighborhood.

By age twelve Don was into gang activities. His involvement
in criminal activities followed naturally from one age to the
next in the appropriate contexts.

> By the time I was out of grammar school ... I was
> already drinking. Uh, I had been smoking some pot
> already. It was just there. I didn't really like pot, but it
> was around ... just something to do.

> I kinda switched whole areas (neighborhoods). I started
> running with gangs ... the whole thing, you know.

> That's when I made the big switch ... and kinda drifted
> out of school altogether. I ran with gangs and, uh, just
> *prowled* the streets and got into things, *drank, caroused,*
> stayed out all night ... that kind of stuff.

Don was way ahead of other youths in his own neighborhood
so he had to drift to another neighborhood (incidentally, the
neighborhood where his father had grown up in the same way)
where he got into gang activities. The other youths from the old
neighborhood admired him for his prowess. Don was too advanced for the youths in his own neighborhood but, at the same
time, he never really felt totally integrated into the gang life of
the other neighborbood mainly because his family background
was different due to his father's success. While he liked the
general gang life-style, some of the gang activities were dis-
tasteful to him.

> I didn't like a lot of the things ... I didn't approve of
> things they did, ... I didn't feel part of them. They were,
> uh, different ... they were much poorer kids than (me)
> for the most part [pause], larger families.

Nevertheless, being in the gang and entrenched in its activities
served the purpose of demonstrating his commitment to being
a "resourceful thief" and an "operator."

> (Gang life) ... was a better thing (than staying in the old
> neighborhood) ... *it was for "procedure"* (just part of the
> training). If we were stealing I didn't have to. I didn't
> need the money.

> ... if we were on a "strong arm" (robbery), the ones
> where a bunch of kids would jump on some poor guy in
> the street or something and take his watch, ... just
> beating the hell out of some guy, ... I didn't like that, I
> didn't like hurting people. I didn't like the violent end of
> it at all. Uh, *but it was necessary* [pause] *in a way, to be*
> *tough!* And I was usually into it. But I had very bad
> feelings about it. I mean I just didn't like doing it.

Don's gang activities were just part of an apprenticeship. Any
activity that facilitated his training as a developing thief was
acceptable to him. This is apparent when Don says some violent confrontations did not bother him, in the gang context. For
example, violence was acceptable when there was an obvious
reason for it—when it was part of the training as described in
the following statement.

> ... but see the (strong armed robberies of) other kids, see
> they were like fights. This was just something that
> happened, ... we would go into a movie theater, ... sort
> of gang territory things, just like little confrontations—
> this kind of thing didn't bother me. I liked the rough—I
> liked being part of that.

When Don was between twelve and thirteen years of age he
was arrested and committed to a school for delinquent boys
because:

> (I) hit some kid and took some money from him [Don
> also had a police record dating back five years at this
> time]. We knew him and it was ... I don't know ... it was
> just something in them days you did, you know. It had
> been done to me.... I didn't really even consider it a
> strong arm robbery, ... more of a personal thing, it was
> a challenge—(to) fight and then as the end result—I just
> took some money (it was regarded the victor's right). The
> kid had, dollar, fifty cents, whatever. But I was arrested
> for it and they sent me to (a school for delinquents).

Don had always gotten off lightly with the police before because of his father's connections, but at this particular time his
father was in prison on a counterfeiting conviction. Don noted
that, even while in prison, his father wrote some letters making
contacts to assure that he was sent to the school for delinquents
rather than the harsher state reformatory. The harsher disposition, seemingly, would have been the more probable of the two

alternatives since Don already had a long arrest record dating back several years. So he believed his father must have "pulled the right strings" somewhere. When his father got out of prison he took Don back to the school for delinquents after a "run-away." Don remembers his father admonished the cottage counselors "not to lay a hand on me or they would answer to him."

Don's stay in the home for delinquents enhanced his "tough" image. When he got out, after a few months of incarceration, he went back to the same gang. They were "into drugs then." Don describes his involvement:

> ... they were into heroin by this time [previously he had smoked pot a few times—"I could probably count the times—it never excited me," he said] and ... I remember, in fact, ... *this is what did it.*
>
> I said, "let's get some pot," or whatever. But like what would happen—they would take money and go get some "horse" ... *it was ... like the group I was with*—and I started right around then [age 13].
>
> ... *a friend was "using" and had been the one I was running with the past couple of years,* his name was LeRoy ... they (LeRoy and most of the other guys) encouraged me *not* to, "Aw, don't do this." But I felt ... "they're trying this because they wanted it all for themselves" or whatever. "What do you mean don't do it, you know, why not?"

So Don took heroin for the first time because it was there, and because the others were into it. He recalled that he did not understand it at first. For example, Don indicated that he did not know what the effects of the drug were the first time he took heroin.

> DON: I didn't understand it, what it was about right away. I didn't even know I was high the first time.
>
> INTERVIEWER: How long did it take before you learned to appreciate heroin?
>
> DON: Oh, within the next day or so, or right after that.
>
> (I figured there must be something I couldn't understand) ... *well must be something happening,* you know, I mean *they were all getting high. ...*

It is important to remember that Don was already deeply committed to the life of a thief. His involvement in drugs was initially just another thing gang members did to demonstrate their prowess. The patterning of Don's drug use and his later career in theft are taken up in the next chapter. In this chapter, we have suggested that Don's initial deviant behavior emerged because values and expectations favorable to being a thief were emphasized in his social milieu. For the most part the facts of this case lend credibility to the socialization approach. But in the two chapters to follow some questions are raised regarding this conclusion.

The Societal Reaction Approach

One of the most common criticisms of the societal reaction approach to deviance charges that it does not or cannot explain the origins of initial instances of deviant behavior.[11] While it is important to note that the question of the origins of initial instances of aberrant conduct has never been explicitly addressed from the societal reaction perspective, there are two studies that deserve mention in this regard. Becker's "Becoming a Marihuana User" and Lindesmith's *Opiate Addiction* both examine one facet of the emergence question.[12] Consideration of emergence begins, in these studies, not with the initial act of deviant behavior, but with events and experiences which contribute to the specific pattern of the particular deviant behavior under investigation.

Becker later suggests the need to analyze the origins of deviant behavior in terms of events which render sanctions ineffective and in terms of experiences which shift conceptions so that the behavior becomes a conceivable possibility to the person.[13] But, Becker's 1953 study of marihuana use, like Lindesmith's 1947 work, was not concerned with origins in the sense of the primary emergence of deviant behavior. Rather, both Becker and Lindesmith were concerned with events and experiences contributing to processes by which persons come to engage in patterns of deviant behavior. In effect, then, these two studies have addressed secondary emergence to the exclusion of primary emergence. That is, they have examined the first instance of a deviant behavior which later became patterned. But they did not consider the first significant instances of deviant behavior in which the individuals had been involved.

This is also typical of recent studies departing from a societal reaction framework.[14] Since societal reaction theories and research typically begin by focusing on immediate factors which lead to particular patterns of deviant behavior, an important consideration is overlooked, namely, the failure to consider the possible cumulative effects of one's prior deviance, and events and circumstances surrounding it, as contributing to later patterns of deviant behavior. Indeed, the practice of considering the first act of a delimited pattern of behavior while excluding prior acts of deviance denies the importance of one's history in the explanation of present patterns.

Nevertheless, it is important to recognize that some societal reaction theorists do address implicitly the issue of primary emergence. By inferring from such implications and logically extending basic societal reaction precepts, a proposition pertaining to initial cause may be derived. That is, we may consider that deviant social behavior results from an individual's acceptance of and conformity to negative expectations inherent in differentiating labels imposed prior to involvement in deviant behavior. It is this proposition that will concern us most in the present section.

A second criticism and perhaps a greater failure of the societal reaction perspective is found in the definition of deviant behavior. The societal reaction definition encourages an avoidance of the important question regarding the cause of behavior viewed as deviant by the individual himself, even when it is unknown to others. For example, Becker's 1963 definition of deviance does not permit consideration of his very significant recognition of the *secret deviant* or one whose deviance is not known to others.[15] Most societal reactionists have, however, adopted Becker's definition that deviant behavior is that which is labeled by others as deviant. Logically, there can be no secret deviance using Becker's definition, and this leaves the researcher in a difficult position. Some individuals regard as deviant some behaviors they have engaged in which never became known to others.[16] In the present study, the respondent's subjective definition of deviance was used to sort deviant from nondeviant behavior. This definition permitted an analysis of both deviance resulting from the imposition of labels by others and deviance resulting from individual adjustments of their secret behavior.

In the following pages one of the two cases from a sample of fifty is presented to demonstrate the influence of societal reaction processes in the emergence of deviant behavior. The negative counterpart of the accolade *good family* is borne out as a differentiating and deviance-inducing label in this case. The label is that of the *no-good* which is native to small or rural communities and carries the insidious expectation of eventual deviance.

Labeled a No-Good:
A Case for
Societal Reaction

In the normal processes of differentiation some individuals and groups are separated out as untitled and generally undesirable. In the separation and appellation process, attributes, not behaviors, of individuals and groups are the bases for appraisal. Some individuals, because of certain social attributes, may be assigned the status "no-good." Albert Mass is a case in point.

Albert's family was poor and his father was a farm-laborer with a reputation for shiftlessness. These affiliations are intricately connected with his exclusion from the conventional community. Initial exclusion contributed to Albert's perpetual low self-conception. This can be seen, in part, in the following excerpt where the respondent notes the lack of positive relationships with others outside his family and hints that he was generally insecure around conventional members of the community.

> Well, as far as family goes, we had a real close—real intimate relationship there. You see ... I didn't have much to do with other people outside the family—except when I had to go to school. ... And I tried to get out of that as much as I could—and I never played with the other children that much. I've always been, you know, *shy of people.* So ... I didn't have much relationship with anyone else.

Albert was "shy of people" for two interrelated reasons. First, he had an "inferiority complex," as he puts it:

> As far as what I thought about myself, uh, I guess I had kind of an *inferiority complex* about being *ugly* and, you know, *skinny,* and uh, *always shy around people.*

A second reason he was shy of people that precedes the inferiority complex in time is that he was generally treated as a *no-good* unworthy of the common compliments to one's sense of dignity and self-conception which are usual in everyday interaction. When asked about his experience with people outside the family, such as community people or people in the school, Albert related one example which stood out in his memory. He described this incident with intense bitterness and emotions still raw from the experience. He was treated as unworthy of common interpersonal niceties, he was a no-good and no-goods do not merit polite consideration in interpersonal relations.

> (This neighbor) was puttin' up hay; son-of-a-bitch—(I)
> hate that sucker—uh, he was puttin' up hay and, uh, ... I
> told him I would drive the tractor for nothin', you know,
> I was real young then and I didn't think he would let me
> drive it. He did, you know—he was paying everyone else
> on the crew, even his sons ... but uh, I got to drive the
> tractor all that day and thought I was "cool." *What I
> remember real vividly* is when it came pay time—why
> he paid everyone there. And I don't know, I took it real
> hard—even though I told him I would work for nothin'.
> When it came pay time I asked him, I says "where's
> mine?" And he said "you don't get any you little
> mother-fucker." "You said you would work for nothin'."
> [Albert indicated that this was said in an unusually
> disrespectful tone.] And if I had been big enough I would
> have killed the fucker right there—made me madder
> than hell!

Albert's anger was not the result of being refused pay; he expected that. But it was the result of being treated with contempt and disrespect, discounting his worth as a person. This kind of denigration is a standard part of the everyday treatment of individuals who are cast as no-goods.

This experience, which Albert remembered so vividly, was not unique. As may be seen in the following remarks, it typified the way he perceived the reactions of people in the community generally.

> ... I would say they was aiming for me, you know—"this
> little bastard." They never would give me a chance—(as
> if I was just a) "mean little mother-fucker," you know.
> And I guess [regretful tone] I was a ... you know, just
> had a *bad name* ... just a *bad name.*

> (people outside the family) never did care for me—"that
> Mass kid, *no-good* mother-fucker"—never that I can
> remember (have people thought anything but the worst
> of me).

Albert was keenly aware of the fact that both he and his
family were cast as no-good and he understood well the standards of judgment involved. His negative self-conception, or
sense of worthlessness, made it easy to accept the negative
expectations to be a no-good. These expectations were inherent
in the reactions of other people. The following statement indicates that Albert accepted the no-good label. As he noted, his
mischief was just one more minus mark on an already totally
negative slate.

> As long as I can remember—as long as I can remember
> I've always been in mischief and somehow people would
> always find out about it. Well, as far as that goes all of
> us Mass' were *no-good*—I guess. Uh, . . . very poor family,
> you know [as if to offer an explanation for being no-good
> and the reason people discovered his mischief.] But uh,
> . . . always moving from one house to another—in and
> out. You know how people are—gossip goes around. And
> uh—just had a *bad name. I just added one more mark to
> my sheet, you know.*

From his earliest memory Albert was treated as a no-good, or
one not deserving of the common niceties of normal interpersonal relations, the niceties that initially permit one to be confident in social presentation and self-image when interacting
with others. His sense of being ugly, skinny, and shy was inextricably interconnected with the way he was reacted to as a
person without worth, and with his perception of being cast as
just another no-good from a family of no-goods.

Albert's only source of security was in his immediate family.
The mischief that he engaged in was wild, joyous, "hell-raising," unconstrained by any concern for maintaining a good
reputation, good name, or conventional relationships, because
he had none of these to maintain. His deviant behavior was
reckless, rash, and carefree. Indeed, it is this kind of deviance
that is generally expected of no-goods.

Being cast a no-good affected Albert in two ways. On the one
hand, he was "shy of people" because he was treated with con-

tempt by others in the community. This denigrating treatment also contributed to his "inferiority complex." On the other hand, being cast a no-good induced him to conform to the negative expectations conveyed through negative reactions from others.

On Being No-Good

No-good is an evaluative category native to small communities in America. It is used rather liberally among small-town dwellers to categorize persons and families for purposes of exclusion or banishment. It is most often applied prejudicially. That is to say, moral difference is not a necessary precondition to being so categorized.

There are some common indicators used in determining who is no-good. Albert began to identify some of the criteria for adjudging someone as no-good: "very poor family," "always moving from one house to another—in and out." And then in regretful resignation he concluded, "just a *bad name*" in general. Other indicators noted by different respondents are: drunken fathers; loud parental arguments; wrinkled, dirty, and tattered clothing; and trashy yards. Being cast a no-good is a total designation of one's self. It is an apt phrase in that it connotes a total lack of personal worth or that there is nothing *good,* whatsoever, about the person so labeled.

The ascription, *no-good,* and the resultant sense of inferiority that frequently accompanies it are not always permanent. As a case in point, when the individual is in a situation where his status as a *no-good* is unknown or can be concealed, it is possible for him to acquire a sense of worth. Self-worth is communicated to the individual by the same processes as *worthlessness,* through the common experience of everyday interaction. The difference is that a sense of worth is acquired through interactional courtesies extended to the individual and his source(s) of association, while a sense of *worthlessness* often results from the lack of such courtesies.

An example of the perceptions of a no-good about community reactions and acquisition of a sense of self-worth follows. This respondent was considered no-good in his home community because his father had a "bad-name"; he was a drunken, ne'er-do-well sort. The respondent recalls:

> I would be playing with some kid ... my age or
> something, you know, and his mother or old man would

> come out and say "get the hell out of my yard you little
> bastard." I mean things like this . . . just because my Dad
> had been in trouble [arrests for drunkeness] they took it
> out on me.

This respondent later, at age thirteen, stayed with a respectable
uncle in a different community and recalled his first experience with people in the community. His uncle had taken him
on an errand with him into the community. The simple experience of being treated on a basis of assumed worth was sufficient
to prompt a personal reassessment of his low self-conception.

> So . . . we went to a filling station . . . like there was two
> guys standing there and they go, "Oh! Hello Little Jones
> — . . . he [my uncle] was very short." So well, they seen
> me—"What you got here?" He goes, "this is 'Little Jones'
> now, this is my nephew." *I mean like they shook hands
> with me. They were very nice, very courteous. But
> nobody looked down at me. . . . I was looked up to just as
> much as my Uncle Joe was. . . .*

As a result of exposure to respectful treatment this youth who
was always regarded as a no-good in his home community began to think of himself more favorably.

In other circumstances, persons who are originally differentiated as no-goods may be able sometimes to neutralize the
negative reactions from others through personal achievement.
For example, some members of no-good families manage to
gain a fragile positive status by exemplary behavior in the
community. But if the individual in this provisional status is
implicated in some misdeed, the negative reactions may be
more harsh and swift. A respondent from a family with a "bad
name" had enjoyed the provisional status of "best of the bunch"
in the small community where he lived:

> . . . people always . . . said I was the best one out of the
> family, you know [as if to say people seemed to think I
> had a chance of being a respectable person].

He got into "a little trouble" for curfew violation, as a minor out
of state, with a group of youths (all sixteen to seventeen years
old) while driving a car around late at night. They were taken
to the police station and, upon discovery that they did not have

enough money to get home, were held in jail a couple of days until their parents sent some money. After his return home the respondent worried about:

> ... the way people thought, what people thought.

When asked what he thought people were thinking he replied:

> That I was (now) *no-good* and all this, you know, (that I) *couldn't be trusted* and all that.

This respondent was aware before this incident that his status was dependent on a flawless public record and that once he let down his guard or got involved in some minor transgression, people would react to him as they reacted to the rest of his family—as no-good. His fear was that people would consider him totally "bad," totally unacceptable, and untrustworthy. Lack of trustworthiness had nothing to do with the transgression which prompted his concern—rather it was a part of the expectation inherent in the label *no-good.* The respondent indicated, in the interview, that while many people were decent about the incident, others tended to act as though a transgression was inevitable and as if "eventually even the best of these *no-goods* will turn bad." After this minor transgression, which became publicly known, the respondent was frequently reacted to as just another no-good.

The question that occupied us in the preceding section was to what extent does the imposition of negative differentiating labels induce primary emergence into deviance. If we may generalize from Albert's case, as we believe the precepts of analytic induction permit, societal reaction theory can be seen to clearly account for some instances of primary emergence.[17] It also appears probable that no-good's, like Albert, are typical of a general class of individuals more vulnerable to the effects of imposed negative labels. Or, perhaps, it is the imposition of ascriptive status that is the key to understanding such cases. In any event, it is probable that Albert's experiences are not unique, but, rather, are broadly characteristic of minority race or ethnic groups, lower social classes, or large numbers of individuals whose group traits and personal attributes render them more susceptible to forced conformity to negative expectations.

A second case where negative prelabeling induced initial deviance can be seen in the case of Raymond. Raymond was one of four children in a lower-middle-class suburban family. His two older brothers had infamous reputations in the neighborhood as wild hell-raisers. When discussing his early life, Raymond recounts his feelings which eventuated in his first deviance.

> RAYMOND: Everything was good, you know, uh, except the neighborhood was kinda skeptical about me because of my brothers.
>
> INTERVIEWER: What led you to believe the neighbors were skeptical of you?
>
> RAYMOND: My friends, kids my age and older would tell me how bad their parents thought my brothers were and that I was going to grow up just like them. They didn't even want me around, around their kids. They was afraid I was going to get them in trouble or something.
>
> I got the impression they felt the same about me. They thought I was going to be a hell-raiser when I grew up.
>
> I could tell, you know, I sensed it. I guess you could say (I sensed what they thought) about who was who around (the neighborhood).
>
> *It didn't bother me too much because, at the time, I was good. And I had to prove I was good, then, too. But then after awhile it got to bothering me,* you know.
>
> INTERVIEWER: What do you mean, you had to prove you were good?
>
> RAYMOND: You know, I did things. You know, I helped people—I helped people out—cut grass for people, helped other people out that lived around there. *You know, being good and everything.* And that's how I proved myself and everything. And that really wasn't myself then. *And then I started hanging around with little groups, little groups of people out there (that were generally mischievous). And we'd go uh, you know.* We had a lot of fun and stuff too, you know, *start fires and things like that.*

Raymond refuted the negative reactions for some time, trying to change them by exemplary behavior. But ultimately he regarded the actions he took to "prove he was good" as overkill and not characteristic of what he was really like. He also tired of these efforts to prove he was not what some others thought him to be. Nor was he necessarily to become like his brothers.

At this point, Raymond accepted the negative *expectations of eventual deviance* and joined a group already established as a deviant group. Subsequently, this respondent became the deviant he perceived others expected him to be.

The Control Approach

Control theorists believe that weak, neutralized, or broken social controls may result in group and individual deviance. Social control is usually seen to have both internal individualistic and external group or associational components; that is, control comes both from within the individual and from without. Internal controls are either internalized norms opposed to deviance or personally pragmatic decisions making deviance impractical. External control rests in the influence others, groups, and institutions have on the individual. While the two general sources of control probably never exist exclusively of one another, they frequently vary considerably in relative strength. Internal controls, which are in large part a product of external controls, are usually considered to be the most effective given the weakness of controls outside the person.

A weakness in or lack of effective controls is generally considered, by control theorists, to be relatively permanent and pervasive in cases where individuals go on to manifest patterns of deviance. Spasmodic situational breakdowns in control and breakdowns in only one of a large number of the individual's affiliational networks (e.g., the family) are usually not discussed by control theorists. However, these sorts of focused situational problems and crises in one or two of an individual's affiliational systems may neutralize these specific controls as well as other controls for a long period of time. Therefore, we have categorized cases of primary emergence resulting from (1) situational conditions having long-term effects and (2) breakdowns in a single external source of control that neutralized other external sources of control as fitting the control model.

Within this broadly defined conception of the control thesis twenty-five of the fifty cases of primary emergence fit the control proposition.[18] In a large percentage of the cases fitting the control model the initial breakdown in control was related to family stress.[19] Three cases involved a breakdown in one associational system that spread to neutralize other sources of control for a period of months or years. All of the remaining cases involved relatively permanent and pervasive breakdowns of effective control in all areas. The case illustrated below is drawn from this latter group of cases.

Hubert: A Case of Lack of Controls

Some individuals deviate because there is no reason not to. They are not motivated by deviant norms and values, they simply are not constrained by conventional norms. Hubert is a case in point. From his earliest memories, both conventional control norms and those who espoused them were alien to him. Hubert's first involvement in deviance was stealing small things from a store on his route to school. He indicated that after the first theft of a squirt gun he had a "flash of guilt" but quickly discarded it. There was no one in his life whose opinions he cared about and, subsequently, because there was no reason not to, his stealing from the store became regular.

Hubert lived with his parents in a small midwestern community until they divorced when he was nine.

> That's when I moved to my Grandma Mart's to stay with her. I stayed with her for about two years, there in that one time, until I was about eleven years old. Then I stayed with my Grandma Bennis up until I was thirteen and then I stayed with my mom till I was, I would say fourteen. Then when I was fifteen I was staying with my Grandma Bennis and that's when I got sent to boys' school.

The first and primary source of control for a youth is, in most cases, the family. Hubert described his early family life as generally intense and filled with turmoil and uncertainty. His voice frequently cracked with emotion as he recalled his early life, relationships, and feelings.

> . . . there was no kind of family thing at all, just everybody going their own direction it seemed. I always felt like uh (I was) either on the outside lookin' in or on the inside lookin out. *I didn't never feel like I was part of anything.*

> (My family) . . . it was always a state of confusion, wasn't any secure ground to stand on. You never knew where you stood.

... there was just no rest, no sense of well-being at all. It
was a rat race all the way through.

When asked about his relationship with his parents, Hubert
recalled:

> (My father) ... you never knew what to look for next,
> you know. He just—everytime he come in he didn't have
> nothin' to say or nothin' to do unless he was going to do
> some damage of some kind. And when you see him
> comin' you took off to the other direction. *He was just
> mean, uh, hard to get along with, couldn't communicate.*

> (My mother) *She was there but uh,* I just remember
> little bits about her. I really don't remember her too good
> and that time there (before the divorce) I uh, just didn't
> have no uh, it was just uh, *something was missin'*
> somewhere all the time. It just wasn't there, you know
> what I mean—*just no relationship at all.* I didn't feel
> that, you know, like most kids uh, that's the first thing
> they do is (go to their mother) if they need something or
> want something. But I never had that feeling. We just
> wasn't close at all.

Hubert's apparent emotional distance from his parents and
a general lack of involvement in secure group relationships
had a telling effect on his personal dispositions and self-feel-
ings.

> *I developed a kind of inferior thing* about ... "to hell
> with everybody" and I just stayed to myself. Most of the
> time I had that unwanted feeling, more or less, you know
> what I mean, *I didn't feel like I was part of the group. I
> got into this hum-drum thing* [which the interviewer
> understood to mean, a listless insecurity and sense of
> confusion] where I just—I would get off by myself and
> that's when I was most happy.

As with his family, Hubert did not feel he was a part of the
community. He responded to a question about the way he and
his family were perceived by the community with the following remarks.

> I would say, to them, it wouldn't make a damn bit of
> difference if we had blew-up right then or what. The
> community, in general, didn't take too much pride in us.

Hubert continued to steal from stores and from his grandmother's purse occasionally, and when there was either opportunity or felt need, through childhood and early adolescence. There was a basic understanding, on his part, that he should not be doing these acts.

> I knew I shouldn't be doing it see—but I didn't feel too
> bad about it.

But, at the same time, he was not attached to anyone who might influence him to abandon the activity. He was not concerned with how anyone else felt about his behavior.

> I'm tryin' to tell you there was none (no relationship)
> between nobody in the family. *I never felt uh, what you
> say, close to anybody—even halfway. Uh, nobody . . .
> never did.*

Beginning in the third grade he became "turned off" by a teacher's indifference and school in general which seemed to complete the circle of separation from and lack of influence by conventional sources of control. Hubert's family, the community, and the school were not reference points in structuring his behavioral repertoire—therefore deviance was available to him. Hubert's case is further developed in chapters 7 and 8.

Summary

This chapter was concerned with the origins of initial instances of deviant behavior, which we have called primary emergence. Three cases of primary emergence were illustrated to provide an empirical comparison against which the three theoretical approaches were examined.[20] Don's strong commitment to beliefs favorable to the type of behavior characteristic of his social milieu lends support to the plausibility of the socialization explanation of primary emergence. The second case is important because it represents an empirical instance of original cause explicable in terms of the societal reaction formulation and therefore casts doubt on the frequent claim that societal reaction cannot explain initial entry into deviant acts. Albert's case provides suggestive evidence that societal reaction can account for some cases of initial cause and that perhaps no-goods are a part of a social type of individuals categorically more vulnerable to the effects of societal reaction.

An Empirical Evaluation

The case of Hubert depicts a youth who was not propelled to deviance by values favoring it but, rather, he was enticed by opportunity or need because he had no ties to conventional sources of control and constraint. In the following chapter we will look at the development of patterns of deviant behavior.

Notes

1. See David Matza, *Becoming Deviant* (Englewood Cliffs, N.J.: Prentice-Hall, 1969).

2. See Edwin H. Lemert, *Social Pathology* (New York: McGraw-Hill, 1951).

3. See Howard S. Becker, "Labeling Theory Reconsidered" in the 1973 printing of *Outsiders: Studies in the Sociology of Deviance* (New York: Free Press, 1973), p. 179. Also, for an emphasis on the behavior of defining agencies, see C. Ray Jeffery, "The Structure of American Criminological Thinking," *Journal of Criminal Law, Criminology and Police Science* 46 (January-February 1956): 658–72, and Austin T. Turk, *Criminality and Legal Order* (Chicago: Rand McNally, 1969).

4. Don C. Gibbons, "Observations on the Study of Crime Causation," *American Journal of Sociology* 77 (September 1971): 262–78.

5. The most notable exceptions to this tendency are Edwin H. Sutherland's "differential association" first conceptualized in 1939 (see Sutherland and Donald R. Cressey, *Principles of Criminology* (Philadelphia: J. B. Lippincott, 1966), and Walter C. Reckless' "Identification of a self-factor" first published in 1943 (see Walter C. Reckless' "The Etiology of Delinquent and Criminal Behavior," Bulletin 50, New York Social Science Research Council, pp. 51–52). Reckless, joined by his colleague Simon Dinitz and students Frank Scarpitti et al., at the Ohio State University, pursued the idea of a "self-factor" or self-concept as a crucial factor in the etiology of crime and delinquency for two decades. For a complete bibliography of the massive longitudinal and related studies see Walter C. Reckless, *The Crime Problem*, 4th ed. Englewood Cliffs, N.J.: Prentice-Hall, pp. 444–57. Donald R. Cressey's *Other People's Money: A Study in the Social Psychology of Embezzlement* (Glencoe, Ill.: Free Press, 1953), and Alfred R. Lindesmith's *Opiate Addiction* (Bloomington: Indiana University Press, 1947) stand out as classic attempts to address the question of etiology with specific types of deviants. While some works in sociology purport to be genetic theories of crime or explanations of the emergence of delinquent subcultures, such as Sutherland and Cohen, most sociologists of the socialization tradition are interested primarily in the beginnings that eventuate in patterned deviance. They are less interested in etiology of deviant acts that do not form a basis for a deviant career. Control theories are far less guilty of this sort of oversight with respect to unpatterned deviance.

6. Etiology is important even to the phenomenologically oriented sociologists since self-perceived causation is important to individuals in the structuring of their lives. When individuals regard their condition as having a "cause," the phenomenological reality of the individual's condition may be understood in terms of the effect of the perception of "causes" on present entanglements. See Carol A. B. Warren and John M. Johnson, "A Critique of Labeling Theory from the Phenomenological Perspective," in *Theoretical Perspectives on Deviance*, ed. Robert A. Scott and Jack D. Douglas (New York: Basic Books, 1972), pp. 79–102.

7. See Edwin M. Lemert, *Social Pathology* (New York: McGraw-Hill, 1951), p. 75.

8. Ibid., pp. 444–46.

9. In the interest of readability we have given a ficticious name to each respondent's life-history illustrated in chapters 6, 7, and 8.

10. See, for example, the view that one behaves in accord with cultural expectations if there are no conflicting alternatives in Sutherland and Cressey, *Principles of Criminology,* pp. 81–82, and Clifford R. Shaw, *The Jack-Roller* (Chicago: University of Chicago Press, 1966), pp. 33–47.

11. See, for example, Jack P. Gibbs, "Conceptions of Deviant Behavior: The Old and the New," *Pacific Sociological Review* 9 (Spring 1966): 9–14; Walter R. Gove, "Societal Reaction as an Explanation of Mental Illness: An Evaluation," *American Sociological Review* 35 (October 1970): pp. 873–84; and Milton Mankoff, "Societal Reaction and Career Deviance: A Critical Analysis," *Sociological Quarterly* 12 (Spring 1971) pp. 204–18.

12. Howard S. Becker, "Becoming a Marihuana User," *American Journal of Sociology* 59 (November 1953): 1–15, and Lindesmith, *Opiate Addiction.*

13. Becker, *Outsiders,* p. 60.

14. See, for example, John I. Kitsuse, "Societal Reaction to Deviant Behavior: Problems in Theory and Method," *Social Problems* 9 (Winter 1962): 247–56; Aaron V. Cicourel and John I. Kitsuse, "The Social Organization of the High School and Deviant Adolescent Careers" in *Deviance: The Interactionist Perspective,* ed. Earl Rubington and Martin S. Weinberg (New York: Macmillan, 1968), pp. 124–35; and Erving Goffman, "The Moral Career of the Mental Patient," *Psychiatry* 22 (May 1959): 123–42.

15. Becker acknowledges the problems with this definition in an addendum to the *Outsiders* in 1973. He notes that we may look at secret deviance as "potentially deviant" behavior, since others would likely label it if they knew about it. Then, Becker indicates, the remainder of his discussion may stand as it is. See "Labelling Theory Reconsidered" in *Outsiders* pp. 180–81.

16. David Matza and Jack D. Douglas have recently considered the *secret deviant* in greater depth than Becker while looking at what Becker tends to overlook even in the 1973 reconsidered version of his theory. They consider the self-labeling process. See Matza, *Becoming Deviant,* and Jack D. Douglas, *American Social Order* (New York: Free Press, 1971), pp. 141–42, for a discussion of the intersubjective judgment of "Being" as an aspect of self-labeling.

17. Analytic induction, as used here, draws on the idea that a thorough knowledge of one or a few cases may serve well as a basis for making generalizations. The logic is the same as for enumerative induction where the base is a less thorough knowledge of a larger number of cases. See Lindesmith, *Opiate Addiction,* p. 21.

18. Sixteen of the instances of primary emergence were not sufficiently explained by any of the three approaches.

19. Eleven out of twenty-five, or 44 percent, of the cases of initial cause resulting from a breakdown in social control involved family stress. This provides some evidence to support F. Ivan Nye's concentration on the family as the primary place for social control of youth. See F. Ivan Nye, *Family Relationships and Delinquent Behavior* (New York: John Wiley, 1958).

20. The three approaches did not subsume all the cases of primary emergence in this study. Indeed, a wide variety of primary sources of deviance were apparent in the data. Some fit other established theories of other disciplines, others seemed to be produced by factors which are typically overlooked by theories of deviance. Those cases that are explained by other theories may be grouped under problems of personal security and neuroses. There is a rich body

of literature in psychology and psychiatry relating to these inducements to deviance. The author is most persuaded by the early works of Karen Horney and Harry Stack Sullivan as explanations of deviance induced by personal insecurity and neuroses. See Karen Horney, *Self Analysis* (New York: W. W. Norton, 1942), for a discussion of problems of disturbed relationships and neurotic needs which develop as a result of anxiety produced therein; Karen Horney, *Neurotic Personality of Our Times* (New York: W. W. Norton, 1937), for coping strategies employed by insecure and anxious persons; and Harry Stack Sullivan, *Conceptions of Modern Psychiatry* (Washington, D.C.: William Alanson White Psychiatric Foundation, 1947) and *The Interpersonal Theory of Psychiatry* (New York: W. W. Norton, 1953). For those cases not well explained by other theoretical frameworks, two factors emerged as important inducements to deviance: practical considerations (i.e., deliberately calculated deviance for some desired end) and situational stress. Don C. Gibbons speculated recently that these factors are more frequently involved in the etiology of crime than most theorists assume. The present data support Gibbons. See Gibbons, "Observations on the Study of Crime Causation," pp. 262–78. Also for a discussion of situation stress as it relates to individual forms of deviance see James E. Teele, "Social Pathology and Stress" in *Social Stress,* ed. Sol Levin and Norman A. Scotch (Chicago: Aldine, 1970), pp. 228–53, and Marvin Wolfgang, *Patterns of Criminal Homicide* (Philadelphia: University of Pennsylvania Press, 1958). Importantly, Edwin Lemert's classic study of "The Naive Check Forger" has shown that this form of deviance may arise out of certain types of *situations* where the actor subjectively perceives a constriction of behavioral alternatives. See Edwin M. Lemert, *Human Deviance, Social Problems, and Social Control,* 2d ed. (Englewood Cliffs, N.J.: Prentice-Hall, 1972).

The Patterning of Deviant Behavior

7

A deviant act is not always followed by subsequent deviance. Once the first deviant act has been engaged in, many individuals do not go on to pattern the deviance. Instead, they regard the initial act as occasional, alien, or unreflective of their better selves.[1] Some may cease after the first deviant act and begin again at a later period, eventually to pattern the same or another form of deviant behavior. Still others may continue the same behavior, or behaviors with similar subjective meanings, to the point of developing a pattern of deviant behavior. Once the deviant act has been committed, then, an individual may or may not go on to a pattern of deviant behavior. Those who do go on to manifest patterns of some form of deviant behavior are the subject of concern of this chapter.

We are interested in *why* and *how* patterns of deviant behavior develop. These are questions which the socialization, societal reaction, and control theorists answer differently. This chapter deals with two broad issues. First, are the three approaches viable explanations of the processes by which deviant behavior may come to be patterned? Second, can they account for all that happens in the patterning process when they are applied to ideal examples of the types of cases they purport to explain?

111

The different theoretical explanations of patterned deviant behavior offered by our three approaches provide a critical point upon which their comparative explanatory power may be evaluated. In the present analysis the approaches are tested in the sense that, following Becker's reasoning, an approach is viable to the extent that it explains the facts in the development of patterns of deviant behavior.[2] Aspects of this development that cannot be explained within the framework indicate weakness in the theoretical approach. Becker's reasoning is extended here to suggest that, since no one of the approaches will be explicable in all cases, a fairer and more direct test is produced when the basic tenets of the approaches are pitted against prototype or ideal type cases which they purport to explain.

It is on the issue of patterned deviant behavior that the question of the comparative viability of the three approaches is most reasonable. This is the case, first, because the position of all three theoretical approaches is more explicit with regard to patterning than it is with regard to the explanation of the emergence or the change of deviant behavior.[3] Second, all three approaches take patterned deviant behavior as a theoretical focal point. Third, the distinction between the three theoretical approaches is greatest and most apparent at this level of explanation.[4]

Theoretical Distinctions on the
Issue of Patterning

Socialization formulations, as noted in chapter 2, explain patterns of deviant behavior in terms of the internalization of norms and values. Internalized norms and values form behavioral predispositions and beliefs. Deviant behavior is patterned, in this view, as a result of the internalization of values favorable to deviance. These norms and values are transmitted through *positive expectations* and, once internalized, the resultant beliefs and behavioral predispositions form the core of the personality structure. Ultimately, deviant behavior is patterned because of compelling forces in the personality and because of support and encouragement in the deviant's social milieu. Stated differently, the individual conforms to internalized norms and values and is usually reinforced by significant others in the social setting. This is the same as the socialization explanation of primary emergence except that social support and encouragement from the deviant's immediate milieu is now added as a factor.

Societal reaction theories explain the patterning of deviant behavior differently. Patterned deviant behavior is the product of induced, or forced, conformity to the *negative expectations* imposed in the process of social reaction. These negative expectations, that is, expectations to be deviant, are inherent in the deviant label and in the corresponding reactions of the labelers. Therefore, as a result of societal reaction the person is treated, and is expected to act, like a deviant in all respects. The individual, once labeled, is *expected* to behave unacceptably. Moreover, the behavior of the labeled person is credible to the labelers only if it conforms to the negative expectations. Even if it does not conform to the negative expectations, the person is still regarded and treated as a deviant by the labelers. This is often sufficient to justify a pattern of deviance, even for an individual who would rather discontinue deviance. This process of induced or forced conformity to negative expectations stands in direct contrast to the *internalization thesis* of the socialization approach.

In essence, the difference between the socialization and the societal reaction approach is the difference between conformity to *positive expectations,* which are internalized and therefore compelling, and conformity to imposed *negative expectations,* which are *not* internalized but are compelling because they are actively expressed in the reactions of significant labelers. Expectations are positive when they reflect the values of the individuals and groups expressing them. Negative expectations communicate the belief that one will engage in behavior regarded as deviant by the persons expressing them.

The socialization approach assumes that conformity to positive expectations is the principal factor involved in the patterning of deviance. These positive expectations are internally compelling because they become part of the personality structure. The personality structure, to the socialization theorist, is in part a set of behavioral predispositions. Once formed, the personality is a major force in determining and shaping individual behavior.

By contrast, societal reaction theorists regard actively imposed negative expectations as the most important factors in causing the patterning of deviant behavior. The labeled individual is compelled to conform to negative expectations by immediate interactional pressures and constraints. The individual is, first, reacted to negatively. Second, there is pressure to be deviant through these negative reactions, since they carry the expectation of additional or continued deviance. Third, the individual is restrained from nondeviant forms of behavior because the labelers accept as credible only indications of deviant behavior. Being treated as totally deviant, along with the refusal of the labelers to accept legitimate behavior, induces one to behave in deviant ways.

This points to the different conception of personality posed by societal reactionists. To these theorists, personality or "self" is heavily influenced by external forces in the interactional context of a point in time. A significant portion of the self is always in the process of forming and is vulnerable to external definitions. It is through this vulnerability that negative expectations, communicated in the reactions of others, are effective forces in inducing and shaping specific behavior patterns.

Essentially, the socialization view assumes an *internally* compelling force based in the personality structure. The societal reaction framework assumes an *externally* compelling force based in the reactions of significant others.

Control theorists, on the other hand, do not see any set of forces compelling individuals to deviance. Rather, the only compelling social forces generally recognized by control theorists are those that bring on conformity. It is the absence of these social constraints that permit deviance, but deviance is not necessitated by it. The control theorists' proposition on patterning is much the same as that for emergence. It is the weakness, neutralization, or lack of social controls that increases the probability of patterned deviant behavior.

To some extent control theorists envision an intervening inducement between ineffective controls and actual involvement in deviance. Matza, for example, considers a *will* to deivance emanating from either frustration or earlier experiences and understandings, making some forms of deviance familiar and available. In Durkheim's *Suicide,* the intervening factor was a characteristic of human nature—we will pursue personal needs, interests, and desires unless otherwise socially constrained. For others, there is a rational component in our behavior which provides the direction when controls are weak or broken. When it is situationally convenient or otherwise practical to do so we might expect deviance where control is insufficient to dictate conformity.

Operational Definitions

The focal questions in this chapter are (1) which of the three approaches provides the most complete account of our life-history instances of patterning, and (2) does any one approach sufficiently explain the phenomenon of *patterning* for the cases which it was intended to cover. It is important, however, to make clear the operational definitions employed in the analysis of the life-history documents before we proceed with the questions.

Deviant behavior is broadly regarded as *patterned* when behaviors with the *same meaning* to the individual are engaged in a number of times in a subjectively delineated period of time. When an individual has engaged in behaviors, to which the *same subjective meaning* is attached, a number of times within a distinct period of time and sequence of events, this behavior is said to be *patterned.*[5]

Diverse behaviors may be subjectively viewed as either *of the same kind* (have the same meaning) or *subjectively different,* regardless of their social and legal meanings. For example, petty theft, shoplifting, burglary, and armed robbery were all subjectively viewed by some respondents as simply "stealing," "gangsterism," or "thievery." When various behaviors were accorded the same meaning by the respondent, it was interpreted as a single pattern of deviance. By contrast, if behaviors such as theft, burglary, and armed robbery were regarded as distinct and their occurrence was frequent in a delimited stage of life, then each set of activities was seen as constituting a separate pattern. The emergence of each form of deviance was somewhat independent, in these cases, and implied somewhat different causes. In other words, one who regards petty theft and burglary as distinct, yet patterns both during the same time period, may do so for different reasons. One respondent, for example, engaged in systematic theft (stealing gasoline) as a matter of course ("everyday hell-raising"), but committed burglary during the same time period only when he was drunk or drinking heavily. He also regarded himself as a "different person" when he was drinking as opposed to when he was not. Therefore, the two patterns of deviant behavior called for separate analysis and implied somewhat independent explanations.

Patterns of deviant behavior begin, become stablized, and end. The beginning of a pattern of deviant behavior is referred to as *secondary emergence.* It is distinguished from *primary emergence,* which pertains to the first remembered instance of deviant behavior, in that *secondary emergence* marks the first acts of a form of deviance that subsequently comes to be *patterned.* When a particular form of behavior was frequent or prominent enough for the subject to view it as a part of his behavioral repertoire, it was said to be *patterned.*[6] *Secondary emergence* and *patterning* are correlative concepts. Deviant behavior patterns always follow *secondary emergence.* The end of a pattern, which is called *change,* is marked by the respondent's indicating that he did not engage in the behavior for some subjectively significant period of time. Patterns end when the behavior is *changed* or *abandoned.* An individual may go through this cycle several times, patterning different forms of behavior or the same forms, at different stages in his life. Most of the respondents in this study completed the cycle of secondary emergence, *patterning,* and change more than once.

Given the alternative propositions and assumptions of the socialization, societal reaction, and control approaches, we are interested in how viable they are when looking at the natural history development of patterned deviant behavior. In addressing this question, the following analysis looks at life-history accounts of patterned deviant behavior. To begin with, Don's case is continued from chapter 6 to evaluate further the utility of socialization theory in explaining the patterning process. Then, several cases, including Albert's, explicable in terms of the societal reaction framework are analyzed. Finally, the control approach is considered as an explanation of the patterning process. Hubert's case is continued from chapter 6 along with Carl's, another case fitting the control model.

The Socialization Approach—
The Case of Don

In chapter 6, it was shown that Don's primary emergence into a pattern of theft and drug use was most appropriately explained in terms of the socialization formulation. The discussion was ended at the point where Don was committed, at age thirteen, to the life of a thief and was beginning to experiment with heroin. At that stage, we argued that Don's emergence into deviance was a clear example of cultural transmission, the acquisition of values favorable to deviance.

Don "got a habit" shortly after his initial experience with heroin use. During this period and continually through the remainder of his life Don manifested, concurrently, two forms of deviant behavior, drug use and systematic theft. These two patterns are sometimes distinct and sometimes complementary. That is, sometimes the patterns had different meanings, to Don, and sometimes they had the same meaning.

Initially, these patterns were distinct. Don's drug use was an aside, decidedly secondary to his activity and identity as a thief. He had accepted the values and beliefs favorable to thievery and regarded himself as a "sneak thief." Taking drugs was separate from that identity, even though he was addicted to heroin at this time. He regarded his drug use as "for kicks," "just something we did," and as a part of the gang life-style.

Gradually, Don's primary identity shifted to that of a "junkie" or "dope fiend" and theft was then complementary to the now dominant activity of drug use. While previously his theft was explainable as a result of internalized values or conformity to *positive expectations* favoring theft, it was now a practical necessity, as seen in the following comment:

> It was just necessary. If you used drugs, it was necessary to be a good thief.

There was, at this point, no distinction made between theft and drug use. They meant the same thing—"theft was money, money was drugs." Don says:

> ... there was no value on money. Money was just something I turned into drugs.

The general nature of his deviance did not change, however. Don still engaged in both drug use and systematic theft. But, now, the theft was for the purpose of supporting a drug habit.

The point is that, when drug use was an aside for Don, theft could be explained satisfactorily in terms of earlier internalized, or at least accepted, values and norms favorable to such behavior. At that early period Don, as seen in chapter 6, aspired to be a good thief by plotting and planning his thefts carefully. However, when drug use became the dominant pattern in late adolescence and adulthood, his theft was more a result of necessity than of internalized or accepted values and *positive expectations.* This observation is supported when it is remembered that it was never necessary for Don to steal before his involvement with drugs. He always had all the money he needed and wanted upon request from his parents. However, once he became addicted to heroin and was discovered by his parents to be a user, he was generally disowned. Theft was then necessary for him. Theft also proved most expedient because he "knew it best" of all available means of acquiring money. Don disengaged from both systematic theft and drug use a few times; however, he eventually revitalized patterns of both forms of deviant behavior on a periodic basis.

Our task here is to examine these instances of patterning in an effort to ascertain which of the competing theoretical approaches provides the most tenable explanation of them. In addition, we will see that aspects of Don's patterned deviance may be noted which do not fit the theoretical system employed in our earlier explanation.

The patterning of Don's behaviors, it will be shown, was less a result of internalized values and norms than of: (1) practical decision; (2) social support and encouragement from his associates in his immediate environment; and (3) conformity to positive expectations, of others which were not, in the strict usage, internalized. The internalization thesis which underlies socialization theories is questioned in this instance. Social support and positive expectations from significant others are integral components of the socialization approach to deviance and are seen to be more prominent factors in the development of Don's patterns than internalized values and norms. While the socialization explanation still is argued to be the most tenable explanation of Don's patterns, the utility of the internalization thesis as an integral part of that explanation is questioned. The key idea of this internalization thesis is that individuals act according to psychological bents or predispositions which result from internalized values and norms. It is argued that the practical decision in the process of patterning deviant behavior, which is apparent in Don's case, is not compatible with the socialization theorists' ideas on internalization. From this it is argued that the socialization explanation in general is, to some extent, weakened by the assumption of internal forces which propel individuals into deviance.

Illustrations of the operation of (1) practical decision, (2) social support and encouragement in the immediate environment, and (3) conformity to positive expectations, in the development of Don's behavior patterns, are presented in the following pages. We will see that while the internalization thesis was a plausible factor in Don's early life of deviance, it is not defensible in explaining his later patterns of deviant behavior.

Practical Decision to Deviate

The influence of practical decision in the patterning of Don's behavior is seen when he recalls a time when theft was for him the most expedient solution to a problem. Don had noted that he did not want to steal at this particular time. He said he wanted to "do it right" and "have a decent life," but, practically speaking, it was more expedient to steal. The following dialogue illustrates that Don selected theft over other means of obtaining money as a *choice*, not because internalized values and norms propelled him to commit theft. His purposive decision to steal was calculated in full awareness of the consequences of being caught, but, in his view, theft was still the most practical means to a desired end.

> DON: I didn't want to go back to prison. ... I don't know why ... other than the fact that jails were starting to get a little tiresome. (I was) starting to get a little worn out and a little tired ... and the sentences were getting longer then.
>
> ... there were mornings, sometimes, when I didn't feel like going out and stealing but *"like I said, I had to!"*
>
> INTERVIEWER: "had to"—for what reason?
>
> DON: For money—and the bills were due—and this is the way I dealt with it. Uh (that's how I got), things I was going to need—or whatever.
>
> INTERVIEWER: Now, you say you needed money, there are a lot of ways to get money. You selected stealing?
>
> DON: Right, this was the easiest way, and I knew (from past success) that I could ("solve the problem most easily by theft" when) under pressure. When it came to it I would come up with something. There was no question about it. ... I would be able to get it.

It is apparent from these remarks that Don re-engaged in theft and continued to steal because it was more expedient for him than other means of obtaining money for general sustenance because he knew it best.

Social Support and Encouragement

On other occasions Don's patterns were primarily precipitated by situational forces such as the encouragement that follows from being "with the old gang again" or in situations where deviance is part of the "style of life" and is thereby socially supported. The following account of Don's return to drug use begins after he had been off drugs for seven months. He was, however, involved in systematic confidence-games which began immediately upon his finishing a prison sentence. In the dialogue, Don describes his pattern of theft, and the final contributing force, as being "back on the scene." His commentary shows clearly that the involvement in a systematic pattern of theft gradually developed into an exclusive involvement with other deviants and situations which generally supported and encouraged the use of drugs.

Don's "con-games" were purposive and goal-directed, but using drugs again was not. Drug use was the result of conformity to the "style of life" encouraged by others in his immediate surroundings.

> Don: I started a lot of confidence-games. . . . I was working with a guy that had been a cell partner of mine. And we set up (a hustle). (We) sold phony loads of hot goods to fences. We would set them up, make a pretense we had a load of whisky—or whatever—and get the money and it would be an empty garage.
>
> Interviewer: Okay, you told them that the goods would be a certain place, collected the money, then took off . . .?
>
> Don: Yeah, . . . we worked a regular system. First we would put out feelers, we would check newspapers for new tavern owners—or whatever—go in ("if we got any rumor that they were a fence") and tell 'em "Look, we got a load of whisky (that you can have cheap) if you are interested." . . . and we would give them some tempting prices. . . . and we would use names like "Tony" and "Rocky" and "Big Frank." And uh, I usually went out as a feeler (because) people felt they could manipulate me, (that) I was going to be easy. . . . then the other guy (my partner) would "corner them up." And he would give them a lot of double talk, plenty of numbers and paper. And figure it out and he'd say "I'll show you where the garage is." First we would tell them we'd furnish a

truck, then we would tell them (at the last minute) that
we couldn't get hold of a truck. "Can you bring one, rent
a trailer—we'll knock it off the top." Anyway the guy
would come ("sometimes they would send someone else")
and then (my partner) would pull them around by a
garage and get them "up very tight" and say, "well,
watch!", "Do you see anybody," "Let me go in and open
the door," "Let me check," "Keep your motor running
and back in when I open the door." You know (he
would) get them pretty well "souped-up". ("Once we got
the money") I would pull the car around front and he
would just come through the gangway—and we were
gone!

... it was very simple, you could go in just about any
store and everybody was pretty keyed so ... (it worked
well).

... (then) I moved back with the same girl [someone he
had lived with previously for a short while. ... I started
doing some pimping ... , I set up a house for call girls
and had five of them living in one house ... some of
them were working the streets ... mostly it was with
protection. I gave them protection (from the police) ... , I
was a source for narcotics for them. We had the money
and I had the connections ... they were making money
so it was a compatible situation. (*I*) *don't know why I
started using (drugs again).* I started getting into a thing
with a prostitute, I had money ... I just wanted to get
high or whatever ... (I had) a bellman's job (too) ... I
don't know *"I was just back on the scene,"* I had money
and I was a [pause] *I don't know why.*

Don's activities shifted gradually from a con-game operated
rather independently with one other associate to a cooperative
arrangement of connections and relationships which involved
him in a deviant culture. Success in the confidence-games
seemed to lead naturally into deeper involvement. The situational forces (being "back on the scene") in the deviant culture
initiated his desire to use drugs again. His situation, associates,
and general surroundings were predominantly deviant, and
this contributed to his decision to take drugs again.

Conformity to Positive Expectations

Another way in which contributory, or causal, forces operate
through continued deviant surroundings and associates may be

illustrated by Don's case. Don was trying to "go straight" while maintaining his associations with deviants.

> ... I worked at this place for about a year, I went to
> work for a guy I knew as a kid. He run the place [pizza
> place, which Don had previously felt was beneath him].
> He paid me well so I really didn't mind it. But I rented a
> place for her [his girl] and ... tried to set up an
> apartment and that. *But it didn't work, she was still
> messing with "speed" and she didn't want to just sit
> home.* She had gotten caught up running with another
> circle of people, using speed and that. I could see she
> didn't know where I fit in their little world anymore
> (since I was trying to stay clean)—*she started using me
> ... and I was having to steal after work* (to keep her in
> drugs and fun).

To maintain his relationship with his girl, who was involved in a "drug using" group, Don felt he had to steal and he felt pressure to use "speed" himself. He was expected to use drugs with the group or suffer being used as someone who did not fit in.

The Internalization Thesis

Our analysis suggests that Don's patterns were always to a large extent motivated and supported by the positive expectations of his significant others. Further support for this interpretation is seen when Don, looking back on his behavioral history, says at the end of the interview:

> I was a Catelli and the whole family was thieves and
> manipulators. *It was expected* (that I be one too)!

In a similar vein his feelings about being a thief late in his career suggest a sense of commitment to deviant values because of the social support and positive expectations in his social milieu. He says after discussing an extensive history in professional theft and an impressive success and versatility with different "hustles":

> ... I finally felt, "well, I've established a name for
> myself, comparative to the rest of the uncles. My cell
> partner at state prison was my uncle, my Dad's brother.

The important question that arises at this juncture is whether Don's apparent conformity to these positive expectations supports or refutes the internalization thesis assumed in the socialization approach. This question asks which model of social action, the involuntary or the voluntary, and which model of personality, the static or the processual, is most tenable in this case.

It can be argued that Don's pattern of drug use and systematic theft in later life were more products of purposive conformity to positive expectations in his immediate culture than of internalized norms and values. The reader should recall here that Don's emergence into deviance was suggested to have been in conformity to expectations and values favorable to theft. If these expectations and values had actually been internalized, Don would have felt some discomfort or psychological stress when not conforming to them.[7] The following statement demonstrates that he did not feel propelled to conform to an inner set of beliefs sanctioning theft, nor did he feel bad when he was not involved in theft or otherwise conforming to the expectations of his significant others. He is describing a period when he and a girlfriend decided to "go straight":

> We regretted (our life in crime and the hassle of it). We wanted to be man and wife, you know. We wanted a decent life. And we realized years were going by. . . . I was working very hard. . . . I was really trying ("to do it right").

Don showed no signs of regret or psychological stress as a result of having failed to follow the compelling force of some set of internalized beliefs favorable to stealing. If he had, in fact, internalized such beliefs, it is reasonable to suppose that any residual dissatisfaction would have become apparent in the telling of his life-history. There were no such indications, however. Don did not reform at this point, but it is nevertheless clear from his remarks that internalized beliefs did not propel him back into theft, "hustling," or drugs. Rather, his associations and his consistent involvement in predominantly deviant situations were conducive forces which eventuated his return to drugs and theft. His girl was using drugs and this required much more money to support her activities than Don was making from working in a "pizza joint." In addition, all of the friends were bound up in the drug culture, taking hallucinogens or hard drugs.

In short, these data indicate that the internalization thesis was not apparent in Don's later patterns of deviant behavior. At the same time, Don's life-history clearly indicates that he conformed to positive expectations to be deviant. The data on primary emergence hinted that these expectations were internalized in his early life. As a result, we are faced with a curious dilemma: If the suggestive evidence supporting the internalization thesis in early life is credible, how is the absence of such evidence to be explained in later life? The involuntary model of social action and the static model of personality assumed in the socialization approach make no provision for the internalization of values and norms influencing behavior in childhood and adolescence, while denying its influence in adulthood.

There are, however, at least two plausible explanations for the lack of evidence even suggestive of the operation of internalization in the patterning of Don's adult deviant behavior. On the one hand, it may be argued that a maturational force was at work, explaining why the primary emergence and early patterns of Don's deviance, as seen in chapter 6, were the result of internalized behavior tendencies, while later patterns, as seen in this chapter, were precipitated by other factors not involving internalization. The maturational argument implies that during his early years, from age seven to thirteen, Don was incapable of exercising voluntary choice in the area of social behavior. Carried further, this argument would suggest that the beliefs which were internalized at an early age were not a compelling force once the individual matured. Instead, the mature person has a capacity to select individual courses of action purposively. But this position requires an abandonment of the static conception of personality.

On the other hand, the absence of internalization in Don's adult patterns is possible if his internalization of relevant beliefs in early life is interpreted to be questionable. The argument rests on the fact that internalization must be inferred, as it cannot be observed directly, from the evidence of conformity to positive expectations. Since Don conformed to different positive expectations (e.g., he conformed to the expectations of his associates, not his family, in the case of drug use) without guilt or anxiety, it can be argued that he did not internalize these expectations but merely conformed to them as a purposive choice in both his early and adult patterns of behavior. By this argument, Don's patterns throughout his life are explainable as a result of conformity to positive expectations which were not internalized but were an integral and ever-present part of his immediate surroundings. His behavior was dependent on pervasive exposure to the expectation to conform to certain expectations, not on internalization of those expectations.

If the internalization thesis is accepted in any measure it must (1) be inferred from, or imputed to, data which concretely support only the presence of positive expectations and behavior in conformity to them and (2) be amended, somehow, to account for behavior in violation of internalized beliefs by normal individuals who remember no remorse, regret, stress, or guilt as a result of not conforming. While this assertion is based on one case, the investigator believes it is a sufficient basis for generalization and the suggestion that the internalization thesis requires reexamination.

The method of analytic induction encourages such generalizations.[8] Morover, this analysis is premised on the view that facts which cannot be explained by theory call for the reexamination of the theory and a search for explanations.
As Becker notes:

> If we assume that expectations to any rule are a normal
> occurrence, we will perhaps not search as hard for
> further explanatory factors as we otherwise might. But if
> we regard exceptions as potential negations of our
> theory, we will be spurred to search for them.[9]

Summary

Don's patterns of deviant behavior may be explained in large part by the socialization framework. The effect of positive expectations from significant others and support and encouragement for his deviance in his most immediate culture are both consistent with the socialization view of patterned deviance. Nevertheless, some of Don's deviant behavior patterns were precipitated primarily by the practical decision that his immediate needs and purposes were most easily satisfied by engaging in various forms of theft. This facet of Don's patterned deviance is consistent with the voluntary model of social action assumed by societal reactionists and some control theorists.

Conceptual Distinctions in Socialization and Societal Reaction Theory

A basic difference between the socialization and societal reaction approaches should be remembered before considering the societal reaction approach on the issue of patterned deviant behavior. The fundamental difference centers on the conception of the nature and role of *expectations* in the two approaches. In the view of the socialization approach the individual is believed to take on, either through natural learning or precariously, the values and norms transmitted in the form of *positive expectations* and to comply, ultimately and routinely, with them. By contrast, the individual, in the view of societal reaction theorists, accepts unquestioningly the prescriptions of the *negative expectations.* The labelers react to the individual as if deviance were an important part of personal character and implicated in all behavior. The individual adapts by conforming to the negative expectations inherent in the labeling reactions, as a forced choice. The deviant, in the socialization view, is motivated by a *psychological bent* favorable to the deviant behavior.[10] This distinction implies the difference between the models of social action posited by the two approaches. The socialized deviant's behavior is involuntary or propelled by internalized beliefs, and the behavior of the societal reactionist's deviant is voluntary or purposively selective within a proffered range of alternatives.

The Societal Reaction Approach— Exemplars

The deviant behavior patterns of ten of forty-two respondents[11] are primarily explainable in terms of the societal reaction formulation. We will see in the following pages that societal reaction (1) is sometimes sufficient to cause patterned deviance; (2) is sufficiently causal at both *minor* and *major* degrees of severity in social reaction; (3) can be sufficiently causal for individuals with both strong and weak self-conceptions;[12] and (4) is sometimes the necessary cause following situational sources of secondary emergence. In addition, a crucial variable which is not considered in the societal reaction approach is identified and discussed in terms of *self-strength.*

Societal Reaction as Sufficient Cause: Albert's Case

Albert's life-history is sufficiently explainable in terms of the societal reaction formulation. After the accounting of Albert's primary emergence into deviance presented in chapter 6, the reader may have wondered, since Albert was a no-good from a family of no-goods and was, therefore, probably not socialized to conventional standards, is it not reasonable that he would have become a thief without the force of negative reactions?

While it is indeed pertinent to raise this question, Albert's account of his deviance, especially the parts pertaining to the patterning of theft, indicates that he would neither have become a thief, nor would he have patterned theft as a behavioral form, in the absence of the experience of continuous negative social reactions.

No-goods, such as Albert, lack commitment to conventional standards because they are initially, contemptuously, and pervasively excluded from ordinary social participation through processes of social differentiation. Subsequent exclusion is further kindled in a cycle of *negative social reaction,* followed by *confirming deviant behavior,* which, in turn, prompts *increasing negative reactions,* which further *induces deviant behavior,* and so on. This cycle is somewhat different from what some societal reaction theories explicitly purport to explain.[13]

Lemert, for example, describes the sequence of social interaction leading from primary deviance to secondary deviance as beginning with a deviant act rather than negative reaction processes. For Lemert, the deviant act initiates the social reactions which precipitate conformity to deviant roles.[14] Yet we have argued for Albert's case, in chapter 6, that the emergence of the first instance of deviant behavior *was the result, not the cause, of societal reaction.* We have extended Lemert's explanation in the case of Albert suggesting that he was attracted to the rewards of deviance because his potential for obtaining conventional rewards was blocked. We will attempt to show in the following pages that the formation and stablization of deviant behavior patterns may, in some instances, result predominantly from exclusionary social reaction processes. For example, as a consequence of societal reaction, Albert's access to conventional roles, statuses, and rewards was restricted and he was left with the proffered status of *deviant* as his only alternative.[15]

The key factor in understanding Albert's patterning of theft is that his *low self-conception* was inextricably related to the way he was treated and reacted to by others. We shall see below that the major factor that spurred Albert into patterned theft was a conscious quest for personal esteem in his social world.

Albert first discovered that deviant behavior would bring him prestige and high esteem among his peers when he was fifteen years old. He and his only friend bought an "old junker car" and drove it around illegally, "wooing the girls and feeling important." Albert and his friend began drinking during this period and eventually broke into a resort cabin "to get some booze." They knew there were frequently "swinging parties" at the cabin and felt confident they would find some liquor inside.

The day after the break-in Albert and his friend were questioned by the sheriff, but they would not confess. So the sheriff, confident that they were guilty, charged them with curfew violation. They were taken to court and fined $15. Because he thought it was unfair and in an attempt to be "tough," Albert did not pay his fine. As a consequence he was put in jail for two days.

Albert did not consider himself "tough," but because of this recalcitrance expressed in his response to the sheriff, he gained recognition from his friend for being daring and tough. In the comments that follow, Albert's defiance seems, in part, to have been spurred by an effort to gain and maintain some admirable personal quality, something he did not have at the time. As he said, "I still had this complex, the ugly complex. . . ." He chose a daring toughness as a mode of self-presentation in this case, but as his reflections indicate, it turned out to be a feeble bravado. For example, he described, in a very quiet and reflective tone, how he really felt in jail:

> (The jail experience) scared me off. I don't know, it was just really horrible in that jail—dark. Boy!—I liked to die in there. And uh, when I got out I didn't go nowhere for awhile. Well, (I) went to work and back home—stayed there! . . . Uh, (I) thought the sheriff was still after me and ("I was still a little scared of curfew").

Following the jail experience, however, Albert received, somewhat to his surprise, recognition and praise for his display of toughness in defying the sheriff. Albert did not discover this for some time after his release from jail, however, because he was scared and stayed home for nearly a month before going to see his friends. During that time he was "scared off" or delayed from both future transgressions and feigning "toughness" by the hard facts of official handling and jail. But when he started running around with his best friend and a few girls in the community, Albert was praised for the "toughness" and recalcitrance he had demonstrated. He had long since abandoned the idea of feigning "toughness" as a "losing game," but now he was being praised for it. Albert did not understand exactly why he was being praised, but this was the first time he had received praise for any action or personal presentation except drunken daring. So he readily accepted the praise and regarded it as a singular indication of self-worth. As he said:

> I was really having it big after I got out of that jail. My image grew to a gangster . . . you see, I thought I was really big now. . . .
>
> I don't know, it seemed like the girls was always commentin' about me bein' in jail—and "what was it like?" And uh, "were you scared?" (And I would say) "NAW! I wasn't scared," you know, stuff like that (or) "jail wasn't so much" . . . I don't know, it made me feel like I had, you know, been around, I had seen more. . . .

With a growing image of himself as a gangster, Albert and his friend broke into the resort cottage on four more occasions, stole a car that the police had staked out as bait for vandals, just for "kicks" and bold defiance, and stole gasoline regularly. In fact, Albert and his friend got into so much mischief that the police knew of their involvement and were just waiting to catch them in the act. Albert and his friend knew this but thought it was "cool." However, after nearly being caught by the police they decided to leave the state. While these adventures seemed to be more or less public knowledge, Albert's deviance did not precipitate any stronger negative reactions from community members than his ascribed status as a no-good consistently evoked. When asked if people in the community treated him any differently during the period he was engaged in these joyful thieving expeditions, he says:

> They never did care for me—"that Mass kid, 'no-good' mother fucker". . . . (So) I wouldn't say it surprised them or their reactions changed in any way. I would say they

was all about the same still. Their feeling about me was
[long pause—as if to say, they always considered that I
was a *no-good* type all along and this behavior is to be
expected from that kind].

So, except for the fact that the police were after him, Albert's
deviance was not costing anything in terms of community
standing. If anything, his gangsterism was a dependable source
of praise from his associates.

After he left his home state, Albert got a job in a large city in
a western state. He was seventeen years old. Albert met a thief
in the apartment building where he was living with a relative.
Soon Albert and the thief became friends and started engaging
in systematic thefts together:

> ... anything we could pick up in yards, garages ... like
> lawn mowers, bikes, etc., ... Nick had plenty of contacts
> and he could sell anything we could get in any quantity.

This activity bolstered Albert's image even more. It was the
first time he had stolen for money and profit. He was working
during the day and stealing at night and "really felt like a
gangster-type, big time!" He bought an expensive wardrobe
which put the "finishing touch" on his growing sense of personal esteem. Gradually, he became involved in sophisticated
daylight burglaries. These were so lucrative that he eventually
quit his job to become a "full-time gangster." His self-esteem
had reached an all-time high. He describes this period of his
life with great satisfaction—not because of his financial success but because theft and "gangsterism" provided a basis for
praise and consequently enhanced his sense of self-worth.

> Smoked some pot and hash, was a ladies man, was
> tough. I changed quite a bit there, to a full-time
> gangster. I really thought I was a gangster then because
> —uh, I had everything (clothes, a mistress, etc.) but the
> gun. I could have had a gun but I never did pack a gun.
>
> I considered myself a good thief, a profitable thief—uh,
> like burglary was fun, exciting, prosperous ... that was
> the peak of my career, you know.

Then things started going badly. Albert was arrested and
spent fifteen days in jail. His partner was arrested a couple of

times also. Another friend wrecked and totally demolished Albert's car. The fear of getting caught and going to prison became a cold reality he considered daily. Albert could not accept the increased risks of arrest and prison, so he packed his clothes and returned to his home town, scared, depressed, and disillusioned.

The return home, however, revitalized an old problem. Albert discovered that his prestige as a thief had not followed him home. He got back his old job as a farm laborer. Shortly thereafter, his old home-town friend was released from a short sentence in prison for statutory rape, and the two immediately resumed their practice of wild, joyous, "hell-raising." For Albert, this renewed activity was obviously an attempt to regain a sense of prestige. They drank to the point of drunkenness almost nightly and started breaking into taverns in a bold and reckless manner, stealing liquor by the case. These reckless crimes characteristic of an earlier period, however, no longer provided a basis for gaining prestige from others in the old group. Ultimately, they were caught, convicted, and imprisoned.

While he was in prison Albert decided to stop his foolish thefts, because "the consequences were too hard." His self-conception was no longer that of a thief or a gangster.

> That (several) months (in prison) really got me down. I
> had made up my mind in (prison) that I wasn't a thief. I
> told myself I would never steal again. And I mean I
> really told myself that. And I tried to better myself, went
> to school (in prison).

But when he got out of prison Albert soon realized that once he abandoned his identity as a thief his self-conception was again deeply rooted in his family's status. The only sense of personal esteem he had even known came from being a thief. His comments indicate that he was now both applying conventional standards of worth to his own family, and realizing that his earlier inferiority complex was inextricably connected to his being from a family of no-goods.

> I got out of (prison) ... and uh, when I got home, comin'
> down the road—I looked at the house—and, uh, boy! The
> thing was in shambles. ("Before I went out west, and
> then later, to prison—my family ... we were a close
> family—and I never did think about us being poor"), you

know. And (this time) I walked in the door and it was all
... wasn't enough room, heated with an old coal stove, no
rugs on the floor—just a linoleum floor, furniture was
old. And uh, the yard was full of stuff that the dogs had
been draggin' in, the kids threw (stuff) out there—and it
looked like a slum. ... I said, "damn it's dirty". And I
don't know, it ("changed my whole outlook, my whole
attitude again").

I don't know ... my image changed again [from not a
thief to a potential thief—when he realized his only
source of personal identification was now tied to the
family and in conventional circles there was a low
regard for people who lived like his family] ... *it really
depressed me. And I said, "well, even if I have to steal
I'm not going to live like that."*

The same night he returned home, Albert began what
seemed to be the surest way to achieve a status higher than the
one afforded by his membership in a family of no-goods. He
planned to commit enough burglaries to finance a move back
out west. In the interim, however, he precariously construed
the community's reserved, but now more subtle or covert, reactions to him as at least some sort of indication of his self-worth.

Uh, (I) believe people were kind of afraid of me ... *it
used to be before I went to (prison) ... people would
come right out with their opinions about me.* Well,
when I got out of state prison they wouldn't say this
[pause] *you know,* they showed respect—to a certain
extent.

And *they would move out ("when I was coming down
the sidewalk") and they wouldn't talk about me where I
could hear them ... and I guess this kinda raised me*
[pause] you know, the gangster thing ... where they
wouldn't come right out and talk about me.

So, Albert accepted the only source of self-aggrandizement
available, that people in the community were now less overt in
their displays of contempt for him. He was "raised," his self-
conception was bolstered. In this slightly changed community
context, theft and gangsterism were more desirable as proffered
roles than reclaiming his place as no-good. Albert realized that
his low self-esteem was not going to be improved by legitimate
activity in his home community because there his name was

irrevocably disreputable. He was now prepared to go back to a life of theft in spite of his resolve not to and in spite of the consequences. As he indicated, "even if I have to steal I'm not going to live like . . ." a no-good and suffer the low self-esteem imposed by community reaction.

Our analysis invites the interpretation that Albert would not have become a thief if he had not been initially cast as a no-good in normal community differentiation processes. As a result of being defined and reacted to as a no-good his sense of worth was rendered inferior. Because of this, Albert decided a pattern of theft and gangsterism was the most reasonable source of self-enhancement available to him. In spite of the cost of legal sanction, the option of being assigned the low status of just another no-good left him with no better alternative than theft. In the end, then, Albert purposively chose the behavior patterns and the life of a thief to avoid the totally denigrating status of a community outcast and no-good. As the societal reactionists indicate, the individual may, when legitimate role opportunities are closed, accept and conform to the proffered role of the deviant.

Ken's Case: Societal Reaction and Identity Transformation

Another example which indicates societal reaction processes are sometimes sufficient to explain the patterning of deviant behavior is seen in the case of Ken. The case is presented in considerable detail in order to show the transformation of identity from a point prior to societal reaction to a point after the imposition of a deviant label, and to give the reader an opportunity to examine the respondent's account in some depth.

Ken had never been in trouble until he was twenty years old. In his words, he was "a model little citizen," "everyone's little pride and joy," "a straight 'A' student, a track runner, a football man, valedictorian in high school—the whole bit." In general, Ken enjoyed his accomplishments, but he says reflectively that the "goody-goody stuff, constant praise, got a little sickening at times."

At the end of his first year in college Ken began asserting his youthful independence. He dropped out of school, worked in construction for a while, and then joined the Air Force. His parents were demanding and wanted Ken to remain in school and continue doing all the "right things."

Perhaps as a reaction to his parent's dominating ways, or perhaps because he had plenty of money, Ken did not keep his checkbook balanced responsibly. He had a reputation for being absent-minded and forgetful in that regard. There was "never any hassle about it" when Ken was in high school. He recalls that this was because the bank "knew I was good for it." They either took the deficit out of his savings account or sent him a notice asking whether he wanted to pay the deficit and a penalty or have the amount withdrawn from his savings.

Ken's parents were financially comfortable and Ken always had a substantial savings account of his own in addition to a personal checking account. When he was twenty years old he got a job in a neighboring town and moved there. He also changed his bank account to the small town where he lived during this period. Soon, Ken's practice of not watching his checking account caught up with him. He was charged with passing an insufficient funds check for $20 and was sentenced to one year on probation.

Ken remembers that he thought the judicial hearing would be "no problem" so he went to court without a lawyer. The "old country judge," however, saw it differently. The judge knew the offense was not serious but he decided Ken needed to be taught a lesson. Ken recalled that the judge told him it was time he learned how to balance his checkbook. So he gave Ken one year's probation for "a lesson." Ken's first reaction was:

> Didn't bother me at all one way or another. To me it was nothing, you know, except a minor annoyance.

The reaction of his friends was disbelief and levity. Ken recalls their reaction was:

> ... well uh, disbelief, really more than anything—you know, they couldn't believe it, (that) I had [pause], you know, "goody-goody two-shoes" there (in trouble with the law—HA!).

Ken's parents, however, were displeased and angry because he did not seek their help and the use of the family lawyer and because he had "broken the law."

> (I) didn't say, "hey Daddy I need help." I just went (to court) and did it myself. I think that's what really got them more than anything.

(But they were also angry because I had broken "the"
law) ... they didn't mince any words on that (they made
it very clear that I had done a dreaded thing).

But it was not the levity of Ken's friends, nor the harsh purist
reaction of his parents, that transformed Ken from a margin-
ally irresponsible youth asserting his independence to an angry, embittered, and defensive youth primed to behave like a
"deviant." Rather, it was the community reaction, the towns-
people, and Ken's own acceptance of common conceptions of
deviants that changed him.

Ken described his home community as a typical small rural
town that was mostly populated by people of Scandinavian
descent. He notes that the community tolerance level for any
form of deviation was low and illustrated this by telling of a
local man who threw rocks through downtown store windows
while drunk and was "*branded* as a criminal the rest of his
life." This illustration was related in an intense and overzeal-
ous manner and was, no doubt, exaggerated. But it does clearly
point to the centrality of the community reaction as a primary
cause, at least in Ken's mind, inducing his identity transformation from a "model little citizen" to a defensive youth suggestible to the negative expectations inherent in labeling reactions.
The reactions of people in the community were harsh and definite. Ken's inclination as a result of these reactions was *to be
what he was defined as being.* He describes the community
reaction and his feelings as follows:

(They reacted like) "you're going to have to watch him
now," "he's a known criminal now," "he's an outcast," or
"you'll have to watch him he could be dangerous," you
know. Completely (banned)!

At first, I just looked at it like, they had to be putting me
on. I mean their reaction was so (unbelievably) violent.
... Uh, my God! what is this? You know, (I just couldn't
believe it was happening).

Then—I thought maybe (the) next thing they would tell
me is I'm a hardened felon, you know, I go out and
knock people in the head for money.—I couldn't believe
it—but *that's the type of community we had. "If you
was good—you was good. If you was bad—you was
horrid!"* Uh, it's just one of those type deals.

... one of the girls I was (dating and) getting very
serious about—was even thinking about getting married
... her parents were just uh, uh, [pause] I went (to her
house) a few days (after I was put on probation) to pick
her up for a date and the reaction was *almost barbaric.*
Really it was, I mean they wouldn't let me in the house,
they refused to let her come to the door, they told me
never to step on their property again.

I mean, what is this—(I asked myself). *It wasn't just a
show for me—they believed it, the community actually
believed it. I mean, (to) these people ... I was a "bad
criminal," you know.* I was *NO GOOD* and will never be
NO GOOD.

INTERVIEWER: Okay, did this alter your own
self-conception in any way?

KEN: It uh, when I got this from the people it started
making me very bitter. ... you know, like, "what the hell
—*if I'm going to be named a criminal I might as well be
one I guess."* I never went out and done anything, I
mean ... but that was my outlook. And getting more
and more so. I mean, "if they're going to condemn me
for that, what was their reaction gonna' be if I actually
did do something serious." Uh, actually I got a little
more defensive from then on. ...

The immediate feeling Ken had with regard to the harsh reaction from the people in the community was to be a "criminal,"
that is, to be what he was defined as being. Ken did not become
a criminal at this time even though his bitter and defensive
disposition beckoned. However, he soon got into trouble again.
He violated his probation by being drunk, out after curfew,
and by being arrested for improper control of his car and
drunken driving. This occurred while he was celebrating his
twenty-first birthday. As a result, Ken's probation was re-
voked and he was sentenced to one year in a prison for young
offenders.
    The treatment he received while in prison contributed fur-
ther to the transformation of Ken's basic self-conception from
"everybody's pride and joy" to a "generally deviant person"
who can be expected to "mess up" if given the proper amount
of time. Ken articulates with intense emotion the impressions
and feelings the prison experience evoked in him.

(When) you get to "X" prison (a prison for misdemeanants and young offenders classified as minimum security), I don't know if you've ever been there or not—it's actually five times worse than this place. Now it's supposed to be for misdemeanors and un-armed felonies but they treat you there like you're a very, very hardened criminal. I mean you're "shook down" every time you go around a corner—I didn't have as much harrassment (at the maximum security, initial classification center prison where I spent the first thirty days) as I did (at "X" prison). They try to lower your personal dignity as much as possible at "X" prison. I couldn't believe it. It's supposed to be a minimum security and actually ... I would almost classify it maximum security.

They got their little fence around there ... (and) I never heard my name used while I was there by an officer—it was always a number. ... At the time when we was visiting you still had to sit behind a screen ("like the felons did"). Uh, I don't know, you're marched here, you're marched there, you're marched to church under a shotgun ... at every opportunity they had, the officers there *made it well known that you were a "criminal."* You was a *"low life's scum"* and you was going to be treated as such.

So you had to say "sir" and when an officer walks up you have to jump to attention. And uh, if you're smoking a cigarette you have to extinguish it immediately—the whole bit ... I *thought* ... "I can't *believe it! I'm not a criminal and yet I'm being treated as a hardened criminal."* ...

Ken entered the prison with his sense of self-esteem already seriously damaged by the community reaction to his being placed on probation. He recalled then that his feeling was "If I'm going to be named a criminal. I might as well be one." However, he qualifies this by saying, "I never went out and done anything, I mean, but that was my outlook."

After the official reaction of the prison staff, coupled with his bitter resentment toward the community's reaction, Ken buckled under to the negative expectations inherent in the general label, "criminal." His conception of "criminal" was of an individual who was hard emotionally, tough to deal with, untrustworthy, and a generally undesirable, tough type.

Uh, well personally, I didn't look at myself as a criminal.
I said, "alright I am not a criminal." (But) by the time I
got out of there I said, *"Well, what the hell, I guess I am
a criminal! I might as well be like these bastards want
me to be."* And that's just the way it was when I came
out of there.

Ken became a "criminal" in the sense that he conformed to
the negative expectations about how criminals ("calloused hu-
manity" to him) act in certain situations. He illustrated the way
he played the criminal role when confronted with a traffic
ticket.

... Uh, when the state police would pick me up for
speeding—where before I was very polite, very nice, very
kind, and we'd usually work it out, (now) I tell them to
"go to hell." It [pause] to me they are just another symbol
of *"authority"*—the men with a badge were just one of
"them."

*(I thought) because I had already been branded—I'm
one of the undesirable elements—I might as well be.
undesirable all the way.* Now that is a very good
rationalization, I realize ... but *unless you have
experienced it, lived it, you just can't believe what the
reaction is.*

Ken also described the community's reactions after his
prison sentence and the impact of this reaction on the way he
handled himself in situations where he was a prime suspect
because of his *record.*

(It was) ... something else then! I mean (they reacted
like) ... "here comes a *criminal,* he just got out of the
jug," you know, and "he was *behind the walls*" and all
this bit [people reacted to me as if I was *tainted*].

He adds: "So I finally got so disgusted ... I moved away for
about three years and stayed away from the community." But
his record and his own damaged self-conception followed him
back to college for his junior year. This, added to his already
weakened "self," was sufficient to bring about hostile reactions
and continued deviance on Ken's part.

I was under the impression before I went in there that when you serve your time you've paid your debt to society ... (that) the ills you've done to ... (society) are paid in full (by) the time you have been deprived of your freedom. NO!—*your time doesn't start until you hit the streets! That's when you start paying your debt to society.* The time you are incarcerated is nothing ... you just cease to exist for that time. ...

(You) start paying your debt when you "go on the streets" [meaning released from prison]. That's when society can get hold of you. They can really "run you down!" They can't do anything to you while you're in the institutions but when you're out there in "free society" that's when they can get *rough.*

An instance of society's roughness is recalled by Ken as he tells of the difficulties after he reentered college. He says the college administration treated him with great suspicion. As a result he confirmed and justified their negative expectations by reacting in ways indicative of how everybody thought a deviant would react in such circumstances.

(I was called in and questioned by the Dean for everything—"since I was the only criminal at that college I had to be involved" by his reasoning.) (And) instead of sitting there and saying I didn't do it, ... (I would) just tell them to "go to hell." If they thought I did it, charge me with it and let's go get it over with ... other than that (they could) "kiss my ass" ... I mean instead of trying to be reasonable ... and trying to reason it out I would just say "piss on you," "you think I did it— FINE!—charge me ... and let's go to court, or kick me out." And, *I mean I was getting so fed up with it, ... that instead of trying to go along and show them that they were incorrect I thought, "to hell with it—this is the way you want to feel, well alright—I am ... I'm BIG, BAD, MEAN like you think I am.* NOW, what the hell you going to do about it.

Ken was, in fact, involved in a couple of college pranks, of the "panty raid" variety with his fraternity brothers. But the college administration took a dim view of this and imputed a deeper seriousness because of Ken's involvement. He was the prime suspect for everything starting from the time he returned to college. The following excerpt illustrates Ken's awareness of the way social reaction processes operate at the social-psychological level. It also shows his gradual and reluctant acquiescence to the negative expectations expressed in the social reaction processes.

> *I mean after a while a person just gets to that point ...*
> *where you "could CARE less."* I mean really, I got to that
> point. I didn't "give a rat's ass" what they thought.

As he says, "after a while a person just gets to that point where —*he couldn't care less,*" in essence he gives up and accepts the label. The tenor of Ken's remarks, however, indicates that it was, in fact, "what they thought" that was making him bitter, suggestible, and thus deviant in the sense that he responded in ways expected of calloused deviant persons.

> You just more or less ... throw up a little shield around
> yourself ... and withdraw into it. You have to, because if
> you put your feelings out on your shirtsleeve—you're
> going to get them *stomped* on quite viciously. *And if you*
> *are a weak person it could* [quiet pause] (it's) *going to be*
> *very telling. You are either going to "go over the deep*
> *end," or you're going to react in some way that's ...*
> [pause] *what everybody thinks you are.*

Ken conformed to the negative expectations of others, bitterly and defensively, playing, as he says, "the big, bad, mean" role of the criminal. In spite of this, however, he finished his college degree and started a small business which did well for awhile but then folded with too much money on the books and not enough left to pay his debtors. One of Ken's debtors took him to court for civil litigation and brought up his prison record as part of the case. Other debtors threatened to do the same thing. Ken had operated a business for three years. He held a provisional status of the kind colloquially expressed in the phrase "maybe he'll make it this time." Then his business went bankrupt. This preceded Ken's last offense—another insufficient funds check. *He felt he was defined as a hopeless bum, so he behaved* like one. While drunk and bankrupt, he wrote a bad check to pay for a diamond ring for his wife:

> (My attitude was) "I guess I was right the first time.
> They're not going to let me forget it, so I might just as

well start *acting like a bum, being one! . . . you keep
hearing (it) and pretty soon you start analyzing. And
"my God maybe they are right, maybe it's true. . . ."* You
know, I mean I guess they are right, I tried it, I touched
it, and it went bad.

Pretty soon you just start going back in again [back to
thinking like a "con"] *you know, "okay, they accept me
as being a "convict" and (I am) treated as a "convict"
again—FUCK THEM! I am a convict, to put it bluntly*
. . . But I guess that's all I've ever been—and that's all I'm
going to be now.

Ken had completely accepted the definition of "bum," "convict," and "criminal" by the time of the interviews with him
because he could not escape the imposition of condemning labels. In effect, his acceptance of the deviant label induced
toughness and callousness in social relations but it did not
prompt a pattern of infractions. Eventually he came to collabo-
rate in the process of labeling to the extent that he defined
himself and his past in terms of his perception of the common
conception of criminals. As he concluded regretfully, "maybe
they were right all along—I am a bum, I will be a convict."

Societal Reaction as
Necessary Cause

There are ten cases, in the present study, in which societal
reaction processes are demonstrable as a necessary cause of the
patterning of individual deviant behavior. Three cases are illustrated in the following pages. In each case, there is a self-
factor which complements the societal reaction process.
Whether an unusual sensitivity brought about by situational
stress, or a "fragile-self" that results from doubting or denying
reactions from others,[16] some self-factor is a usual complement
to societal reaction processes which bring on patterned deviance.

Mick's Case

Mick had never been in trouble or mischief prior to the eighth
grade in school. As he says, "I lived a pretty normal life growing
up." He got along with everyone, got average grades in school,
which he did not particularly like, and got most of his feeling
of being "the best" as a result of his skill at sports.

Two events led to the reordering of Mick's life. He moved across town to attend a new junior high school after graduating from primary school. The junior high was large and Mick soon learned that he was no longer "best" at all sports. He was still good enought to be "first team," but not unquestionably the "best." Consequently, he had to modify his self-conception from "best" to "just good." This was not easy, especially because it became necessary at the same time that a stressful problem hit his family. Mick's mother became very ill and spent nine months in a hospital convalescing. Aside from the emotional strain, this left a heavy burden of responsibility on Mick who had to stay home and take care of his two younger brothers. Family life became very tense, and Mick became moody and belligerent as a result. His moodiness and accompanying "hot temper" alienated some of his friends.

> ... I wouldn't be feeling good [moody, depressed]—well I
> would get nasty and [if somebody said something to me
> that I didn't like] ... (we) would get in a fight right there,
> and there would go one friend. And that's what
> happened to quite a few of my friends, my *regular*
> *friends* that I grew up with. ...

During the school day, and while participating in sports, Mick hung around with the "straight" friends he grew up with and the althletes. But outside of these contexts Mick's relationships with this group had become strained. He found his desire for companionship generally difficult to satisfy. So Mick started hanging around with a couple of tough guys:

> ... I figured if I run around with a couple of tough guys
> ... automatically ... (others) would think I was tough or
> something. ... I don't know what it was, why I wanted to
> build my image up. I never felt I needed an image
> before [but the new school situation and the family stress
> left Mick without a stable self-image—he felt he had to
> "get one"].

> So I led sort of a double life. In the day time through
> school I would associate with ... I guess you would call
> [them] the "straight" people. And then after school it
> seemed when there wasn't any practice for any kind of
> sport or anything—that I just had idle time. ... I would
> resort back to these guys ("hoodlums or gangsters as they
> called themselves"). ... I felt as long as I had something

> important to do, like sports, that I didn't have to be with
> them. But otherwise I guess I just didn't want to be
> alone. I don't know what (it was) for sure but I always
> had to resort back to people like them. . . .

Situational stress caused Mick's moodiness and, indirectly, it caused his need to associate with "hoodlums." All of these things operated in combination to induce Mick's first involvement in deviant behavior.

Mick got into trouble the first time at age fifteen. He was picked up by another youth for a ride in a stolen car while standing in front of a youth center. Mick claims, unconvincingly, that he believed the youth when he said his uncle lent him the car. They were both age fifteen, so at least Mick was probably aware something was illegal about the situation. Mick tried to run away when the car was stopped by the police, but that only convinced them that he was more involved than he actually was.

Mick's initial contact with the police seemed constructive. He seemed sufficiently scared to be deterred from future indiscretions.

> [The police took us to jail] . . . chewed us out more or less
> for 10 or 15 minutes. And they didn't put no charge of
> auto theft, they just put "joyriding" on both (arrest
> forms) and they took us back and put us in a cell for
> maybe two or three minutes . . . locked us in so we could
> see what it looked like. They they pulled us back out and
> called our parents. . . .
>
> Well, I don't know about the other guy but, it put a pretty
> big scare in me. I didn't think much of the jail and I
> didn't plan on wantin' to go back, ever again.

It is significant to note, at this juncture, that Mick did not steal the car and was not with the other youth when it was stolen. The youth who had stolen the car from his uncle was unpopular, not really anybody's "kind of guy," and he had never been in any trouble before. Both Mick and the other youth were sentenced to six months probation. Mick was very bitter and angry about being placed on probation, primarily because he felt he had not done anything wrong and because the official stigma had further reduced his sense of security with the "straight" youths whom he identified as the ones he really wanted to please.

... I don't know, I guess I felt—"an eye for an eye and a tooth for a tooth" when they give me probation for something I didn't do. [I thought] why not ... give them trouble ... you know, get them back—(get) even in some way.

... my image changed ... it had to change. Anybody's would have to change from the time they never been in trouble to the time that they first do get in trouble and get caught. I uh, ... [pause] around my *normal friends* the ones I grew up with from when I was real young, *I was more embarrassed* because they *knew I had been in trouble one time, you know—and had been caught.* And it, more or less, embarrassed me because not one of them had ever been in trouble, the ones I grew up with real close.

And this other group, they more or less cheered me on for getting in trouble, you know.

The social reaction, in the form of reserved and standoffish treatment from his "straight friends" embarrassed Mick, made him feel "categorized," and hastened the process by which he was becoming deviant. This feeling of being considered a deviant eventually rendered him susceptible to the force of negative expectations implied by the reactions of his friends.

("And the other group—the straight ones") ... I felt they was always with their eyes [Mick pauses, lost for words] "mocking me" with their eyes or something. [Mick was exasperated that "mocking" was not what he meant but that he couldn't articulate the precise way he felt this group had treated him]. They would never say nothin' out loud against me because I had been in trouble. It was just the sense of feeling guilty I had (when I was with them). (I felt like) a *convict* or something and I thought they was thinkin' ... (of me in those terms).

You know, I got the other group—they praised you for getting in trouble. Well, you got to resolve (which) one of the two will you follow. And I might as well go with the people that really like me, you know. (I) mean, "they think more of me than this other group." *So I started running around,* off and on, *with these,* more or less, young guys, *hoodlums, gangsters, or whatever they wanted to call themselves. Uh, because uh, the big reason was just because they treated me more like I*

> *wanted to be treated. But they was the wrong people*
> *that did treat me that way. I would have much rather*
> *had it from the other group.*

> But I saw that they (the straight group) just had, more or
> less, things to do that didn't involve me. I figured that if
> that's the way they wanted to be, then, you know, *to heck*
> *with them.* I would just go stay with this group.

Mick then moved completely away from the "straight" group
that made him feel embarrassed, ashamed, and like a member
of a tainted category. He uses the example of feeling like a
"convict" to illustrate his sense of being treated as badly as he
imagines a convict must be treated in the presence of others
who look down on him with obvious apprehension and aloof-
ness. It is this subtle, but very real, social reaction that brought
about Mick's acceptance of the deviant label and subsequently
led him to join, and identify with, the group of hoodlums. The
group applauded his newly acquired status of "one who has
been in trouble with the law."

Still Mick did not conceive of himself as a gangster or a
hoodlum and he had no previous wish to be considered a gangster by others. But, now, he felt he had no alternative since he
was labeled deviant and excluded, however subtly, from more
desirable conventional roles. As he relates:

> ... they were not the people that I truly wanted to be
> with, but *they were the people I had to be with* because
> they were like me. Like, *take a person with leprosy,*
> *nobody's going to be around them.* Well, I had been in
> trouble—none of the other people I had run with before
> had been. *I was different and I was put in a different*
> *category.* And uh, I wasn't one of their kind of people
> and they didn't have nothin' (no time) for me. And I had
> to resort to somebody, I had to have somebody to be with,
> at least I thought I did. *And I had to resort back to them*
> *kind of people.*

> And I knew deep down that they ... liked me because I
> (had been) "in trouble." So I figured I was in the right
> place. *I was with the people I was supposed to be with—*
> *not that I necessarily wanted to be with, but that I was*
> *made to be with, at that time.*

Therefore, Mick made the move away from the reluctant
"straight" group he wanted to be part of, to a deviant hoodlum

group that he saw as the only reasonable alternative. Upon changing affiliation, Mick felt more than ever that the "straight" group expected him to be a hoodlum and to engage in further deviance.

It took six months for Mick to make the complete change in groups and during that time he did not engage in any deviant behavior. On a couple of occasions he tried to strike up relationships witn old "straight" friends who were "just friendly" but distant, and "always in a hurry to get someplace." Mick completed his six months of probation successfully at age sixteen and then immediately started engaging in "small stuff"—stealing hubcaps and tires, siphoning gasoline—generally taking things off of cars for use on his own car or his friends' cars. This marked the beginning of his pattern of thievery and burglary that continued for the next four years. In that time, Mick was sentenced to a total of four years on probation, served a year and a half in prison and was serving another sentence of one to three years at the time of this interview.

Mick conformed to the negative expectations, becoming what he was expected to be, a young hoodlum, because he was reacted to as a hoodlum and because his own conception of deviation was absolute, just as he perceived it to be in the eyes of his significant others. Even though he completed the first probation successfully, Mick felt tainted and he perceived the reactions of others as carrying an inescapable finality.

> (I felt society would) look on as if I was one of them
> (hoodlums or gangsters) because I had been in trouble.
> And uh, *I figured that once you did get in trouble that*
> *society could never look on you again as anything but a*
> *—thief! A criminal, you know* (or some such deviant
> category).

> "You're no good to society, you don't belong here"—And
> that's just the way I had it set in my mind, that they
> would all feel about me.

> *So if they're going to think the worst about me why not*
> *be out doing the worst things. There's no more harm in*
> *that* [Mick believed others thought the worst things
> about him because they were distant and standoffish].

An essential part in the patterning of Mick's deviant behavior is societal reaction. Ultimately, he became a thief and a burglar by accepting the subtly imposed deviant label and by conforming to his perception of the negative expectations conveyed by the standoffish reactions of his significant others. The obvious question then is: Why did Mick accept the label? He was particularly vulnerable to imposed definitions of "self" because the change in schools brought a lowering in his relative status in the group, and because the family stress following his mother's illness produced needs which further damaged his place among friends. Together these two situations contributed to an unstable and vulnerable self-concept. In other words, Mick's identity was "fragile" at the time the societal reaction was evoked, and this rendered him highly vulnerable to the force of negative expectations to be deviant.

Willy's Case

The account of Willy's involvement in deviance represents a second illustration of societal reaction processes as a necessary condition in the development of deviant behavior patterns. For the first nine years of his life Willy lived in a rural area of a southern state. His father was a farm-laborer who frequently drank to the point of drunkenness and caused considerable havoc in the home. Willy, however, was quite secure in the family and remembers his family "had a good name back in South-state."

When Willy was nine years old the family moved to Mid-state where his father worked first as a farm-laborer, then later in a garage. Willy had been accustomed to stealing soda pop with the other youths back in South-state, but he did not steal anything for several years after the move to Mid-state. The family name was not good in the new Mid-state community. Willy did well in school, however, and was able to enjoy, provisionally, the status of being "the best one out of the family." He was very much aware that his good standing in the community was dependent on a continued good public appearance. This is probably the reason Willy did not continue his practice of stealing soda pop and candy after he moved to rural Mid-state.

When Willy was around thirteen or fourteen years old he broke into an old vacant house with three other youths. They did it for fun, excitement, curiosity, and because they had heard the ubiquitous tale about "old houses having lots of money hidden in the walls and cellars." The police caught them in the house. No official action was taken, but it became known in the community that Willy was involved. His chief concern was how this would affect the way people in the community thought about him. The following dialogue illustrates both Willy's recognition of, and his concern for, his provisional status.

> ... after it happened I felt bad about it, you know [in a very sincere tone].
>
> INTERVIEWER: In what way did you feel bad?
>
> WILLY: *The way people thought, what people thought.* ... I always, you know, people (would) always tell my people ... (that) I was pretty smart, you know. And they said I was the *best one out of the family*—you know. I felt bad about that.

Most of the people, "who didn't feel they were better" than Willy, treated him much the same as always after this incident. But Willy indicated, with an embittered snicker, that this transgression gave those people "who thought they were better" than him just what they needed to justify their negative feelings and expectations toward him.

After this experience, Willy felt his reputation was so damaged as to be even more provisional than before. Then a false accusation, a "run-in" with the law followed by more false accusations, precipitated Willy's withdrawal from conventional activities. These incidents also contributed to his patterning of petty deviance. Willy recalls, first, being at a friend's house with two other youths who left before he and his friend did. The friend's father discovered his wallet was missing and accused Willy. Willy's tone and demeanor indicated that this accusation both "hurt him" and made apparent the beginning of the decline of his tentatively good reputation. Willy noted sadly that his response to the accusation was one of regretful and quiet indignation.

> And I told him, I said—"I didn't take the money." I said, "there's no way in hell I would do that," you know.

A second experience that contributed further to Willy's suggestibility to negative expectations involved a confrontation with the law. Willy and a group of young boys were picked up by the police for curfew violation in a community of a close neighboring state. When they discovered the group did not have enough money with them to make the trip home, the police put them in jail to await money from their parents. They were in jail three days. Willy was mildly astonished.

> Well, they had us locked up right there with everybody else (the regular kind of people in jails), you know, right there in jail.

After being released from jail, the group returned home only to be charged with stealing gasoline from a farmer. When the case came to court another youth, not a member of Willy's group, confessed to the theft. This experience, in addition to the three days in jail, provoked a defensiveness with regard to the law. He came to think of the police and courts as "nothing to be afraid of," and as "not so smart." Although he did not admit to it directly, the tenor of Willy's comments about this experience indicates that it was not wholly unreasonable to suspect him, or his associates, of stealing gasoline. Willy showed no signs of indignation about this accusation, as he did when describing other incidents.

For example, on a number of occasions, other youths falsely accused him of thefts at school. These accusations, unlike the former charges, bothered him greatly. Willy eventually quit school to escape the stigma and the negative reactions he received from other youths following his contacts with the police and courts. Willy admits, very reluctantly, that it was the stigma and the reactions from others that prompted his quitting school, as noted in the following exchange:

> WILLY: (School) ... just wasn't the same ... the teachers wasn't [pause] ... (it) just started getting to uh, where uh, you know,—I didn't care about school no more. ...
>
> I mean I wasn't getting along in school as good as I was, you know. ... And I would go to school and would "get into it" [meaning he would get into a fight or argument].
>
> INTERVIEWER: For what kinds of things would you "get into it?"
>
> WILLY: Just [pause] little arguments. I mean uh,—went to school one day and one of [pause] ... somebody said something about me stealing something, you know,

which I hadn't done. So we "got into it," you know. So I
got to where, you know, "to hell with school," you know.
"School ain't nothin' (or important anyway)." So I went
ahead and finished the eighth grade ... and that was it.

These false accusations produced in Willy an emotional vulnerability. The concomitant negative expectations that he
would probably deviate again were compelling.

Well, you know, this made me feel bad, you know. When
something [pause] uh, (*I*) *got the idea if something was
missing—it give me the idea that* ... people was (always
thinkin' I took it). And then when somebody would look
at me I would figure they was thinkin' of that.

Willy later escaped these circumstances by quitting school
and joining another group whose activities were characteristically deviant. By so doing, he took the initial steps toward conforming to the negative expectations inherent in the reactions
of others, namely that he would continue to deviate. He became
defensive and denounced the significance of the accusers by
saying "what I do is my business." When Willy joined a group
of deviant youths, his severance from old school associates was
completed. As Willy notes:

I mean I felt bad about getting in trouble, you know. ...
but uh, I just figured to hell with it—(I can't take this
negative treatment). *What I do is my business,* you
know, (this) *is the way I got to thinkin'.*

In effect, however, Willy was allowing the scrutiny of his
peers to change his general behavior tendencies from conformity to conventional standards to conformity with their negative expectations. This is evident in his joining a group where,
as he says, "we all ... fit together."

(Then) I started hanging around with different people,
you know. ("We all seemed to fit together"). And
whenever I would want to do something ... we would all
do it, you know ... we started drinkin' ..., runnin'
around with girls [they also stole gasoline and petty stuff
for their cars, and engaged in minor vandalism and
pranks].

While his behavior patterns involved rather systematic deviance at this point, Willy was still attitudinally more committed to conventional norms than to the deviant standards of his companions, as he admits:

> ... when I would be alone, you know, I would think about ... why I did it. You know, why I dropped out of school and then ... (the kind of stuff) I was doin' then. You know, what I could be (doin'). You know, it would bother me—what I was doin'.

It was the provisional status in the community that left Willy vulnerable to the negative expectations of significant others. Quitting school, joining a deviant group, and patterning deviance, even though his attitudes and basic beliefs were more consistent with staying in school and conforming to conventional standards, were all a function of his vulnerability to negative reactions. It was simply easier to drop out and avoid these face-to-face negative reactions. In the process he came to accept the definition of being different or more prone to deviant behavior and eventually found some slight sense of security in being with a group that "all seemed to fit together," that is, in which all were deviants.

In summary, societal reaction was a necessary condition in the development of Willy's deviant behavior patterns, but it was not a condition sufficient to cause such patterning. Willy's standing in the group and community, and therefore a large part of his self-conception, was provisional from the beginning. Willy was aware of the provisional character of his acceptance in the community. The fact that his "self" was fragile in this regard was also a necessary and perhaps a crucial condition in the patterning process. It was this basic fragility that rendered him vulnerable to the relatively mild initial societal reaction.

As Lofland points out, the "self" is crucial and must be protected. It must be maintained by relatively direct and continual confirmation from one's peers, or significant others. In their response, or lack of response, to one's actions, or in one's "perception" of social reactions, others confirm, raise doubts, or deny one's status as adequate. Too much doubt and denial causes self-esteem to wither.[17] It was at this point that Willy became suggestible to the expectations implied in the doubtful or negative reactions of others.

What constitutes too much denial, doubt, and negative reaction is dependent on the relative stability of the self-conception. Willy's self-conception was in constant jeopardy because it was dependent on his being extraordinarily good. Even minor transgressions in cases such as his can spark denial in the responses of others. In turn, the individual perceives the responses as denying self-esteem. Ultimately, Willy became suggestible to the negative expectations inherent in the societal reaction.

Orly's Case

Societal reaction processes are a necessary, but not a sufficient, cause in the development of Orly's deviant behavior patterns. Situations in Orly's home and high anxiety and insecurity are other conditions that must be considered in the explanation of his patterning of deviance. Orly recalls that he hated his stepfather who neglected him and that there was much tension in the family. These were the major sources of his insecurity. Orly was regarded, however, as a "decent," church-going, working-class youth by people in the community. He failed the third and seventh grades in school but recalls that things got better for him around the junior high school period.

There were two reasons for this improvement. First, Orly grew to be respected as a good athlete by his classmates during this period. Second, and because of this new-found prestige, Orly learned not to "give a damn" about pleasing his stepfather who neglected him.

> I wanted to make my stepfather realize I was good (as
> an athlete) ... (but) when I seen that this wasn't going to
> be accomplished I just forgot about trying ... and started
> showing the kids in school that "I could do it."

Orly then began deriving self-esteem, and, thus, some personal security from the praise and attention of his peers.

For about two years Orly enjoyed relatively high esteem among his school peers and the community people who followed athletics. Then, in his sophomore year, he got involved with several other youths in the burglary of three buildings after a beer party. Four of the seven youths involved were from "respectable families." Orly remarked knowingly, "their folks had money—let's put it that way." Three of the youths, Orly and two others, were not from "respectable families." The two others who were not from respectable families had been in trouble with the law before, one repeatedly. Orly had had a minor run-in with the police prior to this time.

The experience of being arrested, spending time in jail, and later having to face his peers destroyed Orly's sense of self-worth. First, the police came to the school to arrest him. He described the incident with clear memory and indicated an apparent emotional impact.

> ... they had a warrant for my arrest. So they took me (even though "the principal didn't want to let them take me out of school"). Well all the kids in classes upstairs— it's a two-story building and they're all looking out the windows (watching me being taken away). And (the police) handcuffed me—and take me walking out to the car.
>
> Well this killed me, you know. Cause everybody was lookin' out [pause] ... they seen ... and uh, it was a hell of a feeling. *And I figured, "well" (it's all over for me now, my reputation is permanently scarred).* I was (totally) embarassed—and I didn't want to face them again.

Orly was then taken to a neighboring town and put in jail.

> They took me to "X" town and put me in the juvenile section of jail. And they got me scared to death because all they're talkin' about is (that they are) going to send me to penal farm, or reform school. And they keep talkin' this and kept talkin' this—and I don't know what's going on (because I'm so scared).

Eventually, after three weeks, one of the older kids involved, the one who had been in trouble several times before, testified that Orly was not involved in any of the actual burglaries.

> (So then) they (the judge and state's attorney) were going to put me on probation—not for stealing but for being with the people that did steal [pause] for running with this type of people when I should have got out of the car and come on home.

Orly did not participate in the actual burglaries, but he was in the car waiting while several others performed the three burglaries.

> So I (had to) spend Christmas in jail. *This made me very bitter.*

Orly was in jail for a total of three weeks, including Christmas day. When he got out he was put on probation with only two requirements: go to school, and go to church. The crisis surrounding his arrest at the school had left him fearful and apprehensive; indeed, as he said, it destroyed his image.

> (The probation requirements) ... hurt me more than anything because *I didn't want to go to school and face these people that the police had come and got me from under.* And I just had the feeling that when I walk in school everybody was going to be lookin' at me—and they were going to be watchin' me—and they were going to be talkin' about me [pause] and *it hurt!*
>
> ... *I was scared* 'cause I didn't want to face anybody—I didn't want to face the kids. And I didn't want to leave [pause] uh, (I wanted to) stay at home. And like I say, *it destroyed my image* ... (it) really hurt when it came time to get a date or something. (I) couldn't get a date (sometimes). Because so and so's Dad didn't want her messin' with ... (me), because (I) ... had been in trouble, blah, blah, blah, you know.

The destruction of Orly's "image" was accomplished primarily through the conspicuous degradation surrounding his arrest in full view of his peers at the school. These were the youths that had previously confirmed his high esteem; now they were witnesses to his denigration. Consequently, he now saw them as confirming his low self-esteem, which he subjectively imposed on himself in anticipation of their reaction. Orly's anticipation of the reactions of his peers was accurate. And, subsequently, these reactions were sufficient to induce avoidance as an escape.

> ... I had to face each one of these people every day ... ("it did hurt").
>
> And uh, like I said, ... my morale was very low ("I felt *very low* as a person") at this time. And uh, *I had a lot of people whose kids couldn't mess with me because I had been in trouble,* uh, bad influence. This is what "come back to me." And uh, *I resented this—so uh, I just*

quit school and decided, "well—can't take this, I'll run. I
can quit school and go to the service." So I quit school.

Orly's home life provided no stability and his good standing
in the community was waning, so he "ran" just as he had con-
templated doing. He joined the service and was shipped over-
seas almost immediately. Orly liked the army and, as he says,
"I was buckin' for them stripes," trying to become an officer.
Shortly after being shipped abroad, however, Orly began drinking heavily.

> ... I would more or less say it was homesickness, a
> loneliness. I started "taking up with the bottle." And I
> had never drank anything hard, all I had ever drank was
> beer. ...

He drank continually and always to the point of drunkenness.
Toward the end of his stay in the army Orly got involved, as an
unwitting accomplice, in a theft. He had the apartment key of
a girlfriend and, while drunk one night, he took a friend to the
girl's apartment to wait for her. Orly passed out on the bed; the
girl didn't come home, and the other man stole some money
from her apartment and left. Orly was charged with the theft
and spent thirty days in the stockade. Later he reimbursed the
girl for her loss and was eventually cleared of the charges. The
other man was dishonorably discharged from the armed ser-
vices for stealing the money.

In the process of being charged by the army and the foreign
authority, however, Orly's captain came to suspect that he had
a drinking problem and ordered him to have a psychiatric examination. An army psychiatrist diagnosed Orly's condition as
alcoholism. Orly soon completed his time in the army and was
discharged under "generally honorable conditions."

When Orly first returned home to stay with his "folks" they
were getting along well. The tension between his parents was
now gone. He also got along with his stepfather for the first
time in his life. But then his mother discovered the psychiatric
report that diagnosed him as an alcoholic. Both Orly's parents
began "riding him" to get professional help, but he would not
do it. So they watched him, expecting trouble to follow from his
heavy drinking. His stepfather went with him to bars to see
that he did not get into trouble. His parents' negative expectations that he was bound to get into trouble bothered Orly, even

though it was reasonable to expect such trouble from his previous actions.

In due course, Orly's heavy drinking led him into circumstances where, with a couple of intoxicated companions, he broke into a coin-operated machine. The cycle of deviant action followed by negative reactions was thus begun. He was sentenced to ninety days in county jail where he met some burglars. His parents and relatives disowned him because of this jail sentence. Consequently, when he got out of jail he had no place to stay, and he had no job. He says:

> I got to feeling where, "hell with it," you know. *If they feel this way about it I'll just go my own way.* So this is when I went to see this other guy . . . [a burglar he had met in jail].

> And uh, I didn't really want to steal, but at the time . . . I had to have some money to live on because I didn't have no place to live.

They started drinking, on the other guy's money, and as Orly says:

> I got to feeling damn good and the more we drank the more his idea (about pulling a burglary) sounded good.

> And I just said, "hell with it" and went along with him.

This marked the beginning of a pattern of criminal behavior which included a great many burglaries and other thefts.

Two questions must be addressed before analyzing Orly's behavior patterns—since his history, thus far, is not entirely explainable in terms of any one of the theoretical approaches under consideration. First, would Orly have become an alcoholic if it had not been for the societal reaction which prompted his quitting school? It seems quite possible that he would not have become an alcoholic without this blow to his sense of esteem and security. But, it seems equally clear that the social reactions would not have been devastating enough to evoke a drastic response like quitting school if Orly's sense of security had been less dependent on confirmation from his peers. Hence, both the general insecurity Orly felt as a result of his stressful home life, and the effects of the social reactions it permitted, apparently contributed to his alcoholism.

A second question is: What eventuated the criminal behavior pattern that Orly had begun? The answer requires both an understanding of Orly's alcoholism and the effects of societal reaction on his behavior. Orly was still prone to seek escape when he returned home from the army, just as he was when he quit high school. Even the mild attacks by his parents were sufficient to prompt a resentful splurge of extra-heavy drinking and generally spiteful behavior, such as a disapproved marriage to a "community tramp." The harsh reaction by his family after the jail sentence induced the same kind of escape tendency as previous occasions had, except this time there were no socially established escapes open to him, like quitting school, alcohol, or disreputable women. Orly could not find a job, his family had shunned him, and he had to eat, so he became a burglar.

> Uh, one burglary led to another. . . . I started running
> around then in what you call "X" street in "X" city. And
> it's a known street for the *hoods and contacts.* So when I
> started running around there all the guys started
> knowing me—I was alright, you know. "He's alright."
> "He's a good guy."
>
> . . . I had money in my pocket and had bought a car,
> could eat, had nice clothes, I could pick up the women—
> so I figured I was alright.
>
> Then I got with the bigger guys, and the bigger guys,
> and the bigger guys. And then I thought I was one of the
> crowd, you know. I was living an entirely different life
> then [that is, the life of a "full-time hood"—usually
> meaning rather versatile types of criminals who dabble
> in several varieties of theft].

This style of life really did not satisfy Orly, however. After about six months of the "thieves' life," he tried to return to the "straight life," only to find himself locked out by social reaction. When asked where he fitted in the hierarchy of hoods, Orly confessed his discontent with the life of a thief.

> Uh, (I was just) a middle hood, but uh, I really didn't
> like this life. I wanted out of it—thought about getting
> out of it many times but uh, just never accomplished
> getting out of it.

> (One time) I went back down around my folks and lived
> down there. I didn't live with them, but I lived down
> around that area. And I worked and I was making it all
> right, was living okay! (It) wasn't anything like I had
> been living. But I was making an honest living and I was
> happy. . . . I wasn't looking over my shoulder every day.
> . . .

Then he was arrested and charged with several burglaries he
had in fact committed while running with the hoods. He "beat
all of the charges" of burglary in a jury trial. But in the process
of the arrest and trial, he lost his job and was again publicly
labeled, recognized and treated, as a deviant.

> . . . when I got picked up (there were) court features (in
> the newspaper) and everything. My picture was in the
> paper and all this. (And) even though I was not
> convicted they (fired me from my job). It had all come
> out in the paper. I made front lines.

> I figured if those people want to have it this way, *"to hell
> with them, I'll just go back to the way I was living."*

> . . . I figured, "well I'm 'labeled it' *I might as well live it."*
> And so I started trying to live the life of a thief. But I
> wasn't cut out for it—never have been cut out for it.

> So, like I said I went back to the . . . life (which was
> really the only one available since no one wanted me
> around). And uh, it lasted nineteen days and I was back
> in jail with three counts of burglary all in the same
> night.

Orly resented the fact that his efforts to change went una-
knowledged. So he again spitefully conformed to the negative
expectations expressed in the reactions of his boss, who fired
him, and in the reactions of his family, who continually disowned him. His return to theft was short-lived since he was
almost immediately apprehended for burglary and sentenced
to prison.

The next several years showed a similar pattern of efforts to
change, followed by exasperation over the negative reactions
that touched off another relapse into drinking and theft, and
finally led to arrest, conviction, and prison.

At the time of the interview Orly had spent six of his twenty-
nine years in prison in three different prison sentences. He had

always left prison with the intention of going straight. Recently, he has spent much of his time in prison reflecting on his life's course and its causes. Here is Orly's own explanation of his deviant history.

> Well I started realizing, evaluating different things that had led to the first time I was sentenced, (the) second time, and this time. I don't blame *it all* on alcohol but alcohol had a big factor in all these crimes.
>
> INTERVIEWER: Okay, if you don't blame "it all" on alcohol what other things do you blame?
>
> ORLY: Uh, mostly myself, a resentment, a stupidity more than anything else. Because *when people would say that I was so and so—well, they would "piss me off." So I would just go show them that I was this instead of trying to show them that I wasn't what they thought I was. I would go along with their program.*

It is clear from this that Orly readily succumbed to the negative expectations of his significant others. As he put it, "People would say I was so and so . . . and I would just go show them (for spite) that I was" instead of trying to demonstrate "that I wasn't what they thought I was." Interestingly, Orly separates his admitted alcohol problem from his susceptibility to the lure of negative expectations. This is consistent with the dual explanation offered here. Orly was, first, insecure and engaged in "security operations"[18] and was, second, more susceptible to the effects of negative reactions as a consequence. Harsh social reactions rendered him more suggestible to the negative expectations therein, and generally more defensive and resentful.

In Orly's case, as in the cases of Mick and Willy, a "self" vulnerability in the form of a "fragile-self" or a weak self-conception, which results generally from a lack of social confirmation in interaction with significant others, is also a necessary condition in the explanation of these deviant behavior patterns.[19]

Summary

In the previous section the cases of Albert and Ken were presented to illustrate social reaction processes as a sufficient cause of deviant behavior patterns. Further, these cases illustrated the effect of societal reaction on a community's *no-good* and a community's *pride and joy*. The other cases of Mick, Willy, and Orly showed the operation of societal reaction processes as a necessary cause. These cases provide, in addition, strong evidence to suggest that societal reaction processes are complemented by a self-factor, rendering the individual especially susceptible to their effects. This initial susceptibility may be either the result of societal reaction processes, as in the cases of Albert, Ken, and Willy, or of situational determinants, as in Mick's case, or of abnormal and deficient interpersonal relations reducing personal security, as in Orly's case.

The Control Approach

Control theory, as discussed in chapter 4, tells us that deviant behavior patterns may occur when social controls are weak, neutralized, or absent. We saw in the previous chapter that Hubert's emergence into deviance was essentially the result of not having any reason to abstain. He felt slightly guilty on a couple of occasions following a deviant act, but he was not deterred by this inner feeling because there was no external reinforcement for it. His family, neighbors, and community were not sources of control. Generally, Hubert had no stake in conformity.[20]

Hubert not only had no stake in conformity to conventional norms, but he also felt totally rejected by conventional people and institutions in general. His stepfather hated him, his brother exploited him, there was no attachment to his mother, he felt the people in the community and at school were always looking down on him, and he had no friends ("there were just people I associated with"). From age twelve to sixteen Hubert engaged periodically in deviant acts ranging from petty theft to property destruction and breaking and entering. None of these excursions into deviance resulted in a patterning of the behavior. Most of the acts were engaged in to get revenge for mistreatment, for excitement, or because, as he said, "why not." In a general sense Hubert always felt confused, depressed; nothing made any difference.

For one incident, where Hubert broke into a country club and destroyed the furnishings, he was sent to a juvenile reform school. The combined effect of his perception of the community reaction to the break-in and the reform school experience left Hubert *totally unattached* to the conventional order.

This put me to the point of almost complete
hopelessness, you know, I had a real hopeless feeling
like . . . man, this is a drag, you know. *Nothing had any
meaning.* I had a feeling of lifelessness, no morale, no
spirit, don't want to do nothin'—*don't give a damn about
nothin'.* This put me to the point where I was just about
as close to the bottom as you could almost get . . . [pause]
such a hopeless feeling.

Upon release from the reform school Hubert returned to stay
with his mother and stepfather. There was still no meaningful
relationship between Hubert and his parents. After a short
while he quit school and was working for his stepfather. For no
particular reason Hubert broke into a house one day.

This idea . . . just hit me all at once, it come from no
place, and I didn't have nothing to do anyway. It was in
the afternoon during the summer . . . and so I did—
moseyed over there and knocked on the door and nobody
answered. I just walked on in. I walked through a couple
of rooms . . . into this bedroom and the first drawer I
pulled open had $100 in it—in this little green bag. Just
took a few seconds—walked in, put it in my pocket and
walked out. And as I walked out I picked up a pack of
cigarettes off the top of a shelf and went about my
business—just happened just like that.

This burglary was the first of what became a pattern of house
burglaries over the next several months. Hubert had been involved in a variety of forms of deviance prior to this but none
were utilitarian and none developed into a pattern. The following remarks by Hubert give some insight into why this behavior was patterned by him.

. . . well, that money looked pretty good and it felt pretty
good, you know. And uh, I knew that I was going to do it
again. I knew that this was what I was going to do—go
around and pull some robberies [meaning house
burglaries], keep myself in some money.

I didn't feel bad about it, that didn't bother me too much
. . . but uh, I kind uh, in a sense I felt it was *my due,* in a
way. I mean, hell, all this crap I've been through and
suffered all this time. . . . it's about time something
comes my way.

He engaged in several more burglaries in a short period of time. These were generally not as successful as the first but he frequently netted $20–$30 per house. Hubert spent the money slowly so he was satisfied with smaller finds. Moreover, much of his feeling of satisfaction came from knowing he was enjoying it, increasing his confidence, and doing something which he had complete control over.[21]

> ... I kinda had a feeling that I was ... I felt good to be doing something that nobody else knew I was doing. I felt I was really getting away with something—*gave me a good feeling to know that I was walking in these places and takin' this stuff and getting away with it. And nobody knew it was me.* It was my own little secret. People were running in circles trying to find out who (was doing it). *I got a certain amount of pleasure out of seeing them suffer a little bit.*
>
> ... I was to the point to where I had been getting away with it and *my confidence was getting so strong I was almost ready to just give up everything except stealing* and just steal for a livin', and fun, and stuff like that.
>
> I felt I was beginning to enjoy life a little bit. You know, I was enjoying the life-style—I was beginning to like it. I was getting a lot of pleasure out of it. That's what I say, I could have probably got hung up on it forever if they wouldn't have caught me [pause]. And uh, they did and it knocked me back down to where I was really at. And uh, it put me in that depressed state of mind. ... I mean it took ... the little bit of pleasure out of my life, that I was getting, away. That put me back where I was before I started, and uh, I hit bottom again.

Though the profits from Hubert's burglaries may have been small and the satisfactions may have been simple or vicarious, it is a strong piece of evidence in support of control theory. For what is involved as an inducement in Hubert's behavior is the simple fact that houses were there and easy to burglarize, the money was good enough, and burglary provided him a sense of control and self-confidence. He had never felt control or confidence in everyday events or his life's course prior to this time. Now he was pulling the strings and other people were affected.[22] The point is that, from the control theory perspective, if the bond that holds individuals to society's accepted ways is weak or otherwise ineffective, no special pressure to deviance is necessary. One may deviate for simple or complicated reasons, for whimsical satisfactions, or for practicality, expedience, or socially implanted goals.[23] Hubert was free to indulge his interests or his hostilities in deviance because he had no group or personal relationships capable of effecting social constraint.

Carl's Case

In the following case the effect of broken or absent social control is seen more readily than in Hubert's case. Carl was a forty-five-year-old man who had spent sixteen years of his adult life in prison on four separate sentences. He was one of two children in a family broken up shortly after his birth. Carl never knew his father, and at age twelve, his mother died.

> I don't know, it just stunned me, to a point where, you know, I lost everything. In fact, I remember at her funeral, uh, I was sitting by the grave and after the service was over ... I couldn't move. I couldn't get up— my legs were paralyzed and my uncle carried me to the car. And when we got home he had to massage my legs to get circulation back. And I think, in a way after she was gone—*I didn't care anymore.*

Carl stayed with an aunt and uncle (his mother's brother) who had their own children and were not undisturbed at the addition of Carl to the family. There were periodic arguments about Carl. Their reactions to him, expecially his aunt's, were sometimes contemptuous. As a result Carl recalled:

> I started running around with kids, going out at night. I knew they was bad, *but I didn't care.* My aunt and uncle, they tried to keep me on the straight and narrow but, like I say, *I didn't care.* So eventually I just started going out on my own and committing ... burglarizing homes and things like that.

At age fourteen, Carl was sent to a juvenile training school where he stayed until he was seventeen years old. A few months after his release he was inducted into the army. For two years while Carl was in the army he did not engage in any thefts, nor did he get into any other serious trouble.

> I never stole anything. .... I never made a burglary or
> anything like that all the time I was in the army. I never
> done anything like that either (while I was in the
> service).

In 1947 he was discharged from the army. His relationship
with the aunt and uncle with whom he had lived for a short
period was not strong. The only meaningful relationship Carl
had during this time and primarily for the next several years
was with his older sister. When he got out of the service he went
to stay with his sister who had just been married and set up in
a community. Within a few weeks she helped him get a job and
arranged for him to take a room in a YMCA. He began commit-
ting house burglaries, for the first time since before he was sent
to the juvenile training school, almost immediately after leaving his sister's house. There was a practical reason for burglary
and no active source of constraint in the absence of his sister.

> I liked my job real good. I was working around steam
> engines and it was real good. Still I was twenty-one years
> old and I wanted to run around—I wanted to do things. I
> wanted to be going every night, you know. When I got off
> work why I would go and clean up and I would head for
> East City.

> Especially on weekends I always used to go to the
> McCarthur Hotel over there and stay over Saturday and
> Sunday. And used the, well, at that time they had call
> girls and you get a room and just tell the bellboy you
> want a woman and he sends one up. And it might cost
> $10 for about an hour or so. But that was all the money I
> had. I couldn't spend too much on them and make what
> I had last until next pay day.

> *But living like that, it took more money than what I
> had and that's why I, you know, went into these houses*
> —hoping to find money. I think I was only making $60
> and I think I got paid every two weeks. I think I was
> making a dollar something an hour. *But anyway, I
> needed more money for what I was doing—so I had to
> find some way (to get it).*

Within five months Carl was caught, convicted and sentenced to prison. After twenty-eight months he was released on
parole but his sister would not let him live with her this time.

So he was paroled to another city where he got a job as a welder, a trade learned while in prison. But Carl was alone, unattached, and, as he saw it, not a part of the conventional world. His burglaries began again almost immediately after release.

> CARL: I got a job in a company ... and was doing pretty good. *But again, I was up there (in a strange town),* I was by myself—living by myself—staying in a hotel. And this parole officer, he, you know, (he didn't pay any attention). *(There is) not anybody watching you, seeing what you do when you're by yourself—why you go out and do things.*
>
> *It's usually when I get alone like that* (that I get into trouble). I've always been a loner. I don't mix too good except when I go in taverns I might talk to some people. But generally I would be by myself and drink by myself. *But, when I get by myself I start thinking and eventually all my thoughts start to concentrating on getting into trouble.* Going in, you know, burglarizing houses or buildings or anything like that.
>
> INTERVIEWER: What do you mean all of your thoughts started ...?
>
> CARL: Well, I don't think like some people. When they are by themselves they might, oh, be thinking about: "I'll go to so-and-so's house and see how he's doing—see if he wants to go and have a beer or something like that." I don't think like that. Some guy might say: "I'll go over and call Betty or Jane or see if she wants to go out on a date." I don't think like that either.

Carl was aware that persons who are integrated into the conventional social order are bound by social constraints to respond to being alone in an accepted manner—by calling a friend and doing something conventional. But he neither had the benefits of reliable friends nor the constraining obligations that come with being part of a group. So Carl responded to loneliness by burglarizing houses to get enough money to spend on call girls, hotel rooms, and beer.

> I might be walking down the street and might think: "well, I wonder where there is a house I can get in— wonder where I could find some money," something like that. And so I might walk until I find a street. Then I go down it and start looking at the houses and seeing which

one is dark and which one maybe nobody's there. And
then lot of homes I walk by like that. In the back of my
head, I'm still a little reluctant to go in because maybe
there is somebody in bed or something like that. And I
don't want to get caught but, that's what I thought about
a lot of times when I committed these burglaries. . . . *I
would be my myself and I would start thinking like
that. Well, "I wonder where there is a house I can break
into." And then I would go and I would start looking for
one.*

Carl was soon arrested for possession of stolen property and
subsequently confessed to a series of burglaries which led to
another prison sentence. This time he served five years. When
he was released he went to stay with his sister. Their relationship had improved through correspondence, and her visits to
the prison, and she was now divorced. His sister was the only
person whose opinion he cared about. Interestingly, Carl never
committed a burglary or, for that matter, broke the law in any
other way when he was staying with his sister.

I came down there to stay with her. She was divorced at
that time so I come down and stayed there with her for
about two weeks. Then she helped me get a job. And
when I got a job I went and got a room in a hotel there
and was living there. *Like I say, when I was staying at
my sister's, why, I was doing alright. Then I got by
myself and I started—started going out at nights and
doing things* (burglaries).

Within a couple of months Carl was back in prison, this time
on a one-to-ten-year sentence for burglary and car theft. He
served six years and nine months. At this stage, Carl had been
incarcerated for nearly fourteen years of his adult life. The
only brief periods that he was not involved in theft or burglary
were when he was under the tight control of the military and
the few months in total he spent living with his sister. In both
instances Carl was sufficiently constrained by external sources
of control.

While he engaged in burglaries systematically and consistently when he was not incarcerated, Carl neither liked what
he was doing nor did he consider himself a thief and play out
the role. Rather, what he did for pragmatic needs when not
constrained by the military or his sister left him with a sense

of being different and unacceptable to conventional people. This self-feeling, in turn, operated to bring about his own lack of involvement in, and thus control by, conventional groups.

> I never did consider myself a burglar. I guess that is the technical name for a person who goes in homes and steals. ... I never thought of myself as a thief. As funny as that may sound because I knew it was wrong but truthfully I can't say that I consider myself as a burglar.
>
> INTERVIEWER: Do you think other people thought of you as a burglar or a thief?
>
> CARL: Well, that's funny, I never did. Now the people I knew, they didn't know that I was going out and doing that and I always thought, you know, I always wondered what they would think of me if they knew I was doing this. And I think that's why I feel alone so much because *I know what I am. I know what I've done and I feel strange around people.* Like I told you a while ago, I don't mix very well with people. *It's because I feel different. I feel like I'm not good enough to belong around people because I've done all these things. I've been in prison, and I've stolen, and I've done just about everything that there is to do.*
>
> ... I think, "well, if I'm with a bunch of people and I'm sitting looking at them and they are treating me as one of them. ..." I think, "well, how would they react if they knew what I really was and what I'd done. How would they treat me then? What would they do? Kick me out? Tell me, "well, get away from me I don't want you around here?" And so, I hate to go where there is, you know (conventional people), like in a home or something.
>
> ("I feel this way") ... especially when I get around my sister ... because I know that I hurt her real bad. And I feel like just being around her and her friends just isn't right—and that I don't belong. ... I feel she knows me and knows what I am, and I just don't feel right around her—just like I'm contaminating the environment. I just don't feel right. I feel like I want to get out and *I feel better by myself.*

Further evidence suggesting the credibility of a control theory explanation of this case is presented in the next chapter.

Summary

This chapter examined the extent to which socialization, societal reaction, and control approaches to deviance are viable as explanations of the patterning of deviant behavior. Several cases were presented to suggest the general plausibility but not necessarily the specific accuracy of each of the three approaches.

The case of Don was used to evaluate the socialization approach. In general, the compelling effect of positive expectations, social support, and encouragement in the social milieu of the deviant were confirmed as factors contributing to patterned deviance. However, the internalization thesis was questioned since considerable evidence indicated that Don, while expediently disposed to deviant values, was not compelled to deviance by a psychological bent. Rather, his theft behavior sometimes came to be patterned only because it was more expedient than conventional employment.

The cases of Albert and Ken suggest the viability of the societal reaction explanation as a sufficient cause of patterned deviance. In Albert's case it was seen that social reactions to the ascribed status of a no-good rendered him susceptible to the negative expectations inherent in the "no-good" label. Albert's corroboration with those who labeled him, and the relatively high esteem he received from stealing combined to contribute further to make a pattern of theft the most attractive course of action available to him. In the second case, Ken conformed to the negative expectations of the labelers in demeanor but not in actual behavior. Although he came to regard himself as a "bum" and a "criminal" as a result of societal reaction processes, his conformity was reflected in the tough recalcitrant manner he assumed rather than by the commission of criminal or other deviant acts. Ken's case demonstrates well the transformation of a strong respectable "self" to a calloused, embittered, and insecure self.

The three other cases of Mick, Willy, and Orly involved societal reaction processes as a necessary, but not a sufficient, cause. It was noted that societal reaction seemed to operate as a necessary cause primarily because some "self-factor" such as low self-esteem, provisional status, or emotional stress complemented it. These factors, however, are not always a function of societal reaction. When they are not, societal reaction is less explanatory and must be seen more as a partial explanation.

The voluntaristic model of social action assumed in the societal reaction approach was indicated in all three cases. The processual model of personality was indicated in two of the cases. In Orly's case there was evidence of both a static and a processual quality in his personality.

In both cases in the section on the control approach, the beginning and the continuance of patterns of theft were the result of broken or neutralized social controls. Both men, Hubert and Carl, felt their acts were less than noble.[24] Group and community controls over Hubert had gradually broken to the point that his own feelings of guilt for his deviance were dismissed and replaced with a sense of satisfaction. Hubert's family and the conventional community had no persuasive power over him because neither potential source of control included him within their span of attention and regulation. Hubert's family was disorganized and tension-ridden and, thus, did not provide him with a satisfactory and constraining group experience. The conventional community that was able but, by Hubert's perception, unwilling to include him as a part of it never became a place of control.

Carl was effectively controlled when he was under close observation as when he lived with his sister or when he was in the army. But, when alone and not a part of a social unit or group, Carl was not sufficiently constrained to avoid the pull of easy additional money. Though his own beliefs were contrary to the behavior he patterned, they were ineffective when all external sources of control were absent as when he was living alone. In both cases illustrated as fitting the control model in this chapter, it was shown that deviance may occur where there has been neither socialized values favoring or supporting it, nor inner beliefs propelling it. All that was essential in these cases was that there was no constraining reason to avoid deviance.

There was ample evidence suggesting the utility of all three approaches for certain cases. Ascertaining the comparative explanatory power is, therefore, more problematic. The "internalization thesis" of the socialization approach was questioned and considered to be an over-explanation. The societal reaction approach, in contrast, was shown, without qualification, to be a sufficient cause in Ken's case. In Albert's case, negative reaction processes were shown to induce initial deviance, which was then followed by more harsh reactions, to which he responded with more deviance. Negative reactions are usually seen to follow, not induce, the first act of deviance. In our explanation of Albert's case, however, we have argued that societal reaction processes were sufficiently explanatory of his patterning of deviant behavior.

The control approach was generally more applicable than either of the other approaches, probably because it is less explicit about the process of deviance. Of the twenty-two cases in this study where the control model was, at least, partially explanatory of the patterning process, many different social, psychological, situational, and practical variables eventuated a breakdown in social control. In addition, once social control was broken, deviant behavior was prompted by different factors including stress, rational calculation, expedience, and revenge. The essential aspect of the patterning process, however, involved as much the control that was not there as it did these other factors. Because of the wide variety of motivations to deviance permitted in our coding of cases fitting the control model, it is clear that a large part of its utility is a result of a lack of specificity. Nevertheless, in sum, the present analysis suggests the greater explanatory power of control and societal reaction theories over socialization theories for the patterning phase of deviance.

Notes

1. David Matza, *Becoming Deviant* (Englewood Cliffs, N.J.: Prentice-Hall, 1969), p. 169.

2. Howard S. Becker, "Introduction," in *The Jack-Roller* by Clifford R. Shaw (Chicago: University of Chicago Press, 1966), p. v-xviii.

3. This is, of course, less true of the control approach than either the socialization or the societal reaction approach. Control theory is perhaps the most directly applicable to all three stages of the development of deviant behavior patterns of the three approaches.

4. Charles E. Frazier and Thomas D. McDonald, "Societal Reaction Theory: Postulates and Their Evaluation," in *Alternative Values and Structures,* ed. Swaran S. Sandhu (Moorhead, Minn.: Moorhead State College, 1973), pp. 49–60.

5. Patterned deviant behavior is to be distinguished from "career" deviance as conceptualized by Marshall B. Clinard, and Howard S. Becker, and also from Erving Goffman's "moral career" view of stabilized deviance. See Marshall B. Clinard, *Sociology of Deviant Behavior,* rev. ed. (New York: Holt, Rinehart & Winston, 1963), pp. 204–31; Howard S. Becker, *Outsiders: Studies in the Sociology of Deviance* (New York: Free Press, 1963), pp. 24–25 and 101–2; and Erving Goffman, "The Moral Career of the Mental Patient," *Psychiatry* 22 (May 1959): pp. 123–42. Similarly, the conceptualization of patterning in this study is to be distinguished from Sutherland's classic development of "professional" deviant

behavior in that none of Sutherland's requisites of professionalism must be met by individuals here regarded to have manifested *patterns* of deviance. See Edwin H. Sutherland, *The Professional Thief* (Chicago: University of Chicago Press, 1937).

6. Any behaviors, however frequent in occurrence, which are not regarded as a part of one's potential range of behavior would not be patterned by this logic and definition. It is important to note, however, that there were no cases, in the present sample, where frequent engagement was indicated while the behavior was not subjectively regarded as part of an individual behavioral pattern.

7. See Dennis H. Wrong, "The Oversocialized Conception of Man in Modern Sociology," *American Sociological Review* 26 (April 1961): 183–93.

8. See Florian Znaniecki, *The Method of Sociology* (New York: Rinehart, 1934), and Alfred A. Lindesmith, *Opiate Addiction* (Bloomington: Indiana University Press, 1947), pp. 5–20, for excellent discussions of the logic of analytic induction. Also, see Norman K. Denzin, *The Research Act* (Chicago: Aldine, 1970), pp. 238–40, for a discussion of the use of analytic induction in life-history analysis.

9. Becker, "Introduction" in *The Jack-Roller,* p. xi.

10. See, for example, Robert K. Merton, *Social Theory and Social Structure* (New York: Free Press, 1968), p. 177.

11. Only forty-two cases are considered in this section. Four cases involved occasional offenses where no patterns developed, two cases were considered generally invalid as whole histories, and two were disrupted during the interview affecting the credibility of the account after the point of interruption.

12. Edwin Lemert argues that "deviants are individuated with respect to their vulnerability to the societal reaction because: (a) the person is a dynamic agent, (b) there is a structuring to each personality which acts as a set of limits within which the societal reaction operates." See his *Social Pathology* (New York: McGraw-Hill, 1951), p. 23.

13. See, for example, Frank Tannenbaum, *Crime and the Community* (New York: Ginn and Company, 1938); Lemert, *Social Pathology,* p. 77; and Becker, *Outsiders,* pp. 1–39.

14. Lemert, *Social Pathology,* pp. 76–78.

15. Howard S. Becker's discussion of "gross exclusion" and David Matza's more elaborate consideration of the processes of exclusion are implicated in this statement. A view that differs, in that it posits an involuntary acquiescence to the proffered role of mentally ill, is seen in Thomas Scheff's work. See Becker, *Outsiders,* pp. 33–34; Matza, *Becoming Deviant,* p. 160; and Thomas Scheff, *Being Mentally Ill: A Sociological Theory* (Chicago: Aldine, 1966), p. 92.

16. See Lynn Lofland, "Self-Management in Public Settings: Part I," *Urban Life and Culture* (April 1972), pp. 93–100, for a discussion of "fragile-self." For a different explanation of the sources of bad self-concepts see Walter C. Reckless, *The Crime Problem,* 4th ed. (New York: Appleton-Century-Crofts, 1967), pp. 444–68.

17. See Lofland, "Self Management in Public Settings," pp. 95–96.

18. Security operations or coping strategies are employed by insecure or anxious persons in an effort to become more secure. See Harry Stack Sullivan, *Conceptions of Modern Psychiatry* (New York: W. W. Norton, 1974) and *The Interpersonal Theory of Psychiatry* (New York: W. W. Norton, 1953).

19. See Ernst Becker, *The Birth and Death of Meaning* (New York: Free Press, 1962), for a more intensive look at the idea of "fragile-self."

20. See Jackson Toby, "Social Disorganization and Stake in Conformity: Contemporary Factors in the Predatory Behavior of Hoodlums," *Journal of Criminal Law, Criminology and Police Science* 48 (1957): 12–17, for the original statement on "stakes in conformity."

21. See David Matza, *Delinquency and Drift* (New York: John Wiley, 1964), pp. 88–90 and 188–91, for an excellent analysis of a similar phenomenon called the "mood of fatalism."

22. When the individual turns the situation of always being affected by others' social action to one where the person experiences himself or herself as *cause* and others as *affected,* the "mood of humanism" is restored. See Matza, *Delinquency and Drift,* pp. 188–89.

23. Although the author interprets the case differently, we believe a clear case of patterned deviance as a result of weak and neutralized social controls is presently published as the case of Stanley in Shaw's *The Jack-Roller.*

24. This finding casts some doubt on the view of some control theorists, such as Reiss and Reckless, that internal control is more essential to producing conforming behavior than external control. Our finding is more consistent with Durkheim's early emphasis on external constraints as being most vital in preventing deviance.

Change of Deviant Behavior Patterns

Throughout the previous chapters it has been noted that three phases (emergence, patterning, and change) of deviance are important when examining the explanatory power of the socialization, the societal reaction, and the control approaches. Emergence and patterning were considered in chapters 6 and 7. This chapter is concerned with the change or abandonment of deviant behavior patterns. Change or abandonment refers to the disengagement from deviance. When a respondent disengaged from a pattern of deviant behavior for a *subjectively significant period of time,* his behavior was said to have changed.

This definition of *change* differs from that implied by the terms *reform* and *rehabilitation* in that both of these terms suggest a *permanent* remaking of the individual. Permanence, however, may only be determined retrospectively. To invoke the idea of permanence when considering behavior change is, therefore, problematic. How do we (as researchers, therapists, or deviant actors) know when a change is permanent except by our own subjective estimate of commitment and intent? Our general orientation to valid sources of data, in this work, has consistently depended on the perceptions of the deviant actor. Thus, the actor's abandonment of a deviant behavior pattern was defined as *change* if the respondent indicated it was his intention to permanently disengage from a form of deviance.

This chapter inquires as to whether the socialization, societal reaction, and control frameworks are viable as explanations of the abandonment of deviant behavior patterns. In addition, we will look at the extent to which cases of patterned deviance induced by factors of socialization, societal reaction, or control theory change in ways consistent with their source. For example, we will examine Don's patterned deviance, which was basically a product of factors consistent with the socialization approach, and appraise the extent to which his patterns were abandoned for reasons explainable by the same approach. As we suggested earlier, in part I, consideration of the change phase of deviant careers provides an opportunity to test theories of deviant patterning in a unique way. The forces indicated in the disengagement from a deviant behavior pattern should be subsumable under general principles explaining the patterning if the theory of deviant behavior is to be regarded as a credible general explanation.

The reader should remember that, while the propositions pertaining to emergence and patterning are rather directly derivable from theoretical statements in each tradition, the position statements on change are almost exclusively derived inferentially. Propositions characterizing each approach on change are inferred either from theoretical propositions pertaining to the emergence and patterning phases or from statements of general position by theorists within each approach. Comments on the general credibility of the approaches based in this analysis are, consequently, more problematic than in the case of emergence and patterning.

In spite of the above qualification and the fact that few theorists consider the change process, it is still important to consider change in the evaluation of theoretical approaches. Change completes the cycle of emergence, patterning, and abandonment of deviant behavior which is characteristic of deviant careers.[1] Consideration of change of deviant behavior provides an opportunity to test the logical proposition that stabilized deviance, which is caused by certain factors, changes after elimination or neutralization of those factors. If, for example, deviant behavior is the by-product of internalized norms and values, change of this behavior would logically require the desocialization of the individual, or at least the neutralization of the norms and values which induce deviance.[2] A second reason to consider change of deviant behavior patterns is that this may add to our understanding of the emergence and patterning of deviance. For instance, when an individual noted that he abandoned a pattern of theft because he got married and now had a reason not to get in trouble, he not only indicated his reason for change, but he also implied a source of the emergence and the patterning of his deviance.

Theoretical Distinctions

The basic differences between the socialization, societal reaction, and control approaches on the issue of change are detailed in the general propositions in Appendix A. Implicit in these propositions are the distinctive assumptions about the nature of human social action and the substance of personality which underlie the two approaches.

The proposition to characterize the socialization approach's position on change is as follows: change of deviant behavior patterns requires (1) desocializing the individual to the point that deviant values are dispelled and (2) resocialization to the extent that the individual internalizes values unfavorable to deviant behavior. The processes of desocialization and resocialization are believed to require the removal of the deviant from external sources which support and encourage deviance, and the concurrent assimilation into nondeviant groups whose values are unfavorable to deviant behavior. That is, the proposition calls for eliminating values conducive to deviance, and installing new values conducive to nondeviance. These operations are to be effected by involving the individual in the ordinary processes of nondeviant groups. Since the personality, to the socialization theorist, is a relatively static organization of values and norms that determines the characteristic behavior of the individual,[3] it must be substantially altered in the process of changing behavior.

In essence, then, socialization theorists assume the need to free the deviant from internalized values conducive to deviance as well as from external sources of social support for deviant behavior. This is accomplished through assimilation into an ongoing nondeviant group. The group may be a conventional group, such as a family, that has manifested values unfavorable to deviance,[4] or it may be a specially constituted

therapeutic group.[5] These groups carry out the desocialization
and resocialization through ordinary group dynamics.

By contrast, the societal reaction proposition offered to explain change suggests that change results from a purposive
and volitional decision to disengage from patterned deviant
behavior. An individual may decide to discontinue a pattern of
deviance for a variety of reasons. For instance, the decision to
disengage from deviance may be an attempt to evoke reactions
from others which are more to the deviant's liking, or simply
because of a desire to try another life-style. In any event, the
deviant is believed to be capable of examining alternative
courses of action and of choosing from among them the course
which best suits individual purposes.

Once the deviant decides to change, the ability to do so is
affected by the availability of opportunities to evoke nondeviant "self" definitions from others. Even if the labelers are many
and influential in the life-setting, the deviant must still individually either accept or repudiate their negative definitions.[6]

It is often easier, for the individual, to accept the definition
of deviant and conform to the negative expectations than to
repudiate the definition in the face of persistent denial from
the labelers. In the event that the labelers deny the individual's
change in behavior and persist in negative definitions, the deviant may (1) repudiate their denial in the hope that their definitions will change, (2) change life-setting as well as patterns of
behavior, or (3) accept the label and return to some form of
deviance.

In brief, the societal reaction position differs from the socialization view in that it assumes the ability of the deviant to
change behavior patterns willfully and purposively. Change is
relatively easy if there are opportunities in the deviant's life-
setting to evoke and maintain nondeviant definitions of the
"self." The socialization proposition, on the other hand, assumes the necessity of changing the deviant's values and personality structure before a change in behavior patterns is
possible.

The control proposition more closely approximates the
socialization position than the societal reaction position on
change in that something outside the individual is a prerequi-
site to behavior change. That is to say, the process of change or
abandonment of deviant behavior patterns, for the control
theorists, involves the acquisition of control sources, or the alleviation from situational or other forces that weaken or neu-

tralize usual constraints. The control proposition is also like the societal reaction position in its emphasis on the volitional component to change. That is, the individual is believed to be capable of a voluntary decision to change.

In short, change from deviant behavior patterns, for the control theorist, follows from either (1) increased affiliation in highly integrated, thus constraining, groups or (2) the alleviation of pressures or circumstances which weaken or neutralize existing sources of internal and external control. Most individuals conform because their membership(s) in highly integrated groups provides an ever-present source of constraint, not because their internal value structure forbids deviance generally. In fact, many forms of deviance are inherently enticing and attractive to many of us. And, as the control theorists suggest, if it were not for our involvements in ongoing groups which we are reluctant to risk losing by an act of deviance, we would deviate more frequently.

Even when social control is securely implanted by the regulation of group membership, the effect of this control may be weakened or neutralized. This rendering ineffective of existing social controls may be the result of diverse forces such as situational pulls, temporary stress, or the disintegration or dissolution of a primary group affiliation. The acquisition of new sources of control or the alleviation of forces which weaken or neutralize existing controls is the key to change for control theorists.

New controls may be accidental, therapeutically implanted and manipulated, or purposively sought out by the deviant in a plan to change. Alleviation of forces contributing to weakening or neutralizing existing controls may come about similarly by natural processes and time, through therapeutic guidance, or through deliberately calculated individual action by the deviant.

The differences between the control and the socialization models of change are that (1) the former does not require any desocialization before new or revitalized sources of control may be effective and (2) group membership may be an effective control even when the individual does not internalize group norms. The control model of change differs from the societal reaction view most apparently in the assumption that something outside the actor, such as group affiliation, must become active as a control before change will come about.

The sufficiency of the socialization, societal reaction, and control explanations of change and their comparative utility as general theories of the development and change of deviant behavior patterns is examined below by considering specific cases from our deviant life-histories. Several instances of change will be illustrated in the following pages. We will look first at the changes in the patterned deviance of respondents considered in previous chapters to depict archetypes of socialization, societal reaction, and control deviants. Then other instances of change fitting each theoretical approach in whole or in part will be discussed. Finally we will consider the relative explanatory power of the three approaches with regard to the change phase of deviance.

The Socialization Model of Change

According to the socialization theorists, change from deviant to conventional behavior patterns requires a desocialization of deviant values and attitudes and the installation of conventional ones through a resocializing group experience. While no instance of change in the present sample fits the socialization model exactly, several cases were the result of basic socialization principles. In the case of Don, whose entrance into and stabilization of deviant behavior patterns were primarily explainable in terms of the socialization framework, change did not require a resocialization process. This is important since Don's deviant career, his social background, and all that they imply constitute a textbook picture of a socialized deviant.

Don's Change

The reader will recall that, in addition to being a career thief, Don was also a long-time drug addict. Don made three important changes from his career as a hustler, none of which involved a resocialization process. The changes were, rather, individually calculated, voluntary, and purposive in design. The following account of one change is exemplary. Neither Don nor, interestingly, the girl mentioned in his commentary had ever approached the problem of sustenance except through hustling before.

> ... when Ellen and I came out of (the jail) ... I went to
> work initially and she was kind of insecure. (Because),
> like I say, she wasn't going to hustle anymore. ... I didn't
> want her to hustle. She didn't want to either. I don't
> think, although she never knew ... she never really

knew anything else. And uh, but we were trying to kind
uh, "do it right" [abandon deviant behavior patterns]. So
I worked at a pizza place which wasn't very successful. I
mean I could make the pizza, but I didn't like the job. So
uh, I left and she found a job working at a jazz joint. She
(was a) cocktail waitress and she wound up making good
money. And we rented another nice apartment and
everything and, but the role (I was playing), I didn't
know how to handle it from there.

INTERVIEWER: Do you mean because she was making the
money?

RESPONDENT: No, the whole thing became, boy! It became
(for example) our sex relationship all of a sudden
changed. We played different roles up until then. We had
a very wild sex life, there was a number of girls, there
was lesbian activities, there was two (or) three girls and
me—and her. It was pretty bizarre. And we just assumed
all kinds of roles. And all of a sudden it got strained ...
she was playing a wife and she didn't really know what
a wife should be. And ... I didn't know how she wanted
to be treated now. So it became very confusing.

INTERVIEWER: You said you were trying to "do it right."
Do you mean you were trying to live a straight life?

RESPONDENT: Right, right!

INTERVIEWER: Why? Did you have a change [Don cuts in
here].

RESPONDENT: Yeah, it was just—we were just—[pause] *it
was affection. We loved each other and it (the life we
were living as thieves and addicts) was starting to steal
from us. We didn't want to use drugs anymore.* And I
had gotten involved in a narcotics anonymous group and
stuff like that. *I was trying. She didn't want me to steal
so I didn't.*

This case is especially important because it shows that even
career deviants produced in a subculture of deviance can
change without desocializing and resocializing group experiences. Don abandoned his well-polished trade of hustling without having been desocialized by either a conventional or
therapeutic group. He, and his girlfriend, established for a subjectively significant period of time a conventional-style marriage relationship and occupations without being resocialized
in terms of conventional values. They did it because the style
of life with drugs and theft was, as Don said, "starting to steal

from us." Each of Don's changes was voluntary with some pragmatic purpose underlying it. Desocialization and resocialization were never factors in his changes.

The fact that Don's changes do not fit the socialization model raises some interesting questions. How can one who learns and internalizes values favoring deviance dispel them at will? Was Don a product of his culture, a socialized deviant, at one time and a purposive actor in his own behalf at another time? Or, was Don a rationally purposive actor all the time and simply persuaded and guided by circumstances to choose the courses and patterns of action he did? One thing is clear, if the emergence and patterning of Don's deviance were, as it appeared earlier, the product of internalized values favoring deviance, the desocialization and resocialization process is not necessary in change. But, a more satisfactory explanation of Don's case is that the internalization of or psychological commitment to deviant values assumed by socialization theorists does not operate as a permanent inner source of motivation to deviant behavior. Rather, it appears that deviant behavior is a result of positive social support in a particular situation and life-setting instead of a function of a permanently formed personality. Values appear to invite behavior in conformity to them but they do not compel individuals to engage in only behaviors which actualize their values.

While the desocialization-resocialization process does not surface as a factor in the instances of change in the present life-history data, there are several changes that resulted from group and general influences of the social setting. A group relations principle is an integral aspect of the socialization model. That is, socialization theorists believe behavior change, like behavior patterns, is the product of group influences and support from the actor's social environment. The following excerpts from the cases of Orly,[7] Sony, and Tim exemplify the effect of these group factors in behavior change.

The first instance of change for Orly demonstrates the influence of the group on Orly's deviant behavior patterns, but it does not involve either the processes of desocialization and resocialization or the removal of the deviant from his life setting.

Orly

Orly was around fourteen to fifteen years old when his first change occurred. He had only recently come to be considered for acceptance by a group whose values were strictly unfavorable to stealing. The influence of the group in changing Orly's deviant behavior pattern may be seen in the following statement.

> A few of my friends did find out (that I had been stealing), and uh, this is what made me stop. ... (That is) some of the ... closer friends that I had ... uh, they ... *told me to quit stealing or they was going to "cut me loose because they couldn't run with somebody like this." So I set down and evaluated the whole thing and figured out,* "well, what's the use of stealing, I don't need it." *So I just more or less quit* and I started running with a little better crowd of people than what I had been ... too!

Orly's change is partly a result of group influence, but also it was partly a result of purposive desire to improve his community status. The group had threatened him with exclusion if he did not change. But he was not desocialized (i.e., stripped of values conducive to theft) or removed from his other affiliations. He was simply offered the opportunity to join a "better crowd of people" if he stopped stealing. Orly *decided* the new crowd's offer was worth the change, since the gratifying praise he would get from the new group was important to him and stealing was not.

Sony

This nineteen-year-old respondent describes a change in his behavior which he characterized by vengeful destruction, aggression, and theft. He considered himself "mean," "bullyish," and "violent." Both his behavior and his personality were substantially changed by group influence. The respondent's life-setting was changed in the first instance. In the second instance he drifted into a different group.

Sony was between eleven and thirteen years of age when the first change occurred. His father had given up any hope of controlling him and had asked Sony's uncle to take him to raise for awhile. Unlike his father, Sony recalled, the uncle was "a very respectable man, ... "He was a church going guy, and, there ain't a person in Centerville that won't say 'Hi' to him or look up to him."

So I went to live with (my uncle and aunt) until I was
thirteen. I was doing alright when I first got there, you
know—I was loved, actually. But that was hard on me.
You know, I never had that before. *And I just took it
wrong.* So *instead of ... giving them love back, I started
stealing from them.* Like they had these silver dollars,
for about two hundred years, you know, run down the
family. I stole them—and spent them and just things like
this—anything I could get my hands on I would steal. I
would hide it.

Like, I bought him a square lighter for Christmas. You
know, one of them dudes that you push a button and a
hole opens and you put your cigarette in there—I stole
that from him. I bought it for him and I stole it from
him—I give it to him for Christmas.

Eventually the things were discovered missing. The respondent walked in the house one day when his aunt and uncle were
discussing the missing silver dollars.

They was just sittin' in the living room one day when I
walked in ... they were just all discussin' it. Well, I sit
down and I discuss it right along with them—and I had
done it.

But they didn't suspect me in the least [pause] Well
[pause] that made me feel bad ... what really made it
hurt was that he didn't even act like, you know, he didn't
even ask me if I'd done it.

*At home mom would have beat the shit out of me—even
if I hadn't done it,* she would have made me say I had
done it.

So I finally told them. I felt guilty about it, so I told
them. ... (My uncle said) "... Sony, if I can't have a good
boy I don't want any" *You know, he still wanted me to
stay—so I did.*

That's what really started changing me. You know, he
knew everything I had done and it kind uh, I don't know,
it just made me feel real guilty. I don't know, *it just
made me a little soft* ... see before I never had no
friends ... if I did have and I wanted to steal from them
(I did without any qualms). *But ... (after staying with
my uncle for that time) I couldn't steal off of somebody*

> *I liked.* I wouldn't hit ... (somebody I liked) either, you
> know, I had really changed. *I wouldn't do anything to*
> *make (a friend) mad at me.*
>
> ... *I started realizing, you know, you can't live like that.*
> *You know, that ain't no life.*

This experience with his uncle and aunt induced great
change in Sony's behavior patterns and his personality. He not
only disengaged from stealing and from aggressive assaults on
his peers, he indicated that he had no tendency to act that way.
When Sony says, "that ain't no life (to act like that)," he hints
at a difference between belonging to a group that is disintegrated and one that is highly integrated. Deviance is an unacceptable threat in the latter type of group.

Another example of change is seen when Sony tells how a
friend and his group later deterred him from stealing and contributed to change in his behavior patterns and his personality
structure when he was seventeen years old.

> When I first got out ("... of reform school I was riding
> down the street with a new found friend who had stolen
> only one thing in his life ... and he never stole another
> thing"). I said, "well, I need some cigarettes—I said,
> "well, I'll get some." He said, "where?" I said, "(I'll steal
> 'em) out of some store." He says, "yeah," he says, "go
> ahead but let me out and don't come after me no more."
> Well, I liked him ... see he's a very popular person. You
> know like there ain't no "chick" that won't go out with
> him and nobody that won't say "Hi" to him. And ... I
> respected him for (saying) that. ... (And) by hanging
> around him I've got more friends than I need actually.
>
> I mean I never realized that people could be so friendly
> —and he's the one that showed me that. *That's what*
> *changed me right there. ... And that's what stopped me*
> *from stealing.*

There was no resocialization in this exchange between two
friends, nor was any implied as a result of his general group
experiences, his change was simply a case of acquiring a reason to stop stealing—there was too much to lose in being excluded from the group if he did not change. Thus, we see that
group influence may operate in ways conducive to behavior
change without desocializing or resocializing the deviant actor.

Tim

The following excerpts from Tim's life-history interview illustrate the effect of group or individual influence in changing his behavior. When the respondent was twenty-five years old and had spent almost two years in jail and reform school, on two different charges, and four years in prison, on three different sentences, he changed. As Tim said, though, it was not the prison experience nor the cumulative effect of incarceration that changed him.

> To be truthful about it, I don't believe it (prison) did (change me). I tell you what I think actually helped me was my "rapee" [his partner in the offense for which he was sentenced] (started introducing me to people who had not been in trouble) "cause really I don't know anyone around that town unless it was a criminal or someone I had been in jail with. So he knew quite a few people that hadn't been in trouble, hadn't been in any kind of trouble whatsoever.

> So we went up to this one guy's house—and (he's) married and had a couple of kids—and talked with them awhile, you know. And, for some reason, I went back by myself. You know, just (to) talk to them. And he told me —he said, uh, "if you want a job," he says, "I can get you one." He said, "but uh, there's to be no stealin' or anything like that." So I told him, "*As far as I'm concerned, that's all* over" [as if to say, "So I just decided that was okay—I would quit stealin' if that's what it takes"].

Tim got a job with the help of this honest friend and did well for five months. He stopped running around with his "rapee" and got married to a girl who, as he remarked, "was the type that didn't believe in stealin' or anything."

> ... I think my wife—*just me gettin' married changed everything.* 'Cause after I stopped running around, after I met this other [straight] guy that had gotten me different jobs ... I quit runnin' around with this one guy that I had been in prison with. And uh, *I didn't have* (to) —*uh, run around with them anymore* (that is) *guys that had been in trouble, or anything* (because I had a new group).

Tim not only abandoned his deviant behavior, but also seemed now to feel a part of the straight world. He expressed satisfaction with his nondeviant affiliations and indicated that he "stayed out of trouble" for three years. In this time, he had gained some status in a nondeviant group.

> Well, to me, it seemed like I was getting along better with people—even people I didn't know would, uh speak, would talk to me more. I mean, uh, from different friends that I got to know or different people that I got to meet and everything—(we) got to be friends and everything. And people that I didn't know that these other people knew . . . they would come around. I mean they would just come right over and talk to me. For me, "you couldn't ask for a nicer person" (than these people were). I mean they just acted like I was a *human bein'* for a change, you know. And heck, I, just seemed like I got along with everybody.

Although it is tempting to do so, it would be a mistake to interpret Tim's change as a product of total internalization of conventional values. Because, after a three-year change from a pattern of theft an old prison friend came to his house one day and asked him if he would like to "pull a job" with him. Tim said ". . . I was working. I didn't need the money. I just thought I would help him out a little bit. . . ." So Tim helped his friend with the theft and in a short time he was involved in systematic burglary again. His wife who didn't believe in stealing, now persuaded by the profit motive, joined Tim in a number of burglaries.

Tim's change was influenced by group pressure from conventional persons but there was no resocialization to prevent his return to a pattern of deviance. From this, it appears that commitment to group norms, whether deviant or conventional, are not as strong as the socialization theorists suggest. In two other cases in this study the respondents reported disengaging from deviant patterns as a result of group influence with no indication of commitment to beliefs unfavorable to deviance. One respondent explained the abandonment of a pattern of shoplifting following his family's move to another town saying simply: "I had different friends who didn't shoplift." Another respondent explained his change from destructive gang activities when he moved to another neighborhood in the same city by saying: "It was a new neighborhood. Kids did different things."

What this analysis points to is a reiteration of an observation on the socialization model of deviance made in the previous chapter. The internalization thesis, which combines an involuntary model of social action with a static model of personality, is at least overstated, if not misguided, as a basis for interpreting the development and change of patterns of deviant behavior. There is nothing in the present data on deviant histories to lend credibility to the assumptions of determinism in the socialization approach to change from patterned deviance.[8]

Societal Reaction and Change

The societal reaction position on change permits a wide variety of factors to influence an abandonment of patterned deviance. But two components must be present if the change is to be considered to fit the societal reaction model. The change must meet some individual purpose and it must be volitional. In other words, the deviant actor must willfully select change as a course of action for some subjectively meaningful purpose.

The vast majority of the changes indicated by respondents in this study are primarily willful disengagements from patterns of deviance. The changes were generally goal-oriented and purposive. Below we will examine Albert's changes, three which fit the societal reaction model of change and one which does not. Then two cases, Willy and Ben, are presented as clear examples of voluntary and purposive change. Finally, two cases are analyzed which show the problematic nature of individually structured changes not accepted by significant others. In one case, Ralph's, several attempts to change were aborted by lack of community and official acceptance. A second case, Orly's, shows that even changes that are considered complete may be quickly undone by negative social reaction processes.

Albert

There were three instances of change in which Albert indicated a purposive and volitional decision to disengage from a deviant behavior pattern. The first followed as a direct result of being "scared off" by a confrontation with legal officials. Albert was fourteen years old at the time:

> I think it scared me off a little bit on that ... and uh,
> when I got out I didn't go nowhere ... I was still a little
> scared ... uh, (I) thought the sheriff was still after me....

Later, Albert had patterned a form of deviance characterized by theft, property destruction, and rancorous "hell-raising." However, after he discovered this kind of behavior could have severe personal costs, he decided to change. The self-concept he had established as a "gangster" losts its glamour and he reappraised his activity. Prior to this change Albert had lost his job because he was absent for over a week avoiding the police.

> *I lost my job* (because I had to get out of town before the police came for me) and all that ... uh, (the) *feeling wasn't very good,* you know. So, uh, I don't know—*I'd say I probably didn't want to be a gangster anymore ...* it's just not profitable, (it) *ain't doin' nothin' but hurtin'.*

He changed because of this and moved to another state to live with a relative. Still later in his career, Albert found fear of official consequences and practicality again to be sufficient reasons to disengage from deviance. This time it was a very lucrative practice of systematic burglaries that he abandoned. Two things happened that influenced his decision to leave what he described as a very satisfying life-style as a thief. First, his partner and tutor in crime had been arrested on suspicion. Albert altered his own thefts to a safer variety, after the scare of his partner's arrest. A few weeks later another friend who ran with the group of thieves wrecked and totally demolished Albert's car. Albert attributed the car accident to the life-style he was living. In short, these people (his gangster friends) tended to have no regard for such things as cars, as he did. So, Albert decided this life-style was not worth the cost in things he valued, so he returned home. There he got back his old job as a farm laborer, and changed, abandoning his pattern of deviance.

> Jimmy was picked up on suspicion, ... that scared the hell out of me. I decided, "well, if he can get picked up on suspicion, (I) can get arrested and locked up." ... and (then later) ... Jay wrecked my car, totalled it out. ... there was no hope for it ... that (really) discouraged me. It wasn't long after that that I packed my clothes and ... (left).

That Albert was scared and thinking pragmatically was sufficient to induce the abandonment of this pattern of theft. A final change that was just in the attitudinal stage at the time of the interview is particularly interesting. Albert had changed or abandoned deviant behavior patterns three times prior to the present change. Each time the change involved a purposive decision, but he was never able to establish sufficient reason, in his own mind, for continuing his legitimate behavior once he had changed. There was no group support and no firm emphasis on conventional behavior in these previous changes. They were individual decisions for pragmatic individual reasons.

After being in prison for several months, Albert joined a therapy group which employed transactional analysis as a treatment technique. Roughly, this technique is designed to break down the attributes deemed conducive to deviance and rebuild the individual on the basis of his better personal qualities.[9] But the particular treatment stratagem is less important in this case than the fact that group support and encouragement were now afforded to Albert's basic desire to change.

Albert suggested that he was aware of the stupidity of his acts before this exposure to a therapy group, but he always repeated them. He noted that the same thing would probably have happened again in the future if it were not for the group support he was getting from the therapy group.

> I could see how dumb and ignorant I had been, you
> know, up to now. And I could see that as soon as I got
> locked up. I could see that (at prison this last time). As a
> matter of fact I—(upon entry into prison) I told myself—
> "that was it (no more, this is stupid)." ... before (getting
> into the therapeutic group this time) ... I thought "well,
> I'm always doing wrong. I'm always getting locked up—
> *So I won't do it no more.*" But, uh, I couldn't analyze it
> very good. And TA has helped me to see ... that I have
> really been "fucked-up" and uh, ... (crime is) not for me.
> ... they pounded it into me about (my having had) the
> same thought (about changing) before (and I never
> succeeded). ... (And) *I had this (thought before on a
> couple of occasions). And until I got into TA I probably
> would have gone right back out and done the same
> thing again. But TA has* [pause] I don't know [pause]
> *they're interested in me* [he says this with a sense of
> great satisfaction] *"they've shown me that I'm O.K."*

This last point is crucial for Albert's sense of confidence at the time of my interviews with him. The group had given him a sense of worth apart from his criminal activities. As Albert said, "I know I can make it—TA has shown me as a person I'm O.K." Being considered O.K. is the social support he needed to sustain a long-term change. At the time of the last interview, Albert was attitudinally ready to abandon deviant behavior patterns and take on conventional patterns of behavior. Previously, he was only concerned about stopping the deviant behavior patterns because they were causing him too much agony. He did not have the support of conventional groups previously because no conventional group accepted him. But once the therapy group had defined him as "O.K.," he felt renewed confidence.

Albert, as a consequence of the TA therapy group, now had social support for his favorable definition of himself as a nondeviant. Before this, as noted in the last chapter, Albert received praise and prestige only when his deviance or defiance was exceptionally noteworthy to his cohorts. And he got his only positive social responses from his few companions. Albert had learned long before that his deviance was not the answer to his dilemma, "ain't doin' nothing' but hurtin'," as he put it. But, he had no positive definitions or social support upon which he could establish legitimate behavior patterns and still maintain a sense of self-worth equivalent to that he had known as a thief.

Willy

Willy had changed only once in his nine-year pattern of burglary. In that period he was incarcerated in prison four times for burglary or parole violations totalling five years. Actually, Willy's burglaries were few in number and very unsophisticated, and two of the four periods in prison resulted from parole violations involving public drunkenness, quitting his job, wrecking his car, and breaking curfews. These violations were in bitter and deliberate defiance of the official authority which, he believed, punished him with unreasonable severity for his first offense. After a total of five years in prison he came to understand that he was losing from his attempts to "get even with the law." His change was a purposive choice to "straighten up."

> ... after I did that six months (for parole violation)—
> MAN! *I wanted to straighten up. I didn't want to do no more time. I was sick of it. Made up my mind I wouldn't*

do no more time. So, uh, (when) *I got out I got me a job.*
I got married. (And things) *looked real good.* ...

Willy decided to change because he was tired of being in prison. After five years of increased bitterness, he reasoned that a change in his behavior patterns was necessary to avoid further incarcerations. So, he changed, he decided to "straighten up," abandon burglary, and cease his embittered attempts to get even with the law.

Ben

Ben had been a systematic thief for several years as a youth but stopped stealing completely for four years while in the marines. He was deterred by the threat of swift and harsh punishment.

> I quit stealing while I was in the Marine Corps. I hit the brig for 30 days for being drunk and that cured me (of everything). If "drunk" got me 30 days, stealing could get me 30 years. No way I was going to (risk) standing in line and ask a man for a cigarette for 30 years. But that's the way brigs were run. I never did any more stealing for the rest of my three or four years in the marines. I raised some hell, but I didn't steal ("I never had any qualms about stealing before I went into the Marines").

Ben's decision to stop a pattern of deviance was clearly a purposive choice to avoid prolonged incarceration in the then rigidly run military brigs. Almost immediately after his discharge from the service he began another pattern of theft.

Ralph

In this case a career deviant had attempted change several times. Ralph wanted to change not just a pattern of deviance but his whole life-style. The following excerpt identifies his attempts to change and the kinds of things that defeated them.

> I don't know ... sometimes when you get around people that are in a "square game," classified as "squares" uh, (you) say, "this square ... he goes home every night ..., he don't have to look over his shoulder, he's got a family, he's got a home, he's got a car. Uh, of course, he's got bills and stuff like that but, at least, he don't have to be sleeping with one eye open, tense, nervous, all this here.

You know, (tense) all the time. (It seemed when I would be thinking like this and trying to change and make a go of it") *something would happen that would just change it.*

INTERVIEWER: Like what?

RESPONDENT: (I would) say, "well, I'm really going to give this some really serious thought about going straight—'straightening up' and all this here." ... gettin' a job and settlin' down and really playing the "square john" role. ... And *somethin'* that really does happen, you know. And you say, "damn, that's not supposed to happen—that's not supposed to be."

... a lot of times I would get a good job ... and I would be thinking maybe in those terms ("of maybe, you know, going to be a square guy and straighten up") ... (or) trying to do what's halfway right. And then actually be innocent as hell and be walking down the street and thinking maybe this is it! And (then) have some damn cop run you in or throw you up against a wall, side of a building or something—and frisk you down. And then run you into the police station, bust your head, run you through a big interrogation. And (all of) this on some little "hitch" that you don't know nothin' about. (So you think), "now, what (is) this ... is this ... going to happen all my life even though I'm going to try and straighten up. *And try? It's a big role to try to convince people that you went from this type of life to this type of life.* (It's a) big hassle. Uh, 'cause once you get a record—I don't care if you live to be a million years you would still (have to answer to the record). ... (There are always) people that knows that and (your life of crime) is always down on record.

... you think about doing right and (things just reverse on) ... you. (Then, it) just makes you think, "to hell with all that square (stuff) ... this is my life. I know what's happening here. (But) I don't know what's happening over (in) this (square) life.

While the deviant actor has ultimate control over the decision to change, the community and agencies of social control influence greatly the probability that the change will be continued. Change is a social process involving an intricate set of interrelationships between the actor and the community. For a change to be successful it must ultimately gain social support either at the group or community level. If social support is never achieved, or if something happens to give the actor the impression support has weakened, or that it really is not possible (as in Ralph's case), the probability that deviance will recur is high.

The chances that a volitional and purposive change will succeed for a significant period of time without relapse into deviance depend on a number of social factors that vary in both kind and effect on the deviant actor. The following case illustration from Orly's life-history points to community reaction as a social factor which militates against volitional change. This case also shows the way negative community reaction may affect some individuals in the process of disengaging from a pattern of deviance.

Orly

In the last chapter, we saw that the patterning of Orly's deviance was, in part, related to defensive responses to the rejection of him by others even after his changes. Here two more of Orly's changes are illustrated. His career line rotates from a pattern of theft to disengagement and change, back to another pattern, and then change, and so on through several cycles. Orly was never genuinely committed to any form of deviance, so his changes were frequent and easy. The first change discussed follows a period of incarceration in prison for burglary. After his release from prison he changed, got a job, got married, and, as he said, "settled down." But he could not escape the almost inevitable event when his past would catch up with him, and both official and community reaction would be to his previous behavior rather than his present changes.

> It seemed like regardless of what I was trying to do,
> everytime I turned around the law was on my doorstep
> over something. [Prior to an incident of violating curfew
> while he was on parole] the police had been at my house
> three different times. The FBI had been at my house
> once over a bank robbery and then the cops had been
> there three different times over burglaries ... but I was
> clean. And I was keeping my nose clean but they
> wouldn't leave me alone.

Orly became frustrated by the official suspicions that he had been involved in new crimes. He started going out at night and drinking after this and was quickly picked up for reckless driving and violation of his parole curfew. He was fined $90 and sentenced to fifteen days in jail. When he got out of jail he had been suspended from his job. So, more defiantly now, Orly began drinking and staying out after curfew more regularly. Eventually, old associations with local hoods were renewed which paved the way for his being in possession of stolen property that he had not stolen. His friends had stolen it and used his car to transport it. On a routine stop, Orly was later arrested and charged with possession of stolen property. After five months in jail he pleaded guilty to one count of possession of stolen property and was sentenced to prison for six months.

> (While in state prison) this time I lived the role. I was a hardened criminal, while I was in the "joint." ... Then when I (was) transferred to a minimum security prison, *I started changing. I figured, "well, I hurt my folks—I sure as hell ain't done myself any good—so I might as well just accept this ... (for) what it is, and go out of here and try to make something of myself."* So when I got out I was on parole. I made parole first time up. I got out—stayed straight for ten months.

Orly had made significant progress toward establishing a noncriminal life-style, when he decided to "pull just one" burglary to tide his family over until he was called back to work from being laid off. He was caught, charged with the offense and sent back to prison. At the time of the interviews with him Orly had once again resolved to change, this time once and for all. He said it this way:

> I'm not going to be something I'm not. And I'm not going to be what people think I am. I'm not going to be what they think I am. I've got too much at stake this time and I don't want no more of this damn life. I've had enough. I've given them all the young years of my life—and I've given them enough. Maybe I'll never pay for all the things I've done. But, in my mind, I've paid for it. And I accept that I have been wrong and that I have made mistakes. But, yet, I feel that I have paid for the mistakes. *And I'm not going to let somebody drive my train of thought to going back to this old life* (just for spite)—(or) *to prove to them that I am what they think I am.*

What is important to see in the previous two cases is that change may and does come about volitionally for some actors, but the commitment to change is frequently broken by social factors beyond their willful control. Therefore, we must see that successful behavior change often depends less on altering the will of the deviant than it does on a complex of social factors that weaken the resolve to continue a change. There is, no doubt, great variation from person to person and from situation to situation in the amount of counterpressure required to cause one to give up the idea of change and return to deviance. But, as a general proposition it is probably safe to suggest that the less negative reaction there is from official agencies and significant others to the deviant in the process of change, the less likely the person is to relapse into a pattern of deviance.[10]

In the next section dealing with the control model of change, we will see indications of both voluntarism and determinism in changes brought on by the introduction of external controls.

Control Theory and Change

If patterns of deviance are the result of a lack of effective controls, as the theorists in the control tradition suggest, the change to conventional nondeviant patterns must provide for the initiation of effective controls. But that is all that is necessary as a precondition to change. There is no need to consider resocialization and there is, in general, no concern for solving or curing any human condition[11] believed to be associated with or a cause of deviance. All that is necessary is the effecting of social control where it is lacking, weak, or neutralized.

Hubert

The case of Hubert illustrates an extreme of insecurity resulting primarily from the complete absence of group affiliations or interpersonal relations which confirm individual security. This sense of insecurity was reinforced by the generally negative and exclusionary social reactions received from members of the community. Consequently, there was no place, in his significant world, where Hubert could retreat to security. His insecurity, confusion, and disorientation progressively worsened over the course of his life, eventually manifesting itself in a kind of depressed bewilderment. Hubert's pattern of deviant acts were a mixture of "vengeful striking out" at others who ignored or denigrated him, frustrated "cries for help,"[12] and an

absence of any reason not to deviate. Hubert's case is an interesting illustration of an individual who seems to have gained
insight into his own psychic makeup and who then laid out a
plan for changing his behavior involving independently
directed moves to correct both low self-conception and his lack
of control from conventional sources. The low self-conception
and constant sense of insignificance and worthlessness felt by
the respondent began in childhood and became more acute
with age.

By the time he reached junior high school, Hubert's insecurity and feeling of insignificance were extreme. He described
his state as feeling "totally lost," "numb," "almost dead." He felt
fear, distrust, and ineptitude in association with other people.

> ... it develops and it's something that you can't change—
> you can't no matter what. No matter how much you dig
> down inside you can't come out ... there's just something
> there, you know, an invisible barrier. It's hard to explain
> it.
>
> I kinda feel like I'm "sneaking around" getting to know
> people, you know, I don't want to come in there too fast
> 'cause I don't feel right—don't feel natural ... that
> barrier is there. It is an invisible thing, it's a feeling
> inside. And I don't know what causes it but, it's there.
>
> INTERVIEWER: In such circumstances, as you are
> describing, if you had to guess what others were
> thinking about you—what do you think it was?
>
> RESPONDENT: That's what it amounts to right there—it's
> [pause] I think it's that I'm afraid that they'll accept me
> the way that I am [that is, "sneaking," "fearful,"
> "insignificant"] or look down on me, you know. ... I'm
> afraid they won't accept me [pause] what I'm trying to
> say is—I got this *feeling. I already got this feeling that
> they're looking down on me right from the start.*

Hubert came to know that a change in his behavior patterns
of theft and burglary depended on his becoming involved in a
"meaningful" (legitimate) life-style, and to do that he had to
consciously overcome his problem of insecurity.

> ... see *I'm aware of this* (inferior feeling that blocks
> association and meaningful relations with others) *and
> I'm also aware that it ... has to be done away (with)* if

I'm going to be able to really relax and (change my
behavior to conform with the norms) in a community—
and be able to be sociable. You got to be (somewhat)
sociable in order to get along (and by getting along with
people you become "significant," and when you are
significant you have a reason not to deviate).

He pensively reflected on his life and knowingly unfolded his
personal prescription for change in the following statements.

There's never been, what you say, any real important,
any real *meaningful* things in my life—no really
meaningful and important (things even) to me. Just all
these things here, infamous things, you know,
unmentionables—that's all. The rest of it has just all
been a drag.

I think I've been, uh, what you say, all this time, trying
to figure out who I am and what I want out of life and
how to go about getting it. But that there is something
that's kind, uh, hard to grasp. We just don't reach out
there and get it. ... *I believe if I ever get started on
something I want* ... something I really want *or
something I really enjoy having.* Or *something I really
feel that has some meaning ... (for) my life—something
to keep me going.* [pause]. *Well, (then) I'll be alright.
(Then I'll feel like I'm doing something worthwhile. (I'll
feel that it isn't "hopeless," "useless," "lost in motion").*
... It don't have to be something great or fantastic or
anything. All it has to do is ... be something that is
within reason, within the law, ... *something that will
suppress or completely eliminate this feeling I have
about being* [pause], uh, [pause] ... *"insignificant."* You
see, *I have this insignificant feeling within myself and I
feel very insignificant and always have.* Now what I
finally come to the conclusion of, is *"if I could find some
way to eliminate this feeling of insignificance and feel
that I was significant to myself,* even if I wasn't
significant to anybody else—*it would be enough to make
life worth while.* ... And that's where I'm at right now,
more or less."

Hubert realized that he would have to overcome this inner
feeling of worthlessness which caused his tension and fears in
social relations. He also realized that after breaking down that
barrier (the feeling of insignificance) he would have to find

some meaningful, or socially valued, activity or enterprise by which his worth could be assessed favorably. Finally, Hubert came to consider that the latter might well expedite the former as can be seen in the following comment: "if I ever get started on something that has some meaning . . . for my life . . . (then) I'll be alright." Actually, the two are correlative, as a sense of personal worth and meaningful social activity are invariably related.

But Hubert was still in prison at this time and one can only speculate on whether there was sufficient insight on Hubert's part or sufficient commitment to change to enable him to disengage from deviance. All that is clear is that, from our analysis of Hubert's case in chapter 7 and the above, a total lack of meaningful group or personal relationships leaves one both socially unconstrained and personally insecure. If the control formulation is correct, intimate group and personal associations in highly integrated conventional groups would alleviate both problems and bring on change from deviant behavior patterns.

While Carl's case is not an exact parallel to Hubert's, it involves both a lack of social constraint and a sense of personal insecurity. Like Hubert, Carl had neither conventional group affiliations nor intimate personal associations to serve as sources of control. We can see in the following discussion that the control model of change does fit Carl's case.

Carl

After serving over two years in juvenile institutions and fourteen years in prison, Carl, at the end of his third sentence, knew he would get into trouble again if he did not change. He wanted to change but he knew from a long history of relapses into criminal activity that he needed some assistance.

> When I got out of there [prison—after serving nearly seven years for burglary] I said—I decided I was going to straighten up. (But) *I knew if I got out there, I was going to get in trouble again. And I didn't want to do that—so I decided, "only one thing to do and that's to seek help."* So I went to Dismuss House (a kind of halfway house for ex-cons) and they took me in and told me I could stay there until I was ready to leave. . . . they got me a job. [pause] I had my "downs and ups" though. A lot of times I didn't have a penny in my pocket and I would walk the

streets ... *but I never thought like I did these other
times.* I didn't think about, "well, I'll find me a house
and go in it to see what I can *find*."

A couple of times he was pretty well "down and out," laid off
from his job, his car was repossessed, and all his savings were
gone:

> ... but I didn't turn to stealing or anything like that. I
> went to another place (Volunteers of America) and got
> help there.

The important factor which, at least in part, explains Carl's
avoidance of trouble this time was that he had met a woman
whom he dated for a short time and then married. This relationship gave him a reason to stay out of trouble; he was not
"alone" anymore. She was the needed source of control.

It is significant that, as pointed out in the previous chapter,
Carl recalled thinking differently when he was "alone." He
always thought, he said, "about finding a house I could go into
and see what I (could) find." He added, "when I get by myself
... eventually all my thoughts start concentratin' on gettin' in
trouble." But once he met "this woman" he did not "think that
way" any longer and did not steal, even when his financial
situation was bleak.

> I met her in a tavern. Me and her hit it off pretty good
> and so we just decided to get married—and did ... but
> uh, in a way, she was the cause of me losing my car and
> the money I had (saved). ... Because when I met her
> why uh, I wanted to be with her every night. And uh, I
> spent money on her and when I (would) get my pay
> check—why we would go out on weekends (and) drink.
> And pretty soon I was drawing money out of the bank to
> keep going. And I wasn't makin' payments on the car.
> And finally they took it—and the money was gone too.
> And we didn't have nothin', you know. *But ... I come
> back!* And *it was because I really wanted to. I didn't go
> out and steal nothin'.* I made it *on my own.*

Carl stayed completely straight for six years. Prior to this time,
when he was not directly supervised by either his sister or by
the army, he was never "straight" for more than a couple of

weeks and never out of jail or prison more than a few months at a time. Perhaps the best explanation of his deviant history is provided in his own remarks: "It's usually when I get alone like that ... there's nobody watching you, seeing what you do ... why you go out and do things." Carl made apparent the fact that without group or personal attachments there was nothing to stop him from stealing. The significance of this line of reasoning may be seen when we consider that the only real change from his pattern of burglaries that Carl made followed the securing of a long-term personal relationship with another person. He had made up his mind to change before, but this time there was some reason not to relapse and go back to prison.

Mick

Family stress, problems of personal security, and gradual peer isolation were seen, in the last chapter, to be important factors which prompted Mick's deviant behavior. But "one girl" prompted a change. Mick's problems of anxiety and insecurity were not solved, they were simply neutralized by this valued interpersonal relationship.

> ... what *changed* more than anything was, uh, I started running about with this *one girl.* And, uh, most of the time I would just go out with any ... girl that would come along but ... in this period of time I started going around with one girl—messin' around with her. *And I had no idea of stealing while I was with her.* I didn't want to. (*I was that way*) *if I was with somebody that I truly liked and thought a lot of—I wouldn't steal nothin',* *I had no reason* [because then his tensions and anxieties were low].
>
> And, oh, I guess I went with her for about (a year) ... and I know that every day that I was with her or was going to see her the next day *I never thought of stealing at all.* And I never stole once in all that period of time. *So I realize that (I changed) a little right there. I realized that I didn't have to steal.*
>
> I guess (prior to this time) I just had the *impulse* that I wanted to (steal). (Now) *I just thought "look, I've gone for a year and hadn't stole nothin'—why should I go out when I leave her and steal, steal something anyway.*
> And then (other times) I got to thinking, "well, *I guess I*

just want to do it for kicks, you know—(*to*) *get even
with them* [apparently the respondent means, "to get
even with anyone who has been involved in hurting him
emotionally or has caused him to be anxious." This
seems to be generalized, in his mind, to all of "society."]
You know, (just to) see how smart the police are (for
example) . . . (it was) *just to mess with people.*

I didn't do it for . . . a need to live. I mean I had been
living comfortably! I wasn't rich and I didn't have
everything everybody had but I was living comfortably.
And I had a little money to spend now and then. . . . I
just felt that uh, "why don't I just go out and start
getting all the money I want . . . "And then I says, *"if I do
that I won't have her—if I get in trouble."*

She didn't know about me being in trouble at the time
and I didn't tell her. . . . *And I guess* [pause] *just . . .
didn't want to get in trouble while I was going with her
because she would know about it. . . . I just thought that
she would drop me just like (that) if she found out I got
in trouble. . . . I guess I thought too much of her to go
out and get in trouble. But I never had any desires to do
anything (when I was with her).* So (this way) *I realized,
in my own mind, that I didn't have to do this—'cause if
I did . . . just one mere girl would (not) stop me* from
doing it. *So I knew I had a mind of my own.*

Then Mick's girl moved away after a year and, his source of
control gone, he began stealing regularly again. He says:

. . . *I never did get in trouble while I was going with this
girl,* and, uh, we broke up . . . she had to move and I
guess our being separated—*I didn't care much about
anything anymore.* And, well (I thought) "she don't care
much about me or she wouldn't have moved." But
knowing she had to move I just didn't even want to think
that she had to move. *And I resolved back to start
stealing again.*

This respondent felt an extreme sense of anxiety ("inner tensions," as he recalled) and the girl was his relief and security.
She was an ongoing neutralizer of his problem, in the sense
that his relationship with her was deemed important enough
to bring about suppression of his tensions and anxiety. In essence, she was a source of social constraint operating to reduce

the probability that Mick's anxiety would result in deviance. When she left, this problem of tension was renewed, and Mick reverted to releasing his tensions through theft. He did not have sufficient reason to suppress the desire to strike out against "society" after the girl had moved away, so he began stealing again immediately after her move.

Summary

This chapter considered the extent to which the three approaches are able to explain change or abandonment of deviant behavior patterns. In the socialization view, change of deviant behavior patterns is believed to follow from changes in the personality structure which must be brought about through some resocializing group experience. Socialization theorists generally assume that the deviant must be desocialized and resocialized by (1) removal from external sources of social support and (2) assimilation into groups whose values are unfavorable to deviance. This, in effect, amounts to therapeutic intervention.

First, we showed that Don's changes did not fit the socialization model. This is particularly important because his case was an archetype of the socialized deviant in terms of emergence and patterning. The import of group influence and change in one's life-setting was demonstrated in the cases of Orly, Sony, and Tim. However, while essentially compatible with the socialization proposition, we showed that these two factors did not operate in accord with the socialization hypotheses in any of the cases. That is to say, group influence and change in life-setting did not operate to desocialize these respondents of deviant values and resocialize them in terms of nondeviant values. Rather, these forces operated more in an intervening way to eliminate or neutralize, the factors involved in causing their deviance. We believe that these findings call into question the conception of resocialization. It is possible that this conceptionalization is a theoretical artifact with no empirical reference.

By contrast, the societal reaction position was that change follows from a purposive and volitional decision to disengage from a deviant behavior pattern. The societal reaction position was distinguished from the socialization position on change in that the former assumes an individual can change willfully and purposively without therapeutic intervention or alteration.

Most of the changes identified by respondents in this study fit the societal reaction model of purposive and volitional change. The general viability of the societal reaction explanation of change was demonstrated in five accounts of purposive and volitional change. These respondents changed for a variety of practical purposes including (1) the maximization of individual praise, (2) the high personal cost of deviance, and (3) a specific or general dissatisfaction or disenchantment with a deviant life-style. While the general credibility of the voluntary change model posited by societal reactionists is firmly established by three cases (Albert, Willy, and Ben), two others demonstrate the tenuous nature of such changes. The social cultural context of the change plays a major role in the degree of facility with which an actor may volitionally disengage from deviance and assume a conventional life-style. The more resistence to change perceived by the deviant actor, the more likely is his relapse into deviance and the more likely subsequent efforts to change will abort with even less resistance and rejection.

The general credibility of the control model of change is demonstrated by Carl and Mick's cases. Hubert's plan for change was presented to show the beginning stages of willful change in a case where the usual components of social control were almost completely lacking. In Carl's case, we saw that deviance was usual for him except when his living arrangements involved a source of control in group membership or interpersonal relationships.

Mick's case is perhaps even more compelling as evidence in support of the control model of change because his patterns of deviance involved more than the absence of control. His deviance was motivated by a will for vengeance. Nevertheless, the addition to his life of one secure personal relationship was sufficient to induce the abandonment of a pattern of deviance.

In general, our analysis suggests that (1) the socialization model is overstated but not completely incorrect, (2) that volitional and purposive change, though tenuous, is common and lends much credibility to the basic voluntary social action model underlying societal reaction theories, and (3) that the control thesis is applicable in both cases where there is no motivation to deviance beyond the absence of control and in cases where there is a will to deviance.

Notes

1. There is good reason to believe that all types of deviants cycle through stages of deviance and nondeviance a number of times. In the case of crime, this off then on pattern was noticed as a "zig-zag path" going from crime to non-crime and back to crime again by Daniel Glaser. See *The Effectiveness of a Prison and Parole System* (Indianapolis: Bobbs-Merrill, 1964).

2. This is the general position of socialization theorists. See, for example, Donald R. Cressey, "Changing Criminals: The Application of the Theory of Differential Association," *American Journal of Sociology* 61 (September 1955): 116–20, and Rita Volkman and Donald R. Cressey, "Differential Association and the Rehabilitation of Drug Addicts," *American Journal of Sociology* 69 (September 1963): 129–42.

3. This definition of personality which underlies socialization theories is similar to Allport's definition of personality. This definition was first put forth in his *Personality: A Psychological Interpretation* (1937). See Gordon W. Allport, *Pattern and Growth in Personality* (New York: Holt, Rinehart & Winston, 1961), pp. 28–29.

4. See Clifford R. Shaw, *The Jack-Roller* (Chicago: University of Chicago Press, 1930) and *The Natural History of a Delinquent Career* (Chicago: University of Chicago Press, 1931).

5. See, for example, Cressey, "Changing Criminals," pp. 116–20.

6. Ralph H. Turner, "Deviance Avowal as Neutralization of Commitment," *Social Problems* 19 (Winter 1972): 308–21.

7. The instance of change discussed here is the first of four for Orly. The other three are purposive and voluntary and not directly influenced by group pressure.

8. This is not to suggest, however, that there are no human circumstances or conditions for which an involuntary model of social action and a static model of personality are plausible. None of the respondents in this study would have been likely to be diagnosed as dangerously psychotic. To the extent that the human condition may become overpowered by subconscious forces in the psyche, it is plausible to think in terms of these deterministic models of social action and personality. However, they seem characteristically overstated in cases of so-called normal social behavior—which includes most forms and instances of deviance.

9. See, for example, Thomas A. Harris, *I'm O.K.—You're O.K.: A Practical Guide to Transactional Analysis* (New York: Harper & Row, 1969).

10. In general, all of the social contingencies involved in rendering one susceptible to the negative expectations inherent in deviant labels are implicated in inducing a relapse into patterned deviance after a change. See the discussion of these social contingencies in Thomas J. Scheff, *Being Mentally Ill* (Chicago: Aldine, 1966), pp. 96–97. The primary individual variables affecting the probability of a successful change indicated in this study were *strength of self-concept* and *degree of commitment to change.* The individual's self-conception was also found to be related to the effects of labeling in the case of the physically deviant, for example the blind. See Herbert H. Human, Janet Stokes, and Helen M. Strauss, "Occupational Aspirations Among the Totally Blind," *Social Forces* 51(June 1973): 403–16.

11. Sociologists such as Cloward and Ohlin have suggested deviants are socialized into actors who value their deviance more than nondeviance, or

others such as Parsons have suggested deviants develop "alienative need-dispositions" that predispose them to do deviant acts. Presumably, these human conditions must be corrected before change from deviant behavior patterns is possible. The control theorist might see change as following simply from the addition of control where it was lacking, weak, or neutralized. For the above references to socialized or psychologically disposed deviants, see Richard Cloward and Lloyd E. Ohlin, *Delinquency and Opportunity: A Theory of Delinquent Gangs* (New York: Free Press, 1960), and Talcott Parsons, *The Social System* (New York: Free Press, 1951), pp. 249–325.

12. "Cries for help" signify attention-getting action in instances involving extreme personal desperation. For an examination of important psychiatric works which discuss this mode of action in suicide cases, see Edwin S. Shneidman and Norman L. Farberow, *The Cry For Help* (New York: McGraw-Hill, 1961).

Observations Toward a General Theory of Deviance

9

In part I of this book we looked at three distinct theoretical approaches to the development and change of deviant behavior patterns. Part II offered a general evaluation of the comparative utility of these approaches in explaining three stages of deviance— emergence, patterning, and change. While, in specific terms, our analysis identified some strengths and weaknesses of these approaches, it is not possible for us to judge one approach completely valid or another completely invalid as an explanation of deviance in all its phases.

The socialization approach came under the most criticism of the three. We argued that the deterministic view of social action and personality assumed in socialization theories overstresses the extent to which actors are influenced by social norms and values. Positive expectation, group pressure, and social support are often influential in the development and change of social deviance. However, as our analysis indicates, expectations and social supports are not internalized into the personality organization to the extent that they compel one to deviance. Rather, it appears that because of these forces, deviance is sometimes easier, more satisfying, more practical, more fun, or more expedient than nondeviant behavior. When the actor perceives it to be advantageous to disengage from deviant behavior patterns, change may follow from the simple decision to do so.

While the societal reaction model was shown to be a sufficient explanation of all three phases of deviance in some cases, it was clear from other cases that the overlooked relationship between self-factors and societal reaction is crucial to the causal process. The social variables affecting whether labeling will be successful or not are well elaborated by societal reaction theorists.[1] Self-factors are no doubt, in part and at any point in time, a function of broad social variables. There is, however, variation in self-factors that is independent of the social contingencies usually identified by societal reactionists. For example, low self-conception as a result of undesirable physical size or facial and body features seems unrelated to social variables such as the power differential between rule-breakers and labelers or community tolerance levels. Any theoretical explanation seeking to specify the relationship between negative social reaction and stabilized deviance must account for self-strength variation or fall short of a viable theory.

Control theory was both applicable to more life-history cases in this study and more viable as an explanation of all phases of deviance than the other two approaches. This is probably due, in large part, to the fact that control theory (as we characterized it here)[2] specifies less about the development and change of deviant behavior patterns than the socialization and the societal reaction approaches. There are, as a result, fewer points at which control theory can be tested and, therefore, fewer places to be shown wrong.

When considering the relative explanatory power of the three approaches, it is necessary to look at the extent to which each of the theoretical formulations can explain all three phases of deviance in cases to which they are applicable. Clearly the socialization framework is deficient by our analysis. Both the societal reaction and control approaches were more explanatory of the process of deviance—from emergence and patterning through change in archetype cases. That is, when applying the societal reaction and the control approaches to cases for which they claim to be explanatory, both explain more accurately what happens in a deviant career than does the socialization approach when applied to cases considered archetypal of the socialized deviant. Using these life-histories as negative tests in the evaluation of the comparative explanatory power of the three approaches, then, we see that control theory is most credible, societal reaction is second, and the socialization model is the least viable as an explanation of the development and change of deviant behavior patterns. But it must be remembered that this is a negative test evaluation which is useful in identifying weaknesses in theoretical approaches. We do not know from this analysis which of the three approaches is most frequently implicated in cases of deviant careers. What we do gain is insight into the extent to which each of the approaches explains the facts in the lives of real deviants at each stage in the development and change of their patterns of deviant behavior.

Models of Social
Action and Personality

If our interest in the social sciences is in developing theories more explanatory of the social facts about deviant behavior patterning and change as they occur in the real world, we should look toward a more general theory of deviance to explain more of the deviance phenomenon in more of the universe of cases. The present trend toward more specific middle-range theories of some single form of deviance or phase of it, although aimed to the same goal, seems to have proven ineffective. In an effort to move toward a general theory of deviance, the present analysis has attempted to identify the relative utility of basic parts of each of the approaches in explaining the process of deviant behavior patterning and change. But, acknowledging that there is some credibility to parts of each of the three approaches should not give rise to the hasty conclusion that all that is needed is a synthesis of the most explanatory postulates and propositions, and an addition of the most important variables indicated in each approach. We cannot simply add together what is credible and subtract out what appears theoretically useless from the three approaches. That result would not be a theory but, rather, it would be a simple compilation of propositions and variables found to have empirical support.[3] And even if there were some value to adding these theories together, their competing or alternative propositions or postulates would go untested in terms of comparative explanatory power.[4]

For example, in this study, we see that individuals emerge into deviance and come to pattern various forms of deviance because conformity to negative expectations is a forced choice in an atmosphere of restricted legitimate opportunities and, by contrast, because they had learned values favorable to deviance and are engaging in behavior to actualize internalized positive expectations. We have here human actors voluntarily selecting among alternative courses of action on the one hand, and actors propelled involuntarily by internal motivations on the other. Moreover, our life-history data also show that the same actor at one life-stage may act in ways suggestive of a voluntary and purposive action model, and at another stage the person's social action may be involuntary and compelled from within. In short, there is empirical evidence to substantiate alternative models of social action and personality in different actors and in the same actor at different times.

This finding makes the usual method of addressing the problem of alternative models of social action and personality nonproductive. That is, we cannot simply say that the truth lies somewhere between the voluntary and involuntary model of social action and somewhere between the static and processual models of personality.[5] What is needed is not a model of social action midway between voluntarism and involuntarism or a conception of personality that is not static but not processual either. We need to abstract upward to a more encompassing model that explains how both conceptions are possible for different actors, and for the same actor at different times.

The first step that must be taken to satisfy this need for a more broadly applicable conception of social action and personality is to surrender the idea that there is but one correct conception that fits all cases at all times. Human beings need not be either willful actors, or products of their environment, or some combination of the two. It may be, in fact, that some persons are free calculating actors, social products propelled by inner values, and some combination of the two at different delimited periods of time or life-stages. Any given actor, then, when observed over a period of time, will manifest a number of different degrees of voluntarism in social action patterns.

A theoretically useful conception of social action and personality for the study of deviance must cover all the degrees of voluntarism and process found in actual instances of deviant behavior. Such a conception would call into question the view that deviance is simply voluntary or involuntary. It would avoid the idea that deviant personalities are either fixed or in constant process. Instead, if our observations have been correct, whether deviant behavior takes the shape of willful and purposive action, voluntary or involuntary and compulsive action does not depend on a permanent state of the actor's mind. Rather, the shape deviance is to take depends on decisions by the actor to claim or to disclaim responsibility for patterns of behavior considered deviant.

Both the social situation and the actor's purpose may influence whether a pattern of deviance is to be considered voluntary or involuntary by the deviant. The conception of social action and personality offered here, and one that has been useful in our attempts to understand deviant careers, assumes that *individuals construct a personal reality, within a broad social reality system, guided by a desire to insure, at least, a modicum of psychic security.* The deviant, like anyone, is interested in maintaining a sense of security. This is done in the actor's significant social world which includes all the social meanings the individual knows and understands.[6]

When the behavior of the deviant is understandable or justifiable in terms of the broad system of social meanings in his social world, and when his purpose is served by it, the individual will accept responsibility for the deviance being willful. However, when the reasons for the deviant's behavior are not justifiable in light of the general meaning system, it is paramount to disclaim responsibility.[7] Responsibility is disclaimed, then, because the real reasons for deviance are socially unacceptable or because the claim of responsibility would not further the deviant's purpose or interest in self-presentation—as in the case of change, when the deviant's purpose is to be forgiven. So he contrives an acceptable reason for his deviance by blaming neuroses, alcoholism, commitment to deviant values, or some other condition that is excusable as a source of deviance in the actor's particular social world. That the actor may come to believe his behavior is compelled by some force, rather than as being voluntary and purposively selected, is necessary to complete the construction of a protective personal reality.

By providing a socially acceptable excuse for deviant actions the deviant first protects himself from the negative reactions of others. For example, the adult who steals to call attention to a personal problem may find the reactions from others less severe if the deviant acts are presented to be a result of alcohol problems. This is because alcohol is believed to take charge of people and their acts are somewhat excusable because of this belief. Moreover, alcoholism is believed to be curable while, the "need for attention in adults," the real reason for the stealing, is considered to be neither excusable nor curable. Acknowledging the real reason for deviance would bring continued negative reaction.

Second, the actor protects himself from himself by coming to believe the excuse he has presented for the deviance. That is, the actor may come to believe he has a neurotic compulsion to steal and then continue to steal for that reason. Here we see that an actor may engage in a pattern of deviance voluntarily and for some individual purpose. If we observed the deviant actor at this point we would probably interpret his deviance as being voluntary and goal-oriented. But at a later time the deviant may find reaction to his deviance unsatisfying and seek to regain an earlier level of personal security. If the actor reasons, or otherwise discovers, that the real reasons for his deviance are likely to bring more negative reaction than a contrived reason, he may elect to present his deviance in a way that is more likely to be forgiven. Sometimes the actor may have to even play out a series of actions to demonstrate the new excusable causes because significant others have already crystallized their opinions as to the causes of the deviant's behavior patterns.

One respondent in this study, for example, reassumed a previously abandoned pattern of theft in order to give a new impression of the cause of his deviance. He was sure to be drunk before each theft. At other times he was careful to spread his reputation as a heavy drinker through the community. At the same time, however, he began new patterns to establish himself as an "upstanding citizen and good-worker sort" when he was not drinking. It was necessary to have a forgivable reason for his deviance so he could be accepted back into the community. He had set the stage for offering alcoholism as the source of his deviance because vengeance, the real reason, was neither forgivable nor curable. The community needed only to observe the play, where in the final act the deviant saw a psychiatrist, took the cure (which he reasoned would be considered acceptable in his social world) and was able to regain some self-esteem and personal security while presenting himself to the community as cured of the cause of his history of deviance.

Although the discussion of this vacillating process from voluntary to involuntary action patterns may give the impression that it is an intricately planned and deliberately plotted transition by the actor, we do not believe this to be true. Rather, the individual seems to gradually become, at each stage in the transition, what he is presenting himself to be. By the end of the process the actor's behavior patterns are indeed compelled by the forces he perceives to be the cause of his deviance. It is the same as when, in theater, the actor becomes the character played. Here the deviant actor is the writer who comes to enact his own script.

The process may, at a later period, shift back again to voluntary and purposive action. One respondent in this study made such a change after several years in prison on three different occasions and after the absence of the desired effect of his previous self-presentations. He began behavior patterns that were volitional, purposive, and aimed at avoiding more time in prison. He also simply discontinued his patterns of compulsive deviance. The reverse direction of a change from compulsive to voluntary behavior, therefore, seems to be triggered by the same factors as the movement from voluntarism to compulsion —the social situation of the actor and individual purpose.

It seems logical that a rational actor could convince himself to believe that his behavior is compelled by forces beyond his control. But, now that we see the reverse of a compulsive actor transforming to voluntary and purposive behavior patterns, the reader may wonder how this is possible. How is it that one compelled by unconscious forces at one time comes to do the same behavior voluntarily and for specific purposes at another time? It is possible because the idea or conception of voluntarism is almost always available to us in our significant social worlds. Presumably, if it were not, no amount of pressure could evoke a sense of willfulness in the personal reality of actors. Any of our actions, no matter how bizarre, are thought of two ways. Either they are compelled by some unconscious involuntary force or they are the product of a conscious and voluntary intention.

Both voluntarism and involuntarism are available in the American culture as rationales for our behavior. From the present consideration of the nature of social action and personality, it appears that the shape of deviant behavior patterns are individually constructed. When behavior engaged in voluntarily is more condemned than if it were involuntary, social actors may themselves come to accept it as involuntary. This is done to protect their own sense of self or to make the most favorable presentation possible to others regarding their deviance. If, in addition, the social meaning system excuses involuntary behavior only after the actor has been treated by official change agents, more impetus is given to the actor's willingness to call his behavior involuntary. In time, he may come to believe it and begin demonstrating all the symptoms of involuntary behavior and fixed personality. He does not voluntarily act as though his actions are involuntary. He believes they are involuntary and so voluntary options are not considered.

On the other hand, if the social meanings change to favor and excuse voluntary action, the actor may turn around once more and present his deviance as willful and purposive. This occurs frequently in individuals who have experienced different rehabilitative philosophies in total institutions such as prisons. At one point, they are exposed to a treatment philosophy that cures only involuntary behavior. Their significant others understand deviance only as involuntary behavior. The actor sometimes comes to accept his past behavior as involuntary and approaches situations as though there are not choices of alternative behaviors. He does what a fixed personality type like his would do. At a later point, the actor may be recommitted to an institution employing a treatment program that assumes voluntary behavior. Significant others may become convinced of the merits of the new program. The actor's history is then reinterpreted and his present behavior may again become voluntarily directed. One has voluntary choices of alternative behaviors because he believes he has them.

Patterns in the Development and Change of Deviance

Having said that some aspects of each approach are credible and that the underlying assumptions about social action and personality are empirical facts in the subjective realities of actors, let us move on to examine a number of patterns in the way different theories are implicated in our cases. We have seen in earlier chapters that there is sometimes a mixing of the approaches indicated in the development and change of deviant behavior. That sometimes one approach is explanatory of emergence while patterning and change may be better explained by one of the other approaches is perhaps not surprising. Nevertheless, pointing out that the three approaches were mixed in ten different ways as explanations of our cases, at least, suggests that earlier statements considering alternative approaches as only secondary contributing factors might be understated.

For example, many sociologists suggest that negative social reaction processes constitute a factor in the explanation of deviance—but taken alone they are not regarded as explanatory. Societal reactionists have seen the principles of differential learning structures, blocked opportunity structures, external stress, psychological disorders, and lack of conventional ties in the origins of rule-breaking behavior.[8] But they argue that negative societal reaction processes are the prime forces in the stabilization and patterning of deviance. Control theorists acccpt that a number of factors may contribute to the weakening of social controls and to the decision to deviate but that, ultimately, it is the lack of control that is most important in explaining how deviance is possible. We might expect, from these positions, that once the primacy of one approach has been established as the explanation of a deviant career, the factors characteristic of other approaches would be of secondary importance at all phases of deviance for a particular case. But the fact that an approach explains one phase of deviance does not mean it will explain, or even be implicated in, other phases of deviance. The career histories of deviants in this study demonstrate this point clearly.

Figure 3 shows the way we would expect deviance to proceed if we accepted the idea that one approach is generally sufficient to explain any single deviant career. The causes of emergence, patterning, and change would all be primarily explainable by the same theoretical approach.[9]

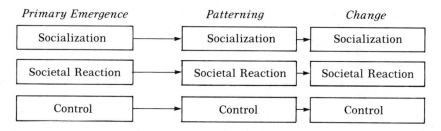

Primary Emergence   *Patterning*   *Change*

Socialization	Socialization	Socialization
Societal Reaction	Societal Reaction	Societal Reaction
Control	Control	Control

FIGURE 3

But, in the actual cases of deviant career development, not only were there cases where one approach was not primarily explanatory of all phases of deviance, but also there were cases where an approach was sufficiently explanatory of one phase of deviance and not even implicated as a factor at another phase. Figure 4 shows the variety of ways the three approaches were implicated as prime explanations of one or more phases of deviance. These patterns of movement through stages of deviance represent the variety of ways the first pattern of deviant behavior developed and changed in our cases.

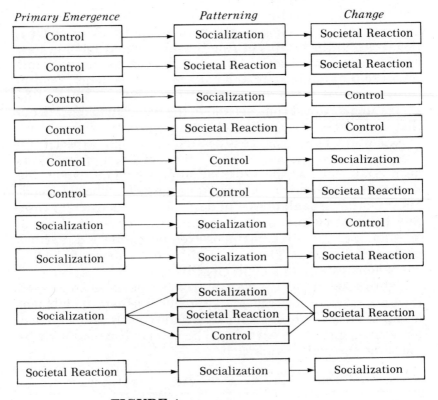

FIGURE 4

We must also assume that other combinations of the approaches are to be found in the empirical world. But our concern is not with how many different ways the three approaches to deviance are implicated in real world deviant careers, nor is it with any particular combination that might occur more frequently than another. The compelling point, and our concern here, is that we find persons proceeding in their deviance along the lines of one theoretical approach at one stage in their careers and then shifting kinds of social action and sources of motivation which bring in another theoretical approach as explanatory at another stage. This seems to be a contradiction, since it would be more consistent with previous thought if the case did not shift from one source of motivation to another.

One way to approach this situation would be to suggest that the human actor is socialized but not too socialized; is rational and purposive in social behavior, but not totally rational; and needs to be controlled, but control alone is not enough to restrict deviance—as situational pulls, stress, or practical expedience may neutralize it. Then we could say that we simply observe what is there at the time. But this dilutes each of the approaches and moves us further away from theory that explains what is there, and why, at any time in a given deviant career. And what might be there are instances of behavior fitting all three theoretical approaches in their pure form.

We feel that our reactions must be correct when we observe socialization at one stage, societal reaction at another, and control at still another—and we believe resultant theories should be developed without qualifying or modifying our observations or our basic and most useful concepts. If deviant careers go together, indicating factors of socialization, societal reaction, and lack of control as single sources of different phases in the deviance process, we must wonder if it makes sense to continue to think of separate theories. Might it be the case that socialization, societal reaction, and ineffective social controls are always available parts of our sense of social reality? Further, might it be that we invoke these principles singly, or in combination, as they serve individual purposes? That is, do we purposely adopt available social reasoning to explain our behavior and then come to be guided by it? Socialization, societal reaction, and lack of control are available in our social meaning system. They may operate alone, together, or with still other causal principles such as psychological disorders.

If there is merit in this argument, then we need a more general theoretical framework capable of subsuming the core conceptions and propositions of the socialization, societal reaction, and control approaches. Synthesis, in this instance, simply makes neat theoretical arithmetic. It does not explain how these competing conceptions and propositions are observed to be singularly explanatory of a particular phase of deviance but not another phase in the same case. Nor does it explain why competing theoretical factors are observed at different life-stages in a single case.

A theory that specifies the most useful variables from all three approaches, and the interrelationships between them, is needed in the sociology of deviance. It is not that previous observations which produced the theories we have now were, or are, all incorrect or that deviance never results from a single set of factors tied to one approach. In fact, the observations upon which the theories are rested were quite probably correct, for the point in the deviant career under study.

But when looking at the life-histories of deviant careers, it is clear that the factors indicated in these point-in-time observations are only a part of the deviance process. In any given case, a number of causal variables identified by socialization, societal reaction, and control theorists may be implicated as primary causes of different phases in the development of deviant behavior patterns. Theorists of deviance have typically missed or overlooked this fact. In so doing they have been guided to the theories of deviance represented by the three approaches in part I.

As such, the theories making up the socialization, societal reaction, and control approaches are not inaccurate so much as they are incomplete. For if our interest is in explanatory theory pertinent to the processes by which deviant behavior patterns develop and change, all of the theories, both taken alone and as approaches, are insufficient.[10]

We need now to formulate a more general theory of deviance. A general theory of deviance would be capable of explaining how actors may be variably rational and compulsive in their deviant behavior, and how factors of socialization, societal reaction, and control emerge and disappear from phase to phase as causes of the development and change of patterned deviance. We feel that a general theory capable of explaining the kinds of facts in the lives of deviant actors reported here must depart from a rational and purposive model of social action. This rational actor may have a static or a processual personality or sense of self at different times. At the same time, the person may be strongly influenced by positive or negative expectations, stress, practicality, expedience, fun, revenge, or pulls of a situation depending on what is available in the individual's social meaning system. In this sense, causes of deviance are causal because the deviant actor accepts the meaning attached to certain social conceptions. One may learn deviance if it is available and if there are social conceptions in the meaning world making the connection between deviance and learning positive expectations. The same is true for any other social conception of cause. Within this context the actor may reinterpret at will the causes of his deviance, and indeed change the source of inducement to it, to as many different forms as there are available social conceptions pertaining to causes of deviance and as many different times as allowed by social situation and individual purpose. Change or abandonment of a pattern of deviance may be achieved through any of the available socially conceived paths to reform to which the actor is willing to subscribe and with which he will be treated.

The sum of what is said here does not, in itself, constitute a general theory of the deviance process. It suggests the need for thinking of deviance as a process that goes through different phases and changes in degrees of commitment, voluntarism, purpose, and even sources. It discusses the need for a general theory of the deviance process and some problems a general theory must address. And, we hope, that it has stimulated some new thinking about the nature of deviance that will be of use to both academics and persons concerned with the official and unofficial handling of individual deviants.

Notes

1. See, for example, Thomas J. Scheff, *Being Mentally Ill: A Sociological Theory* (Chicago: Aldine, 1966), pp. 96–101; Austin T. Turk, *Criminality and Legal Order* (Chicago: Rand McNally, 1969), pp. 53–79; and Richard Quinney, *The Social Reality of Crime* (Boston: Little, Brown, 1970), pp. 15–25.

2. Control theorists, as pointed out in chapter 4, vary greatly on basic assumptions about the nature of social action and personality. In many respects, the view of Reiss, Reckless, and Nye on these issues is closer to the socialization model than the way control thesis is characterized here. But our effort in drawing on Durkheim, Matza, and Hirschi for the underlying postulates of control theory has been to emphasize what is unique in each approach and to attempt to evaluate relative utility of alternative positions. There is no intended suggestion that this characterization is more correct than some others.

3. While synthesis seems to be a natural proclivity among sociologists faced with a number of isolated and partial truths, it is prudent to recall past errors before falling into a familiar trap. In the 1930s and 1940s several researchers abandoned the search for explanatory theory to develop what has come to be called the "multiple factor approach" to deviance. The reasoning was that, since existing theories invariably contained inaccuracies, the factors from different theories shown in research to be causally related to deviance could be profitably combined—ultimately to determine the amount of deviance-causing power contained in each factor. In an additive sense, one researcher argued that a certain number of these factors would cause deviance, presumably in all cases. See Cyril Burt, *The Young Delinquent* (London: University of London Press, 1944). Other references emphasizing the multiple factor approach are Mable A. Elliot and Francis E. Merill, *Social Disorganization* (New York: Harper and Brothers, 1941); Sheldon Glueck and Eleanor T. Glueck, *One Thousand Juvenile Delinquents* (Cambridge: Harvard University Press, 1934) and *After-Conduct of Discharged Offenders* (London: Macmillan and Company, 1945); William W. Wattenberg, "Delinquency and Only Children: Study of a Category," *Journal of Abnormal and Social Psychology* 44 (July 1949): 365; and Lowell J. Carr, *Delinquency Control* (New York: Harper and Brothers, 1941).

For a criticism of this abdication of theory see Albert K. Cohen, "Multiple Factor Approaches" in *The Sociology of Crime and Delinquency,* ed. Marvin E. Wolfgang, Leonard Savitz, and Norman Johnson (New York: John Wiley, 1962), pp. 77–80.

4. van den Berghe's oft-cited article synthesizing functional and conflict theories leaves us without reason to look at the relative strength of competing postulates and propositions. See Pierre L. van den Berghe, "Dialectic and Functionalism: Toward a Theoretical Synthesis," *American Sociological Review* (October 1963), pp. 695–705.

5. In the sociology of deviance, this problem rests historically in the alternative conceptions of free-will vs. determinism in the classical and positive schools of criminology. See George B. Vold, *Theoretical Criminology* (New York: Oxford University Press, 1958), for a discussion of the historical and modern handling of these competing postulates. David Matza, *Delinquency and Drift* (New York: John Wiley, 1964) shows the middle-ground between freedom and constraint in his model of social action and personality that is similar, in some ways, to the one presented in this chapter. One difference, however, between Matza's conception of the actor in drift and the present conception is that ours posits more permanence in periods of freedom and compulsion than Matza's.

6. See Peter Berger and Thomas Luckmann, *The Social Construction of Reality* (Garden City, N.Y.: Doubleday, 1966).

7. Jean Paul Sartre has called this pretense of irresponsibility "bad faith." See his *Being and Nothingness: An Essay on Phenomenological Ontology,* trans. Hazel E. Barnes (New York: Washington Square Press, 1953), pp. 86–116. Also see Peter Berger, *Invitation to Sociology: A Humanistic Perspective* (Garden City, N.Y.: Doubleday, 1963), pp. 143–45, for an excellent brief discussion of "bad faith." Jock Young, in a study of student drugtakers, found that the automatic role of "sick junkie" (learned in interaction with the psychiatrist) is attractive because it allows the individuals to deny responsibility for his behavior. This study is reported in Ian Taylor, Paul Walton, and Jock Young, *The New Criminology: For a Social Theory of Deviance* (New York: Harper & Row, 1974), p. 128.

8. See, for example, Scheff, *Being Mentally Ill,* p. 40; Edwin M. Lemert, *Social Pathology* (New York: McGraw-Hill, 1951), p. 17; and Howard S. Becker, *Outsiders: Studies in the Sociology of Deviance* (New York: Free Press, 1963), p. 28.

9. While there were no cases in this sample where the socialization approach was sufficient explanation of all three phases of deviance, both societal reaction and control approach were completely explanatory of several cases.

10. Insufficiency in explaining the process of deviance should not be seen as a criticism of the specific theories considered in this work because we have in all cases pushed the theories beyond what they were intended by their authors to explain. The definition of the thing to be explained—what we have called the deviance process, including emergence, patterning, and change—has been changed in this analysis. None of the theories were developed to explain deviance defined this way. Moreover, some of the theories were directed specifically at one form of deviance in one set of circumstances and not intended to be employed more generally for all forms of deviance in highly variable social circumstances. However, when generalized upward to basic assumptions and broad theoretical propositions, the general approaches may be seen as inadequate if they fail to explain data on the deviance process.

Deriving Postulates and General Propositions

Appendix A

In the analysis of the three theoretical approaches to deviance we were specifically interested in two things: (1) underlying assumptions about the nature of social action and personality and (2) broad or general propositions representing each approach on the emergence, patterning, and change of deviance. These assumptions are categorized under the headings of *voluntarism, involuntarism* and *naturalism* for models of social action and *static* and *processual* for models of personality. Voluntary social action implies deliberate, calculated, and purposive behavior in pursuit of individual goals. Involuntarism connotes a model of social action where actors are believed to be propelled into behavior by forces beyond their conscious control—namely internalized values. Naturalism is taken to mean action is based on natural desires and personal interests, but it is not compelled by inner motivation or shaped by social constraint.

Models of personality are distinguished in that a static conception implies individual behavior tendencies are relatively fixed at a point in time not to change without prior personality alteration. While the difference is basically a matter of degree, the processual model of personality assumes that the self-concept changes continually in the process of experiencing different reactions from others, new life-settings, and new activities. Therefore, behavior tendencies vary with changes in self-concept which are continuous.

Most theorists did not make completely explicit their assumptions about the nature of social action and personality. The categorization in charts 1, 2, and 3 is the result of cumulative impressions after examining various works by the theorists rather than inference from a few precise statements.

There was not complete consensus on the models of social action and personality assumed by the theorists grouped in either the societal reaction or the control approaches. In fact, in both groups of theories there was wide variation on these issues. Our arbitrary decision was to characterize each approach in terms of the theorists' views that

Charts 1, 2, and 3

Models of Social Action and Personality
Assumed in Theories of Deviance

SOCIALIZATION THEORIES

Theorist	Model of Social Action	Model of Personality
Shaw and McKay	involuntary	static
Merton	involuntary	static
Sutherland	involuntary	static
Cohen	involuntary	static
Miller	involuntary	static
Cloward and Ohlin	involuntary	static

Theories in the socialization approach generally posit an involuntary model of social action and a static model of personality.

SOCIETAL REACTION THEORIES

Theorist	Model of Social Action	Model of Personality
Tannenbaum	voluntary	processual
Lemert	involuntary	static and processual components
Goffman	voluntary	processual
Becker	voluntary	processual
Scheff	voluntary and involuntary components	processual
Quinney	voluntary	processual

The societal reaction approach is characterized as positing a voluntary model of social action and a processual model of personality. Lemert's model of personality has both static and processual components and Scheff's model of social action implies both voluntary and involuntary aspects in social action.

CONTROL THEORIES

Theorist	Model of Social Action	Model of Personality
Durkheim	naturalism	processual
Reiss	naturalism	static
Nye	naturalism	static
Matza	naturalism—voluntary	processual
Reckless	naturalism—involuntary	static
Hirschi	naturalism—voluntary	processual

The control approach is characterized as assuming a naturalistic model of social action and a model of personality that falls between the static and the processual models.

represented the greatest difference from the positions of the other approaches. Therefore, what is distinct about the set of theories was emphasized and the aspects overlapping with theories of the other approaches were deemphasized. If we are to know whether more than one theoretical approach is necessary in the study of deviance and which has the greatest explanatory potential, it is the differences, not the similarities, that must be evaluated.

Thus, the societal reaction approach was characterized as positing a voluntaristic model of social action and a processual model of personality. The control approach was characterized as positing a naturalistic model of social action even though Matza, Reckless, and Hirschi seem to blend their naturalism with voluntarism or involuntarism. A basis for inferring any assumption about the nature of personality is quite difficult in all control theory but the problem is greatest in Durkheim and Hirschi. Chart 4 shows the general propositions derived from a review of the theories representing each approach.

Our analysis of the life-history documents in chapters 6, 7, and 8 are based on these general propositions. Moreover, the conclusions drawn from the analysis, pertaining to the relative explanatory power of each approach, apply only to this particular depiction and not to all that is implied by the various theories making up the approaches.

Chart 4

General Propositions on the Emergence,
Patterning, and Change of Deviance
Representing the Socialization, Societal
Reaction, and Control Approaches.

PROPOSITIONS ON THE DEVELOPMENT AND CHANGE OF DEVIANCE

Approach	Primary Emergence	Patterning	Change
Socialization	Initial deviance results from the individual being socialized into deviant attitudes, interests, and behaviors through participation in neighborhood and intimate group (family or peer group) activities.	The greater the continued exposure to organized social settings and intimate group associations emphasizing deviant values, the more deviant behavior tendencies become fixated (internalized)	Change from patterned deviance must involve (1) desocialization which dispels internalized deviant values and (2) resocialization to the extent that new nondeviant values are internalized.
Societal Reaction	Initial deviance results from the individual's acceptance of, and behavioral conformity to, negative expectations inherent in derogatory social labels imposed as a part of normal group differentiation processes.	The greater the negative social reaction in terms of intensity and pervasiveness, from significant others and control agencies, the greater the probability that deviance will become patterned.	Change from patterned deviance may follow from a reverse of the negative reaction process or through volitional decision.
Control	Initial deviance results when individuals are uncontrolled by membership in disintegrated groups or when they lack constraining group affiliations.	The more detached the individual is from integrated group affiliations and intimate personal associations, the greater the probability that deviance will become patterned.	Change from patterned deviance must involve either (1) the acquisition of control through group or interpersonal affiliation or (2) the alleviation of social situations or forces which weaken or neutralize usual constraints.

Methodology
and
Procedures

Appendix B

The methodology of any study should, in the writer's judgment, meet two requirements: it should be founded upon defensible epistemological grounds, and it should be matched to the problem of study. The central reason for collecting the data discussed in part II of this book was to explore the comparative viability of three competing theoretical approaches employed by sociologists in the study of deviance. In chapter 5, we argued this sort of research problem tends to preclude the use of some of the more standard methods of investigation. In addition, there is no equivalent, in the social sciences, for the classical crucial experiment used by the physical sciences in tests of competing theories. The methods and procedures employed in this research, rather than exactly adopting any one established strategem, were carved out of a number of methodologies and research techniques of the social sciences.

It is necessary then that the reader know what epistemological assumptions were made and the exact way methods and procedures were used. The meaning[1] which individuals subjectively attach to the details of their lives is the *real* meaning, in that their perceptions of forces and experiences (not the theoretical or imputed meaning of them) are the ones which influence their behavior.[2] As W. I. Thomas put it:

... (the individual's) immediate behavior is closely related to his definition of the situation. ... If men define situations as real, they are real in their consequences.[3]

Given this assumption, it is important to establish not only what forces and experiences are involved in the individual's life but also what subjective meaning they had for the actor. To attribute significance arbitrarily to certain experiences or certain forces, ignoring the actor's perception of them, rests on the false premise that they have a similar impact on all individuals. It was important, then, to collect the data in a way that would enable the researcher to determine what meaning certain events had for the respondents.

We assumed that meanings of events to respondents could be apprehended by the researcher. As members of the same culture share common experiences and communication, there are common meanings from which "concrete meanings" (i.e., the real meanings to the individual) can be understood.[4] The awareness of the subjective meanings in the life of the individual is facilitated by sharing specific experiences and cultures[5] with the respondent, and by empathy.[6] This is to suggest that insight into causal motivation must, as Weber noted, follow from understanding at the level of subjective meaning.[7] The reader will no doubt observe that, in general, the research procedures of this study are rooted in the methodology of Max Weber.[8]

The Method of Inquiry

A loosely structured interview technique with no prephrased questions was used to collect life-history data. The course of the interview was left to the respondent so as to insure that the interviewer did not inappropriately impose his own system on the situation or suggest the importance of any particular factors by direct inquiry.[9] Direct reactions were solicited with reference to specific theoretical factors only after the individual implied their significance but failed to elaborate sufficiently. For example, one respondent said, "We never could afford nothin' like that," when describing theft of candy as a small child. In this and in similar circumstances, the specific factor (economics in this example) was pursued more directly by asking the respondent to elaborate, and then by raising the specific question of economics later in the interview to determine whether it continued to be important as a motivating force or as a type of discontent with his lot in life. In all instances the interviewer tried to elicit responses without imputing importance to any condition or circumstance until after the respondent had indicated its significance. When the respondent indicated the subjective meaning of an event the interviewer tried to imply no more or no less import than had been suggested by the respondent.

In some of the interviews, however, this technique was ineffective. The respondent was, in these cases, rendered uncomfortable or uncertain by the lack of specific reference to particular factors. It was necessary, in these cases, to construct an outline of life-stages, events, and relationships upon which to frame more pointed questions such as, "What were the economic circumstances of your family?" or "What was the reaction from people in the community toward you?" In general, responses were elicited on meanings of the emergence, patterning, and change of deviant behavior. Clifford Shaw noted, in his pioneering use of life-history documents, that it was necessary in many of his experiences with delinquents to illustrate the kind of material desired in the written part of the life-history.[10] The illustrations, however, were taken from information already given in a personal interview. To the extent that it was possible in the interview situation, this technique was followed in the present study.

The loosely structured interview procedure was designed to obtain the deviant's own perceptions of the significant forces in his life. In this respect, much of the validity of the life-history responses and, therefore, the creditibility of our conclusions rest on the degree to which the interview technique was effective in influencing the respondent to reply in terms of subjective meanings.

Self-Perceived Life-Histories

The specific technique employed in data collection most closely resembles the life-history or "own story" technique used by both Clifford Shaw and Edwin H. Sutherland.[11] While the life-histories collected in this study were modeled to some extent after Shaw's emphasis on spontaneous reports following the natural sequence of events in the life of the deviants, there are notable differences.

First, many of the "own story" documents collected by Shaw were written by delinquents who were given an outline of behavior problems, delinquencies, arrests, court appearances, and commitments previously obtained from personal interviews.[12] Then they were asked to write their "own story," following the outline. The delinquents were instructed to give a complete and detailed description of each experience, the situation in which it occurred, and the impression which it made. In the present study, on the other hand, all of the information in the life-history document was obtained through intensive interviews.

Second, Shaw believed the accuracy and interpretation of the personal document ("own story") was improved by supplementing it with other case history material such as official records and psychological findings.[13] I have chosen to depart from this recommendation in the belief that the personal account is likely to be more important, for purposes of this study, than the official record, or supplemental evaluations by other professionals.[14]

When there is a contradiction between the official record and the personal account given by the deviant the question of which of these sources is most accurate arises for the researcher. Shaw implies that the official record is most accurate.[15] His position seems to be based on a lack of confidence in assessing the accuracy of personal documents which were obtained in written form. Life-histories need not be obtained this way and the researcher is not necessarily improving the accuracy of the story by checking it against the official record. In fact, the reverse may be true. The answer to the question of which source is accurate in studies of deviant behavior patterns—the personal account or the official record—is almost certainly the personal account. An explanation of this can be seen in the following illustration.

Differences between the personal account and the official record frequently involve confounding circumstances. For example, a respondent might have remembered a particular arrest as having involved a charge of burglary, while, on the other hand, the police record may indicate that the charge was actually loitering. For purposes of understanding the respondent's behavior, it is more important to consider what he thought the charge was than to consider what the police record indicated. The contradiction between the personal account and the official record is easily explained. Sometimes an individual is arrested and charged with loitering, or a similar charge, so that he may be questioned in connection with a different crime. The individual tends to remember what he was questioned about, not what formal charge was recorded, which, in fact, he may not have been told.

It was the interviewer's position that the personal account more accurately described meaningful happenings in the life of an individual than did the official record. And it is the subjectively perceived meaning of events, not an official interpretation, that is influential in the course of social action. By the same reasoning, other supplemental materials, such as psychiatric evaluations and information from relatives, were not used in this study.[16] These sources of information, like the arrest record, were not regarded as significant data when compared to the respondent's perception of events. However, the official records, while not used as data, were used as a guide to career points at times when the respondent had difficulty remembering numbers of arrests, times held in jail, or dates of such events. The interviewer was able to help the respondent develop an accurate chronology by recalling what was recorded in the respondent's official records in terms of such facts as how long the person was held in jail awaiting trial.[17]

Reliability and Accuracy of the Data

Having dealt with the question of what kind of data was used and for what purposes, we are left with a basic question: how does the interviewer know if the respondents are truly representing felt perceptions of their life course? The *own story document,* like the *official record,* can be questioned with regard to accuracy and reliability. Obviously, deviant persons may consciously or unwittingly mislead the interviewer, or other outsiders. Deviants sometimes present "fronts" to manage interaction on their own terms.[18] But steps can be, and in this study were, taken to mitigate and identify distortion, exaggeration, and omission in the life-history interview. By contrast, there is often no way to determine the accuracy of the official record. In the *own story document* the largest part of the question centers on the respondent's honesty in the interviews.

This question of respondent honesty was asked of Kinsey et al., and their answer was that interviewers must use the same common-sense machinery that we all use in everyday life.

It has been asked how it is possible for an interviewer to know whether people are telling the truth, when they are boasting, when they are covering up, or when they are otherwise distorting the record. As well ask a horse trader how he knows when to close a bargain![19]

The good horse trader knows when the best deal has been struck and he also knows whether the horse is worth more or less than the trading price. In interaction with others we usually know when we have as much information as can be obtained and the likelihood that it is accurate, distorted, or abbreviated. This is not to say, however, that there were no other checks on the accuracy of statements or that absolute honesty was assumed. Nevertheless, it is thought that the standard reasons for lying were mitigated considerably by the research design and the interview method. In the research design, participation in the study offered no advantages for the inmate who chose to contribute a life-history nor was there any punishment for declining. Often participation was even an inconvenience. In most instances a rapport was established so that general truthfulness could be reasonably assumed. Even though some good reasons for dishonest or incomplete life-stories can be removed in large part, some personal and situational factors inviting inaccuracy will always remain.

On the remaining problems of distortion, exaggeration, or omission of information the investigator employed several strategies to check the internal reliability of statements. For instance, when the respondent was unconvincing in his remarks and showed discomfort by the tenor of his presentation, the investigator displayed doubt and disbelief. This usually precipitated a more elaborate accounting by the respondent of the event or circumstance being described. In the elaboration, the respondent often acknowledged subtly the inaccuracy in his first description and then cleared it up by a more specific account. The way the investigator showed doubt or disbelief varied with different respondents as the situation seemed to dictate. If a strong expression of doubt was needed to establish the investigator as "con wise" (i.e., not gullible or easily deceived), the reaction was tempered with knowing skepticism.[20] On the other hand, if deception seemed to be a "face-saving" device, for example, doubt was communicated in an expression of sincere and understanding interest.[21] This usually made it easier for the respondent to talk about things that were either humiliating or difficult.

A second internal reliability device was used after questionable information was given. The interviewer waited for an appropriate moment later in the interview and summarily paraphrased the development of events to that juncture, indicating either a lack of exact memory of the questioned point(s), a different explanation of them, or a different degree, number, or whatever from what the respondent had given in his earlier account.

Other strategies were also used such as noting the inconsistencies in two or more points, or remarking subtly that some things just did not tie together, or that something must be missing. The latter strategy is typified by the case of a young inmate who was describing events preceding his involvement in a series of burglaries. He noted that he and "three other guys" lived together in a house. The burglaries began three months after he was laid off his job (the others were either in trade school or not otherwise working). The interviewer asked how they lived, paid for rent and food. He said he sold his car and his records, and that *"friends pitched in on the rent."* When pressed on why his friends would do that, he said that they were "just good friends." The interviewer expressed concern about why they would do this for three months. The respondent said (unconvincingly) that they had a "lot of *drinking* parties at the house," but he said it in a way which communicated, "if you don't accept that answer, as you should not, I'll tell you the real reason." The interviewer reacted with the expected discomfort with that explanation. Then the respondent asked that the tape recorder be turned off, which was more a face-saving device for his attempt at omission than a felt need for secrecy, whereupon he said they had marijuana parties at the house and "everybody chipped in to keep the house in operation."

The investigator's appraisal of the interpersonal and interactional situation and the investigator-respondent rapport was always used to decide "when" and "what kind of" internal reliability device to use, if any. In some instances the respondent was not challenged because only a fragile rapport had been established. In these cases, some statements were identified as unconvincing after the interview and were interpreted accordingly in the analysis.

It is clear from the above discussion that while the life-histories in this study are similar, in many ways, to Shaw's and are in the tradition and spirit of the personal documents developed by him and others, they also differ in some fundamental respects. The primary difference centers around the "verstehen" emphasis in apprehending the data in the present study,[22] as opposed to a heavier dependence on sources other than the life-history documents as reliability checks in Shaw's work. Shaw's interest in other sources was probably a consequence of the fact that the bulk of Shaw's life-histories were written by the respondents themselves.

Procedures

The life-histories in this study were obtained from inmates in two state prisons in Illinois and Florida. Two general screens were initially established in selecting respondents for the study. First, there must have been reason to believe from an investigation of the prison files that the individual had patterned, at some time, a form of deviant behavior. This was usually determined from an examination of the "rap sheet" which listed roughly the number of arrests and the variety of charges and dispositions reported to the Federal Bureau of Investigation.[23] A second screen was a preliminary interview with each inmate selected from the examination of the official files. If the individual expressed an interest in participating in the study and if it appeared from this interview that he had manifested a pattern of deviant behavior at some prior time, he was invited to contribute his life-history.

The category of offenders from the prison population whose files indicated the highest probability of patterned deviance of some form was thieves. Therefore, a list of inmates whose rap sheets indicated considerable contact with the law on a variety of charges involving theft (theft, burglary, larceny, robbery) was developed. Highest priority for selection was given to those cases indicating frequent charges on some form of theft or related charges such as possession of stolen goods, possession of burglary tools, and attempted burglary.

From this list, eighty-one inmates were asked to discuss the study and their possible participation in a preliminary interview. From this group of eighty-one men, seventy-six inmates from the two prisons were asked to participate in the study by volunteering to do a life-history interview. Sixteen declined for various reasons, six were transferred to other prisons before their scheduled interview, and four others either failed to return for the scheduled life-history interview or were mistakenly told by a guard that the investigator was not in that day. In the end, fifty life-histories were obtained.

Once a respondent agreed to participate in the study the earliest future date was set for the life-history interview. On several occasions the life-history interview was done on the same day as the preliminary interview. Normally two to three days passed between the preliminary interview and the first session of the life-history interview.

The length of the preliminary interviews ranged from a few minutes to over an hour. The life-history interviews ranged from one to six hours. In all but four of the cases, the life-history interviews were completed in one sitting.

Following each life-history interview, the investigator wrote or recorded his general impressions and interpretations of: (1) the interview; (2) the respondent; (3) the reliability of the statement; (4) important nonverbal communications; and (5) any outstanding characteristics of the respondent or the interview situation.

The Data and Processing

Approximately 100 hours of tape-recorded life-history interviews were obtained from fifty participating respondents. Eighteen of the interviews were transcribed verbatim. Transcriptions for these cases totalled 1,200 pages and ranged from 35 to 115 pages in length. The average interview was around 65 pages long. The remaining thirty-two life-histories were partially transcribed, drawing out the deviant career line in terms of emergence, patterning, and change of deviant behavior patterns. Approximately 350 pages of notes were produced in partial transcriptions for these cases.

The verbatim and partial transcriptions constituted the raw data. What the data lacked at this stage was the interpretive quality or what we have chosen to call *empathetic interpolations. Empathetic interpolations* include the subtleties of meaning, the inflections, the non-verbal communications; indeed, they include much of the tenor and character of the interview materials as known to the investigator who experienced the telling of the story. Therefore, both the verbatim and the partial transcriptions were further reviewed, this time adding these important data. Each case was reviewed while listening to tapes of the interview session. Hearing the tapes and recalling the interview, the data processing was completed by appending the interpretive data (i.e., the *empathetic interpolations*) to the life-history documents.

Notations were injected when the respondent's intended meaning would have been deceiving and inaccurate by simple literal denotation. In addition, emphasis on certain words and statements and descriptions of the respondent's demeanor were interjected when the literal meaning of the transcription was not the same as the intended meaning. Finally, expressions of emotion and the general tenor of certain comments were added to the original transcription. Each case was finally studied, organized chronologically, and examined in terms of three levels of explanation: primary emergence, patterning, and change or abandonment of patterned deviant behavior.

Notes

1. Herbert Blumer suggests "meaning" is a social product constructed by individuals in the course of achieving a self. It is this meaning which is regarded here as important in appraising individual behavior. See his "Sociological Implications in the Thought of George Herbert Mead," *American Journal of Sociology* 71 (March 1966): 535–44.

2. This assumption stands in direct contrast to a prominent and plausible psychoanalytic assumption which assumes that subconscious motivation plays a significant if not a primary role in shaping one's behavior.

3. W. I. Thomas and Dorthy Swaine Thomas, *The Child in America* (New York: Alfred A. Knopf, 1928), pp. 571–72.

4. This is an assumption based in Max Weber's verstehen methodology. See Max Weber, *The Theory of Social and Economic Organization,* trans. A. M. Henderson and Talcott Parsons (New York: Free Press, 1964), pp. 87–93.

5. Gordon Allport, *Pattern and Growth in Personality* (New York: Holt, Rinehart, and Winston, 1961), p. 516.

Methodology and Procedures

6. Charles Horton Cooley, *Human Nature and Social Order* (New York: Schocken Books, 1964), pp. 136–67.

7. See Weber, *Theory of Social and Economic Organization,* pp. 87–112.

8. For an excellent discussion of verstehen methodology see Peter A. Munch, "Empirical Science and Max Weber's Verstehende Soziologie," *American Sociological Review* 22 (February 1957):26–32.

9. Several questions posed by Rollo May epitomize the investigator's concern in employing this procedure of data collection: "Can we be sure ... that we are seeing the patient as he really is, knowing him in his own reality; or are we seeing merely a projection of our own theories about him? ... how can we be certain that our system, admirable and beautifully wrought as it may be in principle, has anything whatever to do with this specific Mr. Jones, a living, immediate reality sitting opposite us ... ? May not just this particular person require another system, another quite different frame of reference? And does not this patient, or any person for that matter, evade our investigations, ... precisely to the extent that we rely on the logical consistency of our own system?" Rollo May, "Contributions of Existential Psychotherapy," in *Existence,* ed. May (New York: Simon and Schuster, 1967), p. 3.

10. Clifford R. Shaw, *The Jack-Roller* (Chicago: University of Chicago Press, 1930), p. 22.

11. See Shaw, *The Jack-Roller* and *The Natural History of a Delinquent Career* (Chicago: University of Chicago Press, 1931), and Edwin H. Sutherland, *The Professional Thief* (Chicago: University of Chicago Press, 1937). Also see William I. Thomas and Florian Znaniecki, *The Polish Peasant in Europe and America* (New York: Alfred A. Knopf, 1927), and John Dollard, *Criteria for the Life History* (New Haven, Conn.: Yale University Press, 1955), for excellent discussions of this method.

12. Shaw, *The Jack-Roller,* p. 22.

13. Ibid., p. 2.

14. John Lofland, *Deviance and Identity* (Englewood Cliffs, N.J.: Prentice-Hall, 1969), p. 29, points out that if we are concerned with actors and their acts, it is reasonable to take the actor as a central vantage point from which to think about the explanations of his entanglements. The actor may be taken as a vantage point with respect to his *subjective* or *phenomenological* assessment of his acts, his circumstances, and immediate events. If, on the other hand, we are interested in the whole social situation and how the meanings were shaped and shared by others, the perceptions of others become important considerations. See Norman Denzin, *The Research Act* (Chicago: Aldine, 1970), p. 245.

15. Shaw, *The Jack-Roller,* p. 2.

16. For excellent discussions of official records, other professional evaluations, and other sources which may supplement the deviant's own story, see Erving Goffman, "The Moral Career of the Mental Patient," *Psychiatry* 22 (1959):123–42, and *Asylums* (New York: Doubleday, 1961), pp. 323–86; and Jack D. Douglas, *American Social Order* (New York: Free Press, 1971), pp. 42–78, and *The Social Meanings of Suicide* (Princeton, N.J.: Princeton University Press, 1967), pp. 163–231.

17. For a discussion of this use of the official record see Denzin, *The Research Act,* pp. 236–38.

18. Goffman, "Moral Career," pp. 123–42.

19. Alfred C. Kinsey, W. B. Pomeroy, and C. E. Martin, *Sexual Behavior in the Human Male* (Philadelphia: W. B. Saunders, 1948), pp. 43–48.

20. An exemplary instance of this strategy was employed when a young burglar, who was obviously not very sophisticated, told the investigator boastfully: "We were making about $2,500 a month" burglarizing filling stations. The investigator replied: "That must be an all-time record for filling station burglaries ...?" The subject then revised his statement gradually adding: "Well, we stole $800 worth of tools." He finally noted that: "Around three to four thousand dollars (including the worth of stolen merchandise) passed through our hands in a little over three months."

21. See Erving Goffman, *Interaction Ritual: Essays on Face-to-Face Behavior* (Garden City, N.Y.: Doubleday, 1967), pp. 5–45.

22. See Munch, "Empirical Science and Max Weber's Verstehende Soziologie," pp. 29–30, for a discussion of how the verstehen method works. We assume, like Becker, that life-histories of the present kind reveal data (otherwise best obtained through participant observation) and details which sociological theories must ultimately explain if they are to have more than operational and predictive significance. That is to say, our theories must provide a framework for understanding the phenomenon as well as for predicting it. When our concepts can be used in both the understanding and the prediction of the phenomena under investigation, we have produced a credible theory. Formulations that achieve less are and must remain merely plausible. See Howard S. Becker's introduction to the 1966 edition of Shaw's *The Jack-Roller,* pp. v-xviii.

23. The FBI "rap sheet" is an identification record compiled by the Bureau on individual arrests, charges, and dispositions of the arrests. Law enforcement agencies report arrests, by criminal charge and the disposition, of individuals who have an FBI identification on the basis of fingerprints. In many cases, however, the disposition of cases is not included on the rap sheet. It is also safe to assume that not all arrests are reported to the FBI. For example, arrests that eventuate in release or dropped charges are no doubt omitted sometimes.

Index

Emergence: alternative
explanations, 85–86; defined, 6,
83–85; primary, 84–86, 93, 105,
116; secondary, 84–85, 93, 116
Etiology, 83, 84
Expectations: negative, 113, 126,
155, 158, 159, 220; positive,
112, 113, 117, 121, 122, 124,
125, 126, 220

Fatalism, 60

Goffman, Erving, 26, 34, 35, 36,
37, 43

Hirschi, Travis, 49, 65, 66, 67, 68

Identity transformation, 133–41
Internalization thesis, 122–25,
188. *See also* Norm,
internalization of
Involvement, 66–68

Labeling: pre-labeling, 100;
school, 6; tagging, 27, 28, 46n
Lemert, Edwin M., 26, 28, 29, 30,
31, 32, 35, 43, 127
Life-history: accounts, 79; data,
77–78; interviews, 77, 237;
own story document, 233–34;
self-perceived, 78, 233–34
Lofland, Lynn, 151
Lorber, Judith, 5

McKay, H. D., 12, 13, 21
Master status, 33
Matza, David, 49, 59, 60, 61, 67,
114
Meaning, 115, 231, 232, 238n;
real, 231, 232; social, 213, 216,
239n, subjective, 80n, 115, 231
Merton, Robert K., 14, 15, 16, 17,
19, 50, 52, 53, 54, 67
Miller, Walter, 19, 20, 21

Negative case, 78

Neutralization, 59, 60, 168
No-good: labeled, 95, 96, 97, 98;
on being, 98, 99, 100, 101, 102,
129–30
Norm: erosion, 63;
internalization of, 85, 112, 177,
209; retention, 63
Nye, Ivan F., 49, 56, 57, 58, 62,
65, 66, 67

Ohlin, L. E., 14, 15, 17, 18, 19, 20,
21, 26
Outsiders, 31

Patterning: defined, 6, 115–16;
operational definition of, 115,
170–71n; theoretical
distinctions on, 112–15
Personality: models of, 226–27;
processual, 169, 225, 227;
static, 169, 177, 188, 225, 227
Phenomenology, 58
Provisional status, 99–100, 140,
147, 148, 151, 168

Quinney, Richard, 26, 40, 41, 42

Reality: personal, 213; social,
213
Reckless, Walter C., 49, 61, 62,
63, 65, 66, 67
Reiss, Albert J., 49, 55, 56, 57, 62,
65, 66
Resocialization, 14, 17, 20, 177

Scheff, Thomas, 26, 37, 38, 39,
40, 43
Security: psychic, 213;
operations, 171n, 214
Self: factors, 61, 106n, 150, 168,
210; fragile, 141, 147, 157 159,
171n, 172n; security
operations, 171n; self-concept,
33, 36, 41, 62, 151, 171n, 205n,
210; strength, 126, 152, 159,